THROUGH TURKISH ARABIA.

A PERSIAN ASTROLABE

(THE FRONT).

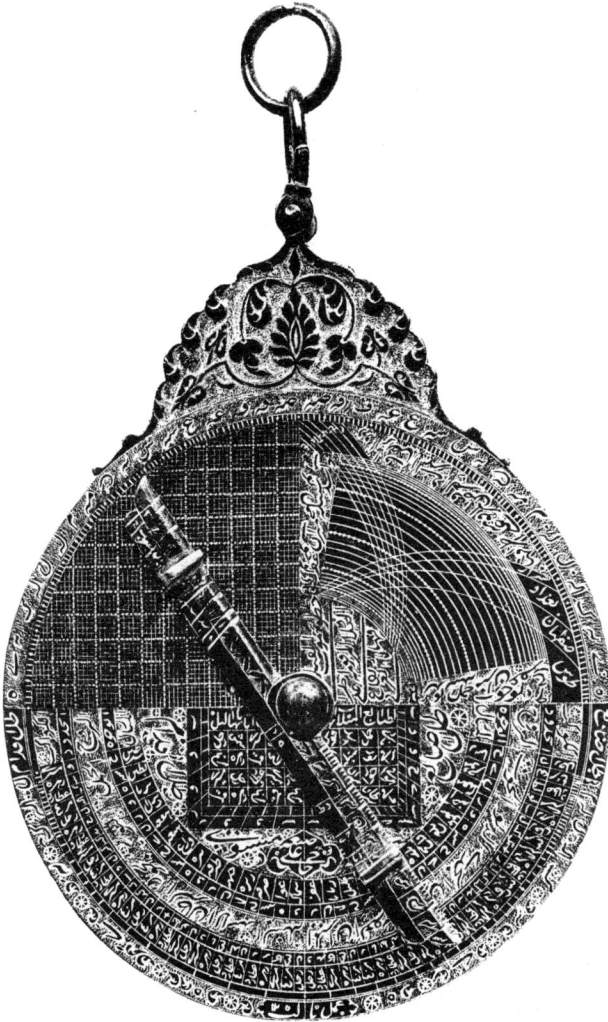

A PERSIAN ASTROLABE

(THE BACK).

THROUGH TURKISH ARABIA.

A JOURNEY FROM
THE MEDITERRANEAN TO BOMBAY
BY THE EUPHRATES AND TIGRIS VALLEYS
AND THE PERSIAN GULF.

BY

H. SWAINSON COWPER, F.S.A.

DARF PUBLISHERS LTD
LONDON
1987

FIRST PUBLISHED 1894
NEW IMPRESSION 1987

ISBN 1 85077 170 7

Printed and bound in Great Britain
by A. Wheaton & Co. Ltd, Exeter, Devon

PREFACE.

THIS volume is the plain record of a solitary journey from the Mediterranean to the Persian Gulf, by the valleys of the Euphrates and Tigris, the two great rivers of Western Asia. As such it must be taken up by the reader, whom I forewarn to expect neither a narrative of scientific exploration, nor to look for the flights of fancy which embellish the book of the globe-trotting bookmaker. Therefore I humbly deprecate the criticisms of those who would fall foul of me for want of systematic observation, or absence of style.

As far as I am aware, the so-called Euphrates caravan route from Aleppo to Bagdad has been described but once in a modern book of English travels, namely, in Lady Anne Blunt's delightful " Bedouin Tribes of the Euphrates." Of the great valley itself, we have of course the scientific and

statistical works which were the outcome of the
Euphrates Valley Expedition of 1836. But these, as
the expedition was by river, do not bear upon the
road, and have not, as was not indeed to be expected,
had any effect in opening up the valley to the travelling Englishman; so that to this day the Euphrates
and its surroundings remain practically a *terra incog-
nita*, and, with the one exception above mentioned,
without any popular descriptive literature.

The reasons for this are obvious. The traveller
wishing to make his way from the Mediterranean to
Bagdad or the Persian Gulf, finds that an easier and
more entertaining route lies by Urfa, Diarbekr or
Mardin, and Mosul. True, these routes are not, as
the Euphrates road is, except at midwinter, all sunshine, but as a set-off against this disadvantage, are
the stories in circulation about the perils from maraud-
ing tribal Arabs of the Northern Arabian desert,
which suffice to deter many a cautious wayfarer from
the road. As a matter of fact such danger appears
much exaggerated, but this is not universally known:
and the supposed difficulty cannot be avoided by
travelling by water, as over the greater part of the
river between Meskineh and Feluja there is no navigation of any sort. Another substantial objection to

the road is the scarcity of provisions, which is such, that the Euphrates road is practically a desert journey, except that it has an ample supply of water. Again, the dare-devil who snaps his fingers at "ghazus," Arab thieves, and small rations, makes the straight rush from Damascus by the old post route, or by Palmyra, and if he be "stuck up" by the Anazeh, or others on the road, he cares but little, as his baggage is scanty or *nil*, and the adventure, on his return to civilization none the worse, will surround him with romance, and a reputation (amongst some) of an Oriental traveller.

For these reasons I have ventured to reproduce, perhaps in rather tedious detail, that portion of my journal which relates to this part of my journey. It must be remembered that the valley has before it an important future, if not as an Indo-European railroad line, at any rate as a route of steamboat traffic.

Though well aware that, in these days of scientific travel, a book of this character cannot claim more than a certain amount of attention, I trust that some of the matter will be found of practical use to others. Such, I venture to think, will be the itineraries of the roads between Aleppo and Bagdad, and between the latter town and Babylon and Kerbela. Next to scientific geographical observations, careful itineraries, kept in

hours, are of the most value for wayfarers on the old
Eastern caravan roads.

My fellow-traveller on the last mentioned of these
routes (Mr. H. J. Coningham, of the Leinster Regiment), is now unfortunately in India, after eighteen
months' journeying in Persia and Central Asia, so that
I am unable to submit to him before publication, as I
should have wished, those pages which treat of the
short but interesting journey which we undertook in
company.

The journey from Bagdad to Bombay is of course
civilised, and sufficiently well known, but I hope that
the reader will find in the part relating to it some
matter of interest.

In the spelling of place names I have conformed
as well as I could to the code recommended by the
Royal Geographical Society. In the name Bagdad,
however, I have not adopted the " gh," which is
generally used to represent the Arabic " ghain " غ
as in the pronunciation of this name there is none
of the roughness which usually accompanies the
letter, as for instance in غزو " ghazu "—a raid ;
where, however, the English " gr " would more truly
represent the sound.

With regard to the title of the volume, I hold with

Mr. Wilfred Blunt and others that the imaginary line drawn from the Gulf of Akaba to the mouth of the Shat el Arab is not the true boundary of Arabia to the north. On the contrary all the desert east and west of the Euphrates, which is inhabited by Arabic-speaking nomads, is as purely Arabian as Hadramaut or Yemen. The Euphrates is indeed held by the Turks, and Bagdad and Busrah are Turkish towns; but the surroundings are none the less Arabian, and the journey from the gates of Aleppo to where the brown stream of water rolls out to the sea at the head of the Persian Gulf, is step for step " through Turkish Arabia."

More than a due amount of ill-health sapped my energy and compelled me to abandon plans which, if carried out, would have materially added to the interest of the journey. Such were the routes to Meshed Ali, and that of the newly opened river Karun. May it be my lot to traverse them some day in future.

H. S. COWPER.

Hawkshead,

    October, 1893.

CONTENTS.

CHAPTER I.

FROM LONDON TO SCANDERUN.

PAGE

My Plans—Preparations—The Levinge Bed—Cholera and Influenza—Departure on the *Orient*—In the Mediterranean—Cairo—The Khedive's Tomb—Moolid of Sitti Zeyneb—Leave for Syria—Yafa—Beirut—Approach Scanderun ... ...　1

CHAPTER II.

SCANDERUN TO ALEPPO.

Scanderun—A Syrian Hotel—Bad Weather—My Carriage and Four—Beilan—Jaleel—Kara Khan—The Plain of Antioch—Syrian Ladies—El Amk—Hammam—Khan Afrin—The Greek Consul and my Bedroom Companions—A Chilly Start—Reach Aleppo... ...　24

CHAPTER III.

IN ALEPPO.

The Azizia Hotel—An Earthquake in Bed—Jaleel—Turkish Cookery and Arak-drinking—The British Consulate—Routes to Bagdad—Servants in Aleppo—The Story of a Student—Decide on Euphrates Route—The Takht-i-rawan—Delays and Vexations—Preparations and Provisions—More Troubles—I Buy a Bishop's Coach—Teskerehs and Passports ... ...　47

CHAPTER IV.

SOMETHING ABOUT ALEPPO.

History—The English Factory—Description—Dimensions—Walls and Gates—Interior of the City—Streets and

PAGE

Houses—Bazaars—Mosques—The Citadel—My Visit
to it—Khan al Wezir—Heraldry—Suburbs—Ceme-
teries—Wells—Sheikhu Bekr—Mixed Population in
Aleppo—Politeness in Aleppo—Slumbering Fanaticism
—Costume—Climate—The Aleppo Button—Street
Life   68

CHAPTER V.

ON THE ROAD.

Make a Start—Bakhshish—Jebrin, a Beehive Village—
Cruelty to Caravan Animals—Sabbakh, a Salt Lake
—Arrive at Deir Hafr—The Khan—My Zabtieh's
Yarns—Fleas—My Takht-i-rawan—Order of March
—My Attendants—A Ferocious Lizard—Bedawi
Sheep Stealers—First Sight of the Euphrates—The
Anazeh Camp—Meskineh—Balis—Skeikh Ghana—
Abu Hureira and Kalah Jaber—We Meet my Men's
Uncle--Turkish Police—Leben Butter and Dates   ...   115

CHAPTER VI.

CONTINUATION OF JOURNEY.

Anazeh Arabs on the March—The Haudaj—Costume and
Arms—We Sight Rakka—Arabs on Inflated Skins—
A Mudir Effendi—A Howling Durwish—Unwelcome
Visitors—Bathe in a Backwater of the River with bad
Results—Camp in Robber Infested District—Reach
Deir—The Khan—Description of the Town—Its
Poverty—Its Agriculture—" Cherrids "—Arab Popu-
lation—Its Political Importance—An " Englishman "
Turns up—His Account of Himself, and his Pecu-
liarities — Woodfuel Fishing — Altone again — The
Terrible Desert—Visitors—Arrival of the Pasha—
Haji Mohammed's " stiff Stomach "—Hardihood of
Muleteers   147

CHAPTER VII.

DEIR TO ANAH.

Leave Deir—Mirage—The Castle of Rahaba—" Rehoboth
on the River "—Mayedin—More Cats—Pass Salahieh
—A Sand Storm—The Mules Cry—Cold Weather
—Wandering Durwishes — A Bedawi Escort—Abu

PAGE

Kemal—An Ingenious Beetle—An Extensive Ruin—
El Geim—An Anazeh Ghazu—I am Asked if I would
like my Throat Cut—Danger on the Road—Fall Ill—
Desert Wadys—Wild Pig—Pass Rhowa—And Reach
Anah   177

CHAPTER VIII.

FROM ANAH TO BAGDAD.

Anah, an Arabian Sydenham—Illness—Wady Fahmin—A
Dispute—Haditha—Wady Bagdadi—A Thunderstorm
—Arrive at Hit—A Dirty Town—The Bitumen Springs
—Ramazan — My Men Catch Two Thieves — Kalah
Ramadi — In Touch with Civilisation — Get Among
Marshes—A Mule Sticks Fast—An Accident to the
Takht—The Euphrates Ferry—Kofa Boats—Feluja
—A Night March—Lose our Way—The Babylonian
Canals—Akar Kuf—Sight Bagdad—More Bogs and
Difficulties—Arrive at Bagdad...   206

CHAPTER IX.

BAGDAD.

Situation of the City—Advantages of the Site—Its Walls
and Gates now Destroyed—Old Guns at the Barracks—
The Streets—Houses—Architecture of the British Residency—Serdabs—Coffee-houses — Bazaars — Shopping
in Bagdad—Money—Mosques—The Tomb of Lady
Zubeidah...   241

CHAPTER X.

MORE ABOUT BAGDAD.

Kazemein—A Bagdad Tramway—The Mosque of Imam
Musa el Kazem—Its Gilded Domes and Minarets—
Population of Bagdad—The Plague—The Arabs—The
Jews—Benjamin of Tudela's Account of the Jews—
The Armenians—Christian Churches—Climate—Ex-
ports — Present Condition—Ramazan — A Bagdad
Hotel—The Date Mark—Yusuf Antika—Prepara-
tions for a Journey to Babylon and Kerbela   263

PAGE

CHAPTER XI.

HISTORICAL SKETCH OF BAGDAD.

Foundation—The Early Caliphs—The Buyides—Degradation of the Caliphate—First appearance of the Turks
—Removal of Bagdad to the East Bank of the Tigris
—Ghenghis Khan—Al Mostanser—Hulagu—End of
the Abbasides—Persecution of the Christians—Tamerlane—Shah Ismael—Capture of the City by Amurath   286

CHAPTER XII.

BAGDAD TO BABYLON AND HILLAH.

Leave Bagdad—Khan Ez Zad—Khan Mahmudieh—Pilgrim
Caravan—The Kajaweh—Khan Birunus—Reach Khan
Haswa—Architecture of Persian Khans—Sleep in a
Coffee-house and are Worried by Fleas—Leave Khan
Haswa—Sight the Ruins of Babylon—Meet Two
Americans—Reach the Ruins—Babel—The Mujelibe
and Kasr—Amran ibn Ali—Leave for Hillah—Knock
Down an Old Woman   301

CHAPTER XIII.

HILLAH AND BIRRIS NIMRUD.

Arrive at Hillah—Sayyid Hassan—Hillah—Start for Birris
Nimrud—Remarkable Appearance—We meet Russian
Travellers—The Birris—Description of the Ruin—
View from the Top—Benjamin of Tudela's Account—
Theories about its Origin—Borsippa—Nebbi Ibrahim
and Arab Traditions—Disappearance of my Umbrella
—The Power of the British Name—Return to Hillah
—Visitors—Yusuf's Horse Makes some Pressed Beef
—Road to Musseyib—Owlad Muslim—Arrive at
Musseyib...   329

CHAPTER XIV.

THE PILGRIM ROAD.

Musseyib—The Pilgrim Traffic—A Storm in the Night—
Meshed Husein—Kerbela Stones—Fanaticism—The
Martyrdom of Husein—Corpse Caravans—Kerbela—
We Visit a Nawab—Martyrdom from Mosquitos—

PAGE

An Awkward Incident—We part with our Host—
Leave Kerbela—Musseyib again—A Hot Ride—Khan
Iscanderieh—Reach Bagdad—Rumours of an Arab
Revolt on the Tigris—The Barber of Bagdad—The
Hunchback of El Busrah—Go on Board a Tigris
Steamer   357

CHAPTER XV.

BAGDAD TO BUSRAH.

Steam Traffic on the Tigris—A River Steamer—Chaldæan
Sailors — Itinerary — Leave Bagdad — Ctesiphon—
Arab Tribes—Paucity of Traffic—Flooded-out Arabs
—Amara—Sabæans—Deck Scenes—The Revolt of
Sheikh Saud ibn Munshid—Ezra's Tomb—A Scare—
Kornah—The Shat el Arab—The Port of Busrah—
Visit the Town—Escape of Prisoners—Historical
Notes—Health of Busrah   385

CHAPTER XVI.

THE PERSIAN GULF.

Mohammerah — Native Craft — Fisheries — Shusteris—
History—Fow—Crossing the Bar—The Persian Gulf
—Piracy—Climate—Winds—Health — Bushire — A
Persian Whiteley—Description of the Town—" Killi "
—Reach Bahrein—Submarine Fresh Water—The
Pearl Fishery   420

CHAPTER XVII.

THE PERSIAN GULF.

Mountains round Lingah—Lingah—Water Supply—The
Straits of Hormuz—Situation of Bunder Abbas—The
Town—Tremendous Heat—The Island of Hormuz—
Its History—Old Accounts—Beautiful Scenery—Fly-
ing-fish and Sea-snakes—Turtles and Black-fish—
Bombay—Leave for England—Wild Weather in the
Red Sea   441

APPENDIX.

I.—Itinerary of the road between Scanderun and Bagdad.

II.—Khans on the pilgrim road to Kerbela, and on the road to Hillah, with the distances from Bagdad in hours.

III.—Abu Nawas, the jester of Harun al Rashid.

IV.—An Astrolabe purchased at Bagdad.

V.—Chaotic weights and measures.

VI.—Balbi's journey from Bagdad to Busrah.

VII.—Hamilton's account of Busrah.

VIII.—Romance of the Persian Gulf.

LIST OF ILLUSTRATIONS.

	PAGE
A Persian Astrolabe (two views)	*Frontispiece.*
Cairo	11
Itinerant Musicians on road to Aleppo	24
Palms and Pyramids...	48
Sheikhu Bekr...	68
Anazeh Camels at Meskineh	115
Beilan	139
Anazeh Arabs on the March	147
The Haudaj	148
My Camp	158
Khan at Deir	162
Anazeh Horseman	177
Arab Ghazu	196
My Takht-i-rawan	206
Nahura at Anah	207
Mosque of Zacharias, Aleppo	229
Gateway of Citadel, Aleppo	243
A Bagdadi	271
Bagdad and the Bridge of Boats, from the West Bank ...	299
Khan Ez Zad...	301

PAGE

On the Waters of Babylon 321

Persian Pilgrims at Musseyib 357

My Host and his Son 365

A Street in Bagdad 386

A Ballum of Busrah 414

A Tower of Silence, Bombay... 458

MAPS.

The Author's route from Scanderun to the Persian Gulf   At end.

The Persian Gulf ... ... To face p. 428

THROUGH TURKISH ARABIA.

CHAPTER I.

FROM LONDON TO SCANDERUN.

My Plans—Routes—Preparations—The Levinge Bed—Cholera and
Influenza—Departure on the *Orient*—In the Mediterranean—
Cairo—The Khedive's Tomb—Moolid of Sitti Zeyneb—Leave
for Syria—Yafa—Beirut—Approach Scanderun.

AFTER spending a most delightful winter in 1889-
90 on the Nile and at Cairo, I formed, on returning
home, a resolution to visit the other great Arabic-
speaking town of the East, namely Bagdad, the
romantic Baldac of the early writers, for I conceived,
until some study of books had undeceived me, that
there should be much of interest to see, and many
things to be learnt from a visit to a city which
formerly played so great a part in the Eastern world.

On coming to examine the writings of modern
travellers, I found I was mistaken; I gathered that

B

the interest of Bagdad lay only in its historical past, and in its romantic connection with the " Alf Lailah wa Lailah"; I found also that access to it was not easy, unless the journey was made all the way by sea, a voyage of about five weeks. The more instructive, though infinitely more difficult route was to land at one of the Syrian ports and make one's way overland to Bagdad, a form of travelling of which I had had hitherto no experience, and which my study of books of travel showed me is beset, to say the least of it, by difficulties to the inexperienced.

However, I had made my resolution, and I decided to abide by it. I had no idea of going out by sea to Busrah, as of all forms of travelling, that by sea is the most conducive of several evils, of which I will adduce but three, biliousness, fat, and ignorance. It remained, therefore, for me to consider the overland routes; of these several presented themselves, of which it is necessary at this stage to specify only two, namely, that by Beirut and Damascus, and that by Scanderun or Alexandretta, and Aleppo.

The first of these routes did not engage my attention long. Although approach to Bagdad this way might be made to embrace the celebrated ruins of Palmyra, it entailed a weary camel ride of a dozen days at least across the desert from that place to the Euphrates, an experience I had no stomach for, although as events turned out, I bettered myself but slightly by adopting another line. I decided accordingly to make my way in the first instance to Aleppo, and to leave it to fate to decide there, whether I should proceed by the direct Euphrates road or make my way to Mosul and the Tigris.

My preparations and outfit were not extensive. I bought a small tent, 8ft. by 6ft., from Messrs. Piggott; in shape it is square, having two upright poles and a ridge pole; when packed the whole weighs only sixty-five pounds, and the three poles being socketed take up but little room. I also invested in a strange appliance known to the initiated as a Levinge bed. This consists of a linen sack, to the open end of which is attached a long mosquito curtain, which is ingeniously contrived, so that it can be expanded into quite a respectable little room by means of bent canes. The entrance into the sack is by means of a neck of linen, the mouth of which can be closed by tapes. It is best for the user to pull this neck into the sack after him, and to lie upon it, and then tolerable security against all things creeping and flying is

obtained.   The top of the muslin curtain is attached
to a nail or rafter.   Although this is a most admirable invention for use in the khans and caravanseras
of the East, where all kinds of vermin swarm, and
one to which I must confess that I am indebted for
many a night's sound sleep, which would have been
otherwise unattainable ; it must be allowed, that
when sleeping in the khan of a wild, and perhaps
fanatical Arab village, with no lock to your door, it is
anything but a pleasant sensation to feel yourself so
carefully tied up in a bag that extrication in an emergency would be almost impossible in less than a
minute or two.   In times of peace it requires the
greatest presence of mind, foresight, and clear-
headedness, to get safely out of a Levinge bed without tearing it.   Under the influence of "alarums and
excursions" I tremble to think what would be the
fate of the luckless occupant.

A roll of bedding, a waterproof sheet, two big
leather bags containing my personal effects, and a
" Gladstone " completed my baggage. When all
things were ready, I went down to the country to
spend Christmas, hoping to leave England on
January 14th, on the Orient liner, *Orizaba*.   The
cholera, which, during the summer, had been pretty

bad at Damascus and Aleppo, and had more than once threatened to overturn my plans, seemed, according to the papers, to have so materially decreased, as to form no obstacle to the expedition. But the " best laid schemes o' mice an' men gang aft agley," and I managed at a Christmas ball to contract a bad attack of the epidemic of influenza, which was then at its worst. In consequence of this, I was compelled to transfer my passage to the ss. *Orient*, sailing on the 29th of the same month. I had decided to go in the first place to Cairo, where I hoped to ascertain which Syrian ports were in quarantine, and also to get definite information about the various lines of steamers plying along the Syrian coast.

Accordingly, on the 29th January, I found myself installed in a cabin on board the good ship, *Orient*. The influenza was raging as bad as ever, and each passenger looked nervously at his or her cabin companions to ascertain if they showed any symptoms of that fell disease. My mates were a young Irish solicitor, and an aged naval bo'sun, the latter being in a state of utter collapse due to drink, grief on parting with his family, and a recent attack of the " blight." He seemed to be only half through the latter, or, indeed, any of his ailments, and passed the whole of the first afternoon, between sleeping on the sofa, drinking, and begging my pardon. When not thus engaged, he was in floods of tears. As he kept the port closed, and had all his meals in the cabin, we did not find him an edifying companion. To our relief he moved elsewhere on the following day.

The steamers of the Orient line, are, as every one knows, among the finest that run between England and Australia, and although a comparatively new line, are in no way inferior to the P. and O. liners in accommodation and fittings. The *Orient* herself was built in accordance with the requirements of the Admiralty for ships, which, in case of war, may be turned into armed cruisers, and is, in fact, the oldest of the eight Orient liners, which are over 5,000 tons burden. Her horse-power is 6,000, and her registered tonnage 5,400. She carries four masts, and two funnels, and draws 27 feet. And her saloon, music, smoking, rooms and boudoir, though, perhaps, not quite so gorgeous as those on some of the later ships of the same line, are the acme of comfort. The upper or hurricane deck forms a charming promenade, and is the arena of many a well-fought match of ship's cricket.

The Bay of Biscay behaved itself better than we expected. A slight roll and an hour's fog being the sum total of its offences; and by the time we were across, we found ourselves in such a genial climate, although it was the beginning of February, that we were enabled to sit on deck till ten or eleven at night without any inconvenience from cold. Capes St. Vincent and Sagres had the effect of massing all the amateur photographers whom we had on board to obtain pictures of these fine headlands, the last of which especially looks very well from the sea, with its bold cliff and caves, and the white signalling station perched on the top. The *Orient* passed within half-a-mile. In front a beautiful lateen-rigged fishing boat, with a big eye painted on its bows, danced gaily on the green waves. The Portuguese fishermen held up for us to see an enormous fish, apparently a big eel. A glorious breezy day was it at Gibraltar; so I went ashore and visited the Spanish town, the dirt of which one pardons for the sake of its picturesqueness. On leaving we had a gale astern, which was very pleasant in that quarter, but would have been uncomfortable in the extreme had it been ahead.

On February 7th we woke to find ourselves steam-

ing slowly into Naples Bay. Above the town hung a
thick haze, for the weather was warm, and over
Vesuvius lay heavy white clouds. At half-past seven
the anchor was down, and our olfactory nerves were
immediately assailed by a stench fit to wake the
dead.

At Naples we lost a lot of our nicest passengers.
This is the rule at sea. Warm friendships rapidly
formed are of necessity put an end to, perhaps for
ever. Yet at sea there are, I think, perhaps, more
lasting friendships made (in proportion) than on
land. I and a party of three had a long day ashore,
visiting and renewing our acquaintance with the
wonders of Pompeii, the Museum and the Opera.

Stromboli proved clear. In the Straits of Messina
the Italian coast was bathed in sunshine, while the
Sicilian side lay in haze and gloom. Of Etna we
caught but a fleeting glimpse at sunset, as most
of the mountain was buried in dense black clouds.
On February 11th we were at Port Said, and the
following morning at three a.m. we got to Ismailia,
where, at the hotel, I found my old Nile cook acting
as servant. On the evening of the 12th I was
installed at the Hotel du Nil, at Cairo.

As soon as I had arrived, I commenced making

inquiries at the tourist and steamer agencies as to
the condition of cholera in Syria, and to ascertain
what ports were in quarantine. The replies I got
were most conflicting. No one seemed to know
anything. I was told that neither the Khedivial nor
the Austrian Lloyd steamers were touching at
Alexandretta, and with regard to the Messageries
line, Messrs. Cook & Sons assured me they did so,
while on the opposite side of the road Messrs. Gaze
informed me they did not. In despair I wired to my
friend, Mr. R. J. Moss, of Alexandria, whose information on such subjects I knew by experience to
be only equalled in excellence by his courtesy and
hospitality, and promptly received a reply that the
Messageries steamers were touching at Alexandretta.
Accordingly I booked my passage by the *Senegal*,
leaving Alexandria on the 21st. Of cholera I could
ascertain nothing. Tourist agencies, officials, and
everyone professed profound ignorance on the subject. It was still supposed to linger, but probably
in very diminished form, and at this time of year was
not likely to increase. It was useless to attempt
to gain any decisive information on the matter, so
I dismissed it from my head, resolving to take
matters as they came.

Whilst I was at Cairo, I was fortunate enough to witness a very curious and characteristic ceremony. Mohammed Tewfik Pasha, Khedive of Egypt, had died on January 7th, and, in accordance with the custom of the country, it was necessary to distribute to the poor a meal of bread and meat for a period of forty days. I heard that this ceremony was only to take place for one or two days more, and accordingly, on February 14th, I set off on foot in the direction of the tombs of the Caliphs, where his late Highness was interred. A small but persistent donkey-boy attached himself to me, and I retained him as a guide. After struggling over the mounds on the east of the city to the tombs of the Caliphs, we arrived at a point behind the beautiful tomb mosque of Kait Bey. As we approached, we were joined by knots of very poor people, who were making their way to the rendezvous to receive the accustomed bounty. A few carriages also passed, carrying Europeans, or well-to-do natives, who were on their way to visit the tomb. On arriving, I found a tawdry structure, of great ugliness, to the door of which my boy led me. About this doorway, which was draped with curtains, stood several soldiers, who with great solemnity bowed me within. Entering, I

CAIRO.

found myself in a covered passage, hung above with cloth, and on the right-hand side of which were chairs, occupied by several individuals, mostly English. On the left-hand side of the passage, opposite the chairs, was a door, which was the entrance to the late Khedive's tomb. An official courteously handed me to one of the chairs, and I was immediately served with an excellent cigarette and a cup of Turkish coffee. After a short pause, I was requested to sign my name in a book kept for that purpose, and having had large slippers placed over my boots, I was ushered into the building, in which was situated the tomb itself. This consisted of two chambers; in the centre of the first, plain and ugly, was a large tomb-like structure, covered with flowers, near which sat some men, engaged in a dolorous chant—I presume from the Koran. From this room I passed to the left into the second room, in which was the usual sort of royal tomb, floridly painted in the Turkish style, and this I was permitted to pass round and inspect. The few ornaments in the room were vulgar and commonplace, and there were hung about a few glass chandeliers. In this room there were also three men chanting.

After seeing this, I passed out, and having gone

round the building I came to the door of a large
court, in which the food was being given away. The
proceedings here were under the charge of soldiers
and several effendis. Entering, an extraordinary
spectacle met my view. Filling the large yard sat,
in messes of about ten each, an enormous crowd
of expectant Arabs. I reckoned them up and calculated there must have been about a thousand. The
left-hand side was occupied entirely by men, while
on the right were only women. Many children were
also present, and all were evidently, from their
wretched clothing, of a very poor class. To begin
with, bread and vegetables were served in large metal
dishes, one to each mess, and these rapidly disappeared. In many cases a second ration was served,
and then the meat (mutton and buffalo beef) was
dispensed in like manner. The meat was cut into
rough chunks, one for each person, and it was almost
affecting to see the way the thin brown hands of
the children clutched at their allotted shares. Yet
all was orderly, and there was no gluttony, no thieving
or pilfering from one's neighbour's trencher, nor
squabbling of any kind; although a good deal of
noise naturally accompanied the proceedings. A
good many English people witnessed the dole, as

this was the last but two of the prescribed forty days.

I finished my day by a walk to the top of Gebel Mokattam, accompanied by my boy, whose importunity that I should go the next day on his donkey to what he called the " buttonified " forest (petrified forest), I resisted.

Another characteristic sight during my few days in Cairo was the festival or moolid of the Seyyideh or Sitti Zeyneb the daughter of Ali and Fatmeh. and granddaughter of Mohammed. The mosque is in the south-west quarter of the city near the Khaleeg, and at the end of the Derb el Gamameez. I rode there after dinner on the same day I had visited the Khedive's tomb. As we approached the quarter, the streets, which near the Mousky were dark and empty, began to assume a more lively aspect, being lit up and hung across with little red flags. Shops were open, especially those at which extraordinary coloured sweetmeats were exhibited. Although sold at a religious festival, these sweets are mostly in the shape of human figures, thus breaking the Koranic edict about depicting life : and the designs of some are even coarse in the extreme. At the mosque itself the crowd was fairly intense, and the slight glimpse we could get through the door revealed nothing but a glare of light. Inside, however, zikrs were being performed. In the streets in the immediate vicinity the illuminations were extra bright, and besides the flags, the streets were hung with festoons of immense glass coloured balls, and quantities of glass chandeliers. Following the road from here, we passed through the Bab Sitti Zeyneb, and just outside, the scene was more merry if not more brilliant than that near the mosque. On each side of the road, which is here among the mounds, were numerous booths and tents erected. First there were swings and roundabouts of various construction, exactly similar to those seen at English fairs. Next on a mastabah (or raised platform) sat two musicians, twanging their rude string instruments as they chanted an Arab romance. Beyond this was a large booth like a circus, which, indeed, as far as we could make out from the backs of our donkeys, it was. On the opposite side of the road stood a tent, in which we could see a dancing girl performing, and close to it another in which there was a male dancer. A little below on the left we came on a man habited in a Roman helmet and with a sword in his hand, whose coarse buffoonery and antics had attracted a large crowd, and was creating much merriment. Beyond this again were numerous small booths and tents, each with some sort of amusement or spectacle. Before every one of these shows stood a throng of people (among whom were many Copts), and the road was so crowded that we had difficulty in forcing our way back. The swings and roundabouts were all going, and although the noise here was considerable, the utmost good temper and order prevailed. As we returned home we passed a house where a zikr was being performed, and stopping to watch it through the open window, the owner of the house came out and presented us with little cups of a hot spiced beverage of which I do not know the name.

On the 20th I went on board the Messageries ss. *Senegal* at Alexandria, where I was given to understand I was the only saloon passenger. It was accordingly anything but a pleasant surprise to find my cabin occupied by two or three dozen other saloon passengers in the shape of Alexandria mosquitos, who worried me so abominably the first two nights, that my forehead assumed the appearance of a phrenological bust. After this I erected my Levinge bed over my berth, and so avoided the bites of these little pests.

The *Senegal*, though advertised to leave on the 20th, did not leave till the following morning, and in the forenoon we were off the Rosetta lighthouse. The water here, off the "*Bouches du Nil*," is turbid and brown; and Egypt, as seen from the sea here, is but a streak of yellow sand devoid of beauty, picturesqueness, or interest. It turned out that there were a few passengers, none of whom, however, were English. Among them, though, there was an Italian, who informed me he was also bound for Scanderun and Aleppo. He also assured me that there was a *diligence* running between those places, a thing I had never heard of before. As besides our national tongues we both spoke only a little French and Arabic, our conversation, carried on in a mixture of those languages, was very limited. At Port Said we remained ten hours coaling and lading, and when we got away, we had on board a pack of American tourists bound for Yafa and Jerusalem.

We arrived at Yafa early on the morning of the 23rd, and after breakfast I went ashore with my Italian fellow-traveller, who, however, got into a scare as soon as he was ashore, and fearing the sea would get rough and difficulties arise about re-embarking, at once returned on board. It must be allowed that the

C

entrance to the celebrated harbour is sufficiently
alarming in calm weather. A semi-circular breakwater
of natural rock projects in front of the quay, and the
entrance to the calm water is made through a passage
about twice the width of a broad rowing-boat. In
rough weather, it is easy to see, that it must be very
dangerous. Although my companion had impressed
upon me that the town was " mauvais pays " and not
worth seeing, I found it extremely interesting. The
first thing coming from Egypt that strikes you is the
difference in costume. Very much less of European
dress is seen than at the Egyptian ports ; although,
to my horror, I noticed that one of my boatmen had
his nether extremities encased in Highlander's trews.
These and a kaffieh formed a most fetching costume.
This last head-dress with the camel's hair band is
seen on many of the inhabitants, for it is not, as is so
commonly supposed, peculiar to the desert Arabs, but
is extremely common among all classes both in Syria
and Turkish Arabia. The very tall and exceedingly
ugly tarbush is also very much seen at the Syrian
ports and Aleppo ; it is chiefly confined to native
Christians.

With one of my boatmen I took a stroll through
the town, and to the orange groves behind. The

streets are narrow, crowded, and chiefly vaulted over ;
above the vaults are dwelling houses. Most of the
streets, especially those near the harbour, are extremely
steep ; and the little " suks," or markets, are full of
characteristic Syrian scenes. A charming walk in an
orange grove behind the town and a peep into the
plain of Sharon completed my excursion. In one of
the streets I met an Englishman, who, I was delighted
to find, was coming on to the *Senegal, en route* for
Constantinople.

Both Messrs. Cook and Gaze have agencies and
hotels here, as this is the starting point for the Holy
Land trip. That of Gaze is pleasantly situated near
the orange groves at the back of the town, and seems
a comfortable and clean little establishment. Here
I first became acquainted with the Turkish currency,
mostly of base metal. I have no idea how many de·
nominations there are, and I should think no foreigner
has ever mastered the subject ; I was in Turkey
altogether three months, and I doubt if I ever made
any transaction in which I was not, in a greater or less
degree, fleeced. Even the native shop-keepers, when
purchases are made, often find it necessary to work
out a little sum on paper, and then it is generally
found impossible, in spite of the great number of de-

nominations, to make up the exact sum, or to give the
right amount of change.

Yafa from the sea is something like a small bit of
Malta.   All round it lies yellow sand, but in the distance, a range of blue mountains adds beauty to the
landscape.

In consequence of the final removal of quarantine,
notice of which we only received at Yafa, we found
ourselves early on the following morning (the 24th)
at Beirut.   The Bay of Beirut is in some ways as
beautiful as the Bay of Naples, which it immediately
brings to memory.   From the sea, the mighty
Lebanon towers in rear of the town, with noble
snow-clad Sanin as its lord.   In front, and to the
right upon the sea, lies the busy and commercial
(although Eastern) town.   For the inhabitants of
Beirut are, for some reason, far more go ahead than
most Orientals, and only a small portion of the town
retains its old Eastern character.   This is, of course,
chiefly due to its being the port of Palestine, in
constant touch with Mediterranean commerce and
civilisation, and situated at the end of the Damascus
road.   There is a very good little hotel kept by a
native, at which I obtained an excellent lunch.
Close by this I sat down in a little rocky bay to

smoke a pipe, and hardly had I done so, when two native women passed me, and having squatted down on the rocks close in front, proceeded to gesticulate to me wildly. At first I could not make out what they were after, until one came up to me, and, as far as I could understand, gave me notice to quit, as they wished to bathe. Upon this I prudently arose and decamped. After my lunch, I passed through the narrow and crowded bazaars, and emerged into the open space on the east side, known as Canon Place. Just here at a street corner I came on a man lying in the road on his back, clad only in a pair of patchwork breeches and a ragged waistcoat, which was thrown back, exposing his chest and abdomen. Just below his ribs there were several deep incisions in his flesh, through which were secured pieces of thread or wool. From his eyes, nose, mouth, and ears quantities of blood were emerging, and his head lay in a pool of clotted blood. At short intervals he groaned and struggled, throwing about his arms and legs as if he were dying, or at least in great suffering. A small crowd had collected, and were placidly gazing at this unpleasant spectacle, but the shopkeepers in the immediate vicinity and the majority of bystanders took absolutely no notice. A young man was walking about among the people round, and collecting alms in a tarbush, in which, when he came to me, I noticed there were a few small coins. I put a small alms in, and then enquired of a bystander what was wrong; but my knowledge of Arabic was insufficient to understand his reply. In answer to another query, I was told he was not a durwish. The spectacle was most disgusting and painful, and I do not know now whether the man was in some fearful sort of fit, or if the whole affair was some humbugging durwish trick. At any rate it was a queer sight in civilised Beirut. I left the place and passed up the Damascus road, which, close to the town, has weavers' shops on either side; and getting clear of the houses, I had a delightful walk out to the Pines, at the back of the town, whence I got a charming view of the Lebanon range, and the bay between the town and the Nahr el kelb. On my return he of the fits had disappeared.

Beirut is full of missionary institutions and schools, which, if they have not improved Muslim morals, are successfully elbowing from the town the final traces of picturesque Eastern life. A staple trade at the present day seems to be woodwork, and shops are seen full of locally made furniture of French style.

We were at Tripoli early the following morning, and at Latakia the same afternoon ; but our stay at these ports was too short to allow of my landing. We were informed that we should be at Scanderun early the next day. Beside myself, there were for this port the daughter of a late English Consul at Aleppo, a French family, and two native Christian ladies, all bound for Aleppo. The Italian before mentioned, for some unknown reason, changed his mind at the last minute, and instead of landing at Scanderun, remained on board and proceeded to Constantinople.

ITINERANT MUSICIANS ON ROAD TO ALEPPO.

CHAPTER II.

SCANDERUN TO ALEPPO.

Scanderun—A Syrian Hotel—Bad Weather—My Carriage and Four
—Beilan—Jaleel—Kara Khan—The Plain of Antioch—Syrian
Ladies—El Amk—Hammam—Khan Afrin—The Greek Consul
and my Bedroom Companions—A Chilly Start—Reach Aleppo.

WILLEBRAND OF OLDENBURG, who travelled in the
thirteenth century, states that Alexandretta, now
called by the inhabitants of the country Iscanderun
or Scanderun, was founded by Alexander the Macedonian for his steed Bucephalus. Legend or fact
as this may be, there is no doubt that this Alexandria
the Little owes its origin in some way to Alexander
the Great. Rochette, in his " Hist. des Colonies
Grecques," tells us also that the place was fortified
by the kings of Armenia, but no fortifications exist at
the present day.* The town is situated within an
extensive bay, the gulf of modern Scanderun and

---

* Ainsworth: " Personal Narrative of the Euphrates Expedition,"
1888.

ancient Issus, and upon a marshy and unhealthy plain, to the east of which rise the noble Amanus hills and other mountains, the modern names of which are given so differently in maps that it would be only confusing to reproduce them.

Another traveller, Moryson, who journeyed here in 1596, describes Scanderun "a poor village built all of straw and dirt, excepting the houses of some Christian factors, built of timber and clay. . . The pestilent air of this place is the cause that they [the factors] dare not make any stay there. For this village is compassed on three sides with a fenny plain, and the fourth side lies upon the sea. On the east side beyond the fen is a most high mountain, which keeps the sight of the sun from Scanderoon ; and, being full of bogs, infects the fenny plain with ill vapours. On the other side towards the north (as I remember) in the way leading to Constantinople, the like fenny plain lies, and the mountains, though more remote, do bare the sight of the sun, and the boggie earth yielding ill vapours makes Scanderun infamous for the death of Christians."* Van Egmont, who travelled in 1759, tells us that there are scarcely sixty houses

* See " Natural History of Aleppo," by Alex. Russell, M.D., 1794 (2 vols.).

at this place, but that the English house makes a " handsome appearance, and adjoining to it are some stately warehouses built by the Turkey company." Also, "most of the inhabitants of Alexandretta are Greeks; it is likewise the residence of a Greek bishop; the fathers of the Holy Land have also a convent here."*

On the morning of the 26th we found ourselves lying in the beautiful bay of Scanderun. There had been heavy rains in the night, and over the mighty Taurus range to the north hung black and angry clouds. Beneath these, high up on the slopes, the glistening snow told us that summer was not yet come, and that on the journey to Aleppo we might look out for a taste of winter. From the sea this noble amphitheatre of hills, with the little town standing out on the plain in the foreground, forms a very beautiful picture. About ten o'clock we made our way ashore, and after a little judicious bakh-shishing to get our baggage through the customs, I found myself at the tail of a long line of red-booted porters, making my way down a road, ankle deep in

* "Travels through part of Europe, Asia Minor, etc.," by the Hon. Mr. Van Egmont, Envoy Extraordinary from the United Provinces to the Court of Naples; and Mr. John Heyman, Professor of the Oriental Languages in the University of Leyden. Lond., 1759.

mire and water, to the office of Messrs. Belfante &
Catoni, the latter of which gentlemen acts as British
Vice-Consul. He was, however away, but Mr. Belfante showed me every courtesy in helping me with
arrangements for the trip to Aleppo. I found it was
true that a good carriage road now existed, and
although I had wished to ride, the almost incessant
deluges of cold rain at last decided me to engage a
covered carriage, which was to be ready early the
following morning for me, with four horses. After
lunch with Mr. Belfante, I proceeded to engage a
room for the night at a wretched place called a hotel,
kept by a Levantine. In so far as the rooms contained
bed, chairs, and furniture, and that the worthy host
would undertake to cater for you, it might deserve
this name. But the approach to it was through a
quagmire of filth, the bedroom was dirty and anything
but sweet, and the bed had evidently been occupied
for no inconsiderable time without any change of
linen being considered necessary. Fortunately I had
my own bedding with me. The old man in charge, on
being interrogated, told me his extortionate charges,
but as I could not make my bed in the foul puddles
outside, and as Mr. Belfante, being in bachelor
quarters, had no accommodation to offer me, I was

compelled to submit after giving the old gentleman
my mind.   Luckily, Mr. Belfante's hospitality saved
me from having to eat my meals in this "hostelry,"
for which I was truly thankful.   The afternoon was
spent rambling about in the wet, buying provisions
for the journey, and seeing the sights.   Truly, Scanderun does not seem to have improved since the days
of Moryson and honest Van Egmont.   I failed to see
a solitary building which had a "handsome appearance," while the unpaved or half-paved roads, swimming in water and mud, made locomotion among the
dirty bazaars and shops anything but pleasant.   I
found, however, one or two fairly good Greek shops,
and in company with my landlord, I laid in for the
journey a couple of chickens, half an oke of biscuits,
a tin of kippered herrings, and cheese, bread, and
oranges.   The red embroidered cloaks and legging-
boots of the peasants, and the strings of shaggy
Turcoman camels, which are continually entering the
town from Aleppo, are certainly of some interest to
the newly-arrived stranger ; but apart from this, there
is nothing to relieve the absolute dead-aliveness of
Scanderun.   Mr. Belfante is, however, of opinion that
it is much more healthy now than formerly.   After
dining with that gentleman, I wandered back to the

"hotel," picking my way through puddles by the illumination of incessant lightning, and to the music caused by the croaking of millions of frogs in the surrounding marsh. I was already so heartily sick of Scanderun that I longed to be out of it.

After a fearfully wet night, I was all ready for a start at nine o'clock, the hour appointed for the carriage to be ready. It was, however, still drenching with rain at intervals, and although I sent word to the proprietor of the posting establishment that I was ready, no carriage turned up. At last, in despair, I sallied forth to find the stables and hurry up the people myself. The proprietor was a stout, well-to-do Armenian, dressed more or less in European clothes, who the day previously had been particularly anxious that I should engage his carriage, not only to Aleppo, but through to Bagdad, a proposal at which I naturally stared, as I knew there was no regular road. He stated, however, that he had done it before, and Mr. Belfante corroborated him. This person I at length found, and having accompanied him to his stables, I made them get the carriage out and put to the horses before my eyes. The carriage was a "ramshackle" old coupé brougham which had seen better days at Beirut or Alexandria. The wheels and other portions had been renewed in unpainted wood, probably at Aleppo, and most of the paint had been knocked off the original portions. It had no appearance of having been cleaned for several years, and presented such a shaky appearance that I felt great apprehensions whether it would ever get through the journey. The nags, four willing-looking little chestnuts, were then brought out and harnessed in abreast, like a Roman quadriga, in which operation the rotten harness had to be supplemented by a great deal of rope and string; and lastly, my baggage, consisting of three big bags, a tent, and roll of bedding, was brought forth and secured as best it might, behind, in front, and inside the vehicle. At ten o'clock all was in readiness, and having settled my account with my host and bidden farewell to Mr. Belfante, I took my seat inside and was whisked off in a halo of mud towards the mountains.

And now I felt fairly started upon my journey; Scanderun, a Mediterranean port, filthy and uncivilised as it seemed, was the connecting-link between Western civilisation and the semi-barbarism of modern Asia. Behind me lay the blue Mediterranean, with steamers and smiling coast; before me

Asiatic Turkey, with its caravan tracks and its squalid cities. I confess that, as I pulled up the rickety window against an icy shower, and, coiling myself up in the corner, lit my faithful pipe, some doubts entered my mind as to the rationality of thus undertaking alone an overland journey of a month's duration with all its troubles and vexations, with no more definite object in view than that of seeing the country.

The road first wound over a wide expanse of marsh, from whence arose a most foul miasmatic odour, which made me close the other window and puff my pipe with redoubled energy. Fortunately, the weather was improving, and although it was damp and chilly, the sun was struggling through the clouds and warming in some small degree the moist air of the plain. Still, on the mountains before us lay the heavy clouds and the snow.

Over the plain the road is in very good order ; it is about six yards wide, and as one ascends the mountain, it is cut out of the rock—here apparently a sort of mudstone. Evidently the caravan traffic over it is very heavy, and there is plenty in this way to see, for as many as sixty or seventy camels are often passed in ten minutes. Besides the camels, caravans

of mules and asses, jangling with bells, and flocks of
sheep with wild-looking shepherds, came trudging
down the steep road, many evidently suffering from
the biting cold of the wind. Amongst them I
noticed one man with a long spear. After winding
about on the mountain side, we reached a curious
village called Beilan. This place, which is used as
a sort of health resort by the inhabitants of
Scanderun, and even of Aleppo in the hot season,
is placed near the top of the pass, at an elevation
of 1,580 feet above sea level. It is built on the
hill-side on both sides of a steep ravine, and the
houses being situated one above the other, the
village looks like a sort of big wasps' nest. Coming
from Egypt or Palestine, one is struck by the fact
that all the houses are roofed with tiles, showing, as I
had already experienced, that there is here a heavy
rainfall. It is said to be the modern representative of
the Pinara of Pliny and Ptolemy, and the Erana of
Cicero.*

At Beilan we halted to give the horses a rest, and
my Jehu took the opportunity of refreshing himself
with coffee and bread at the shop of a friend. I
went to see if I could obtain a drink of milk, as I

*Ainsworth : " Personal Narrative of the Euphrates Expedition."

had foolishly forgotten to bring with me any form of drink; but the people seemed sulky and unsociable, and not inclined to get anything for me. After the pleasant politeness of the Egyptians, this was a change for the worse, but the people of Beilan are probably a mixed lot, of half Turcoman, half Syrian blood, with few of the good qualities of the civil and intelligent Arab. There is said to be a fairly good khan here, but I did not see it. In the gorge over which the town is built, are to be seen the remains of what are considered Roman aqueducts and forti-fications.

While we were in Beilan another carriage from Scanderun drove in, containing the French family. On the box was a quaint-looking native boy in a tarbush, and as his thin clothes formed but a poor protection against the piercing cold, I made room for him in my coupé. He was delighted at this turn matters had taken, and proceeded with the utmost *sang froid* to interrogate me in French as to my name, occupation, and the object of my journey. Having satisfied his curiosity, I ascertained from him that his name was Jaleel, his age fourteen, that he was of Syrian Catholic family, but that his mother's father was a Frenchman. He had been at

D

Beirut for some time, partly for health, and partly for education, and was now returning to Aleppo to his family. Being unable to hire a carriage for himself, he had arranged to pay three mejidies and to occupy a spare seat on one of the carriages. Jaleel could talk French, Italian, Arabic and a good deal of Turkish and Armenian, and was well able to take care of himself. He also told me that he had two brothers in Egypt, one a soldier at Aswan. As he sat opposite me sucking an orange, and blinking at me with his great round dark eyes, he looked the very incarnation of Oriental happy-go-luckiness. I instructed him to address me only in Arabic, and we soon settled down to be very good travelling companions.

Soon after, we reached the summit of the pass, over 2,000 feet above sea level, and just as we were commencing the descent, a wild storm of hail burst over the mountain. The road on this side is less steep than on the Beilan side, and we made our way down at a fair speed. The slopes are in places beautifully wooded. At three o'clock we were clear of the mountains and on a level with the plain of Antioch. An hour and a quarter later we drove through a funny little village built of log and stone huts, and situated on the edge of a brawling stream. There were two khans, from which the village takes its name of Kara Khan, situated about one hundred and fifty yards apart. The French carriage drove into the first, and we went on and entered the further. Kara Khan is situated at the base of the mountains which we had just passed over, and which were still wrapped in clouds. In front lies the plain (El Amk) and the marsh, which extends north-east from the lake of Antioch. Away to the north and north-east beyond the plain I could discern a low range of purple mountains.

The khan to which I went consisted of a square courtyard, surrounded by a low wall, with a dirty stable on one side and a wooden building of two stories on the side facing the road. The lower part of this edifice consisted of two rooms, inhabited by the khanji, between which was a passage through for caravans to enter the khan from the road. Above, approached by an external stair, were two or three rooms for the reception of travellers. The one I was shown into was, of course, entirely without furniture, but it was clean and comfortable. A piece of matting to spread my bed upon and a charcoal brazier to warm the room were brought by

D 2

the khanji. At my request he also produced some excellent " leben," a preparation of milk somewhat like buttermilk. A chair and a little table standing on a sort of balcony outside my room were brought in, and I ate my first dinner in comparative comfort. This khan, and that at Afrin, where I stopped the ensuing night, are the ones at which, since the carriage road has been formed, carriages always stop, both going and coming; and in consequence they have been somewhat improved, and are better in accommodation than the khan on the ordinary caravan route.

While I was lighting my solitary pipe after my early dinner, a man came to tell me that the carriage containing Miss B—— and the two native ladies had arrived and that they were installed at the other khan. Miss B—— had stayed with Mrs. Catoni at Scanderun, and in consequence of the stormy morn ing had left a couple of hours later than myself. I walked up the road to pay my respects and to enquire how the ladies had stood the fatigues of the day; after passing through a large dark room, where a crowd of muleteers and carriage drivers were sitting over a brazier, I was shown into a room very inferior to mine where the three ladies were. All (Miss B——

included, in the absence of chairs), were seated on
cushions, taking their after-dinner coffee. I was introduced to the two Syrian ladies, and to the best of
my ability entered into conversation with them.
The elder was rather a striking-looking old woman,
whose face was a mass of wrinkles, and who, during
the whole of my call, puffed fervently at a big narjileh. The younger (I believe her married daughter)
was a fine-looking young woman, who, as far as the
face went, might have been English : her features
were regular and pleasant, and her eyes large and
expressive; her figure, however, was somewhat stout
and clumsy. Both ladies were dressed in a sort of
mongrel European costume, which probably at Aleppo
was considered the height of European fashion among
the Syrian Christians. The husbands of both were
at Bagdad, or Busrah, and they were returning from
a journey to those places, having both gone and returned by sea. They were much astonished to hear
that I intended to make my way to Bagdad by land,
and could not understand why I should choose the
overland route instead of the long but comfortable
journey by sea; it only puzzled them more when I
told them, through Miss B——, that I wished to
"farraj" (see the country), and they decided that I

must be very rich, and also, no doubt, though they were too polite to say so, very mad to undertake such a journey for pleasure. According to their account Bagdad and Busrah were paradises, where there were dates " Keteer, keteer, keteer " (very abundant), and where English was the chief language, and river steamers, manned by English tars, were as plentiful as on the Thames at Charing Cross. Being in the East I was permitted to light my pipe, and with a cup of excellent coffee I spent quite a pleasant hour in chat. When I turned out to return to my khan I found it had got about among all the muleteers below that I was the Englishman for Bagdad, and a dead set was made on me by one or two to engage their services for the route. One of these accompanied me down the road, and was particularly vehement in his demands that he and I should perform the journey " Sawa sawa " (together), at the same time placing his two fore-fingers side by side to represent master and servant, a very common sign used by Arabs when they wish to be engaged.

After a fair night's sleep, I was making my toilet preparatory to a start, when I saw from the window the carriage with the French family pass, and immediately after Jaleel burst in upon me, with a

lump of bread in his hand, and breathlessly informed
me that it was time to start. Although I had not
invited him into my carriage for this day, he knew
what was comfortable, and had evidently made up
his mind to accompany me. I paid my bill for the
night, two francs, and after a tiny cup of coffee, off
we went at seven, munching bread and hard-boiled
eggs by way of breakfast. It was a beautiful
morning, and in the sunlight the plain of Antioch
looked extremely beautiful; it seemed by a rough
calculation to be about eight miles wide, and perhaps
twelve long. At half-past eight we stopped at a
village among the marshes, which are here crossed
by a causeway and several long and carefully constructed bridges, close to which were big mounds,
apparently old sites. Concerning this, Van Egmont in
1759 writes: " It is called Amurat's bridge, in honour
of a grand vizier of that name, who built it. This
causeway begins with a bridge of three arches, and
is continued to the length of half an hour in a series
of low small arches, very difficult for horses, being
originally ill built, and kept in no repair."

This causeway, built by Amurath, or Murad, crossed
the Kara Su or Black Water, which here flowed
through the marsh. Ainsworth in 1835 navigated this

river up to this point in a boat. The mound close by he notices by the name of Gul Bashi. At present the bridges seem to cross nothing but the swampy plain, owing, no doubt, to the river having changed its course, and also to its being much lost in the marsh. It is said that these works replace similar ones of Roman date, and probably part of this earlier construction still remains. Great quantities of water fowl could be seen on the surrounding plain, amongst which the lubberly pelicans were to be distinguished by their size.* At this halt all the carriages which had left Scanderun the previous day, were together, no less than four in number. There was a carriage containing the Greek Consul at Aleppo, somebody Effendi, and a cawass; the carriage of Miss B—— and the Syrian ladies; that of the French family, and my own. Each carriage had also its driver and an attendant sprite, who

---

* "Tavernier mentions two rivers between Alexandretta and Aleppo; over the first of which, he says, is a bridge very long and strongly built (Book II., Cap. I.). But in this he is mistaken, the bridge and causeway being laid over the bog above mentioned. The other he calls Afrora, and says, that upon rains it is not fordable: this is the Efrin, the fording of which does frequently so much damage to the bales of goods, that our Turkey merchants, some years ago, proposed to build a bridge over it at their own expense; but the Turk would not consent, and so the design was dropped."—From the Geographic dissertation in Edward Spelman's "Expedition of Cyrus," 1740.

acted as groom, so that we were quite a formidable caravan.

Soon after leaving, we got clear of the plain, and ascended gentle grassy elevations on its eastern side. At half-past ten we arrived at Hammam Khan, where we all stopped to rest the horses for an hour, and to have a substantial meal. While preparations for this were in progress, and a small table and a variety of boxes to sit on being brought out, I ran to the top of an adjacent hill of very considerable size. Close to the khan is a curious hot sulphur spring, where I obtained for the first time that day a refreshing (though steamy and odoriferous) wash. After this I joined the very merry luncheon party, representing the English, French, Syrian, Greek, and Turkish nations. Roast fowls, keubbes (a sort of hard sausage in shape like an egg), bread, butter, cheese, oranges, and dates were dispatched like lightning. The party had about three knives and forks among them.

From Hammam we had a long and weary ride over a tableland; at half-past three we came to a small stream, probably an affluent of the river Afrin. After another hour and a half the road became very bad; in fact, for some time we were simply driving through a ploughed field, although a good road was being constructed. The plain still continued on our left, but away to the right was a low range of limestone hills. At six o'clock we drove into the courtyard of the Khan Afrin, situated on the right bank of the small river of that name.* The khan was much like Kara Khan, but much dirtier. At the top of a rickety wooden stair were three rooms for the accommodation of travellers. One was taken by the French family, the next by Miss B—— and the Syrian ladies, and I found myself in No. 3 with the Greek Consul, the Effendi, the cawass, and an aged and very dirty Turk, whom we had seen several times in the day jogging along on an old white pony, equipped with blue goggles and a big umbrella. The Consul and his friend had, with true Oriental politeness, spread their beds upon the raised platform for that purpose, which was provided with matting, leaving me to " pig" on the dirty floor alongside. At the kind invitation of the ladies, my hosts of Kara Khan, I joined them at dinner, and hearing that an early start would be made, I returned to my room to turn in. The appearance of my room did not look favourable to

* Ancient Arceuthus.—Ainsworth.

slumber. The Effendi indeed had retired, but upon the edge of the platform, in front of the brazier, sat the Greek Consul in his big fur coat, with a wild and excited eye, and hair upstanding, " like quills upon the fretful porcupine." He had evidently been dining not wisely but too well, and the room savoured of arak. He greeted me with three words of English, which he launched at me in a husky roar the moment I entered : " Are you sleepy? " He then told me in French that we had to start at two in the morning, and suggested that as it was not worth while to go to bed, I should accompany him to a neighbouring apartment where he had refreshments. He then retired, followed by the cawass, and I sat over the brazier smoking my pipe. Soon after, one of the carriage attendants entered, and beckoned me to follow him, at the same time making signs that there was plenty to drink close by. I, however, turned in, and after various interruptions caused by the noise of the revellers, and a cat which persisted in forcing open the door and letting in an icy blast, I got to sleep. I did not seem to have been asleep ten minutes when I was aroused by the Consul and his friend making preparations to depart, and

the cawass shaking my foot gently to awake me.
It was only two o'clock, and I regarded this as a
practical joke on the part of the revellers, and
turning over, snored lustily. Immediately after,
however, the sprite who attended my horses as
groom, came, and having also pulled my toe, began to
remove my baggage. This brought me out of bed in
a "jiffy," and I found that in very truth everyone was
making preparations to start. Although aroused
thus early, the start was not made till a quarter
past four, and all the intermediate time we had to
wait about watching the baggage packed leisurely
on to the carriages, in a most bitterly cold wind.
At last we were off in the darkness, and when the
day dawned about six, I found myself so numbed
with cold that I got out and walked up a long
hill to get warm. Although I ran up this hill in
a great ulster, I found it difficult to restore
circulation. The grass was covered with hoarfrost,
and the pools of water were solid ice. The road
passes on the left of Jebel Simon, and from the
high ground a beautiful view was obtained of the
snow-covered hills we had passed on our first day's
journey. The road now led on to a high desolate

desert-like tract of country. At half-past nine we stopped at a wayside khan for coffee, where three wild-looking wandering minstrels gave us a performance. This so wrought upon the feelings of the carriage attendants, who owing to last night's arak had been skylarking and bear-fighting at every stoppage, that they formed a ring and hopped about wildly to the music. Leaving this, we passed a conical mound, perhaps eighty feet high ; and in less than an hour the village of Tel-el-Fadr, with a large cemetery. The character of this place is very like an Egyptian village. From here the appearance of the country became more truly desert, and at a quarter to two we caught sight of the citadel and minarets of Aleppo, lying in a hollow. Close to the road at the entrance to the town are two or three well-built houses in European style. The traveller arriving is deluded by these into the belief that he is entering a town into which the light of European civilisation has come, but in this he is mistaken, as with the exception of these the whole town is purely Oriental. These houses were built by one or two enterprising pashas, and are now empty or tenanted only by workmen.

Soon after passing these we rattled over a bridge,
over the Kuweik Su or Aleppo river, and winding
round to the left entered the suburb of Azizia,
where I took up mine inn at the hostelry called,
somewhat pretentiously, the Azizia Hotel.

CHAPTER III.

IN ALEPPO.

The Azizia Hotel—An Earthquake in Bed—Jaleel—Turkish Cookery
and Arak-drinking—The British Consulate—Routes to Bagdad
—Servants in Aleppo—The Story of a Student—Decide on
Euphrates Route—The Takht-i-rawan—Delays and Vexations—
Preparations and Provisions—More Troubles—I Buy a Bishop's
Coach—Teskerehs and Passports.

OWING to all sorts of unseen delays, it was eleven
days before I left Aleppo, and during that time I was
able to ramble about the town. I therefore postpone
such descriptive notes of the place as I was enabled
to make, to a later chapter, and devote a page or two
to my own proceedings during my stay, as it will
afford intending travellers in the East some idea of
the difficulties that beset one's path when once off
the tourist track in Syria.

The so-called Azizia Hotel, at which I took up my
quarters, is situated in a new suburb of that name on
the west of the town. It was kept by an Armenian,
and, although it hardly merited the European name
of hotel, was very comfortable. From the street one
entered straight into a little courtyard, in which was

PALMS AND PYRAMIDS.

a well, and having to the right and left a building of two stories. The upper stories, which had only just been added, were occupied by about four bedrooms each, all of which opened straight on to a balcony which ran in front of them, and to which access was gained by a staircase from the courtyard. Beneath were the offices of the house, and the only public room, the dining apartment. When I arrived the rooms were all occupied but one, very clean and nice, but which had not yet been furnished; and on my arrival the landlord at once sent to the town and obtained a neat iron bedstead and other requisites to make me comfortable. The bed was erected while I was busy in the town, and I retired early, tired with my long journey, and anticipating a good night in the comfortable-looking little bed and clean bedding. Unfortunately, Carabet, the Armenian handy-man of the house, had in his haste or in his ignorance, omitted to secure at their ends the iron laths which sustain both the bedding and the sleeper; so that I awoke some time in the night feeling very uncomfortable, and curled up like a prawn, with my feet and my head at their proper elevation, but with the rest of my body deposited on the floor; the centre of the bed, owing to the giving way of the laths, and to the

E

force known as the attraction of gravity, having softly and silently subsided. When I ascertained the real cause, pleased at finding that I had not just arrived in time for a repetition of the 1822 Aleppo earthquake, I strengthened my situation to the best of my ability, and passed a fairly comfortable night. The other occupants of the Azizia were mostly Turks; there were two army doctors (one a Greek), and several tarbushed Effendis, one or two of whom were in business in Aleppo. Lunch and dinner I took with these gentlemen downstairs. Breakfast was a moveable feast, partaken in the bedroom. When Carabet asked me what I would have for breakfast, I replied, "Coffee, bread, butter and eggs." Now boiled eggs are a dish unknown in the Armenian " cuisine," so that the five eggs which were brought, I discovered, when I scalped them, were still in their interiors in that liquid form in which they had first seen the light of day. I remonstrated afterwards with the worthy Carabet, but he had never before boiled an egg, and my remonstrances were ineffective. The Arabs have a peculiar term for smoking; they talk of drinking their pipe (shrub narjileh), or tobacco: so, although I object strongly to cold liquid eggs, I drank my five eggs to breakfast every morning in Aleppo. I could not possibly have altered Carabet's cooking, unless I had stood over him and his brazier in the courtyard, with a watch in one hand and a drawn sword in the other.

Although I had picked up odds and ends of Arabic two years previously in Egypt, and had taken lessons in colloquial Arabic from a Syrian in London, I found the Aleppo dialect so different, that my slight knowledge of the language was even of less use than I expected. The people in the hotel also, talked almost entirely Turkish and Armenian, so that I was glad when little Jaleel turned up, wishing to engage himself to me as servant to Bagdad. Of course it was out of the question to take a little delicate boy like him for an eight or nine hundred mile journey overland, but I found him very useful during my stay in the town. He was an amusing, bright little chap, full of larkiness and fun, but troublesome on account of his insatiable curiosity and avarice. He would carefully examine my Norfolk jacket and knicker-bockers—a garb, perhaps, never seen before in Aleppo, and then ask, " How much did these cost, Mr. Cowper ? " a question which would be imme-diately followed by, "Will you give me *something*

to remember you by, when you go to Bagdad, Mr.
Cowper?" The idea of Jaleel, with his great black
eyes and shrewd Eastern face, in knickerbockers
and Norfolk jacket and red tarbush was so scream-
ingly funny that, had there been an English tailor
in the town, I should almost have been inclined to
have fitted him out.

Jaleel could also lie—lie with the grace and
facility which can only be found in ingenuous
Eastern boyhood. Once I asked him if he could
read an inscription in ancient Arabic on an old
Saracenic well. Without a moment's hesitation he
scrutinised the writing with an earnest gaze; writing
which was about four hundred years old; and then
gravely informed me that it contained the name of
Sultan Abdul Hamid Khan, the reigning monarch.

Lunch and dinner at the Azizia were respectively
at six and twelve o'clock, Turkish time—a muddling
arrangement for a European, as Turkish time starts
from sunrise, and therefore the meals were a little
earlier every day. The cookery was Turkish, and
very good of its kind, the chief dishes being pilaf,
kubabs, and yoghurt.* Wine was, of course, not

* Pilaf, rice with small portions of meat; kubabs, or kabobs,
meat prepared on skewers; yoghurt, a preparation of sour milk,
called by the Arabs, leben.

drunk at the table, except by myself and the Greek
doctor, but the Effendis often had a little arak
party together just before dinner, at which meal they
would then appear strangely jovial and elated. It
is a question whether their custom of coming
"jolly" to table is not preferable to ours of getting
up "jolly" from it. One young Turk asked me if
I drank arak. I replied, "No; is it not a sort of
wine?" At this he was piously horrified, and
solemnly informed me that it was a bitter, or rather
what we call in England a digestive or stomachic.
The house, being used by Turks of the new school,
boasted table, chairs, knives, forks, and spoons,
though these latter were somewhat scarce. The
table-cloth was the worst feature in the entertainment, as each guest reached across and helped himself indiscriminately from the dish, in doing which
a portion of the helping generally fell on the cloth,
which, as far as I could ascertain, had never been
washed since the opening of the house. I found
the Beys and Effendis courtesy itself, always pressing
me to help myself to each dish first. One or two
of them could speak French.

I made no arrangement as to charges when I went
to the Azizia, and my bill was eight francs a day,

TTA-C*

board and lodging. No doubt if I had made an arrangement it would have been less.

One of the first things I did on arrival was to call on our Consul, Mr. Jago, and to the hospitality and kindness of him and Mrs. Jago I owe much. Mr. Jago, indeed, put me in the way of making my arrangements, and during several pleasant walks we had together, in and about the town, gave me much interesting information concerning the district. The Consulate is a pleasant bungalow-built house close to the Azizia quarter, and standing in a pleasant garden of its own, and there were few days of the eleven I remained in Aleppo when I did not spend a pleasant hour at the Consulate.*

I was pleased to find on my arrival that the cholera, which had been bad at Aleppo, was now at an end. The previous year there had been nine hundred deaths from this cause, and the year before about fourteen hundred. The influenza, which was devastating England when I left, was still lingering in a milder form at Aleppo, and was funnily termed by natives, "Abu Rakab," *i.e.*, the father of the knees, because after an attack the patient feels so weak in

---

* At the Consulate there is a memento of the Euphrates Valley Expedition, in the shape of some old guns dated 1817.

those members. Mr. Jago told me that I was the first European traveller who had arrived in Aleppo for about six months, which shows how completely off the track the town is.* Although there are families of most of the European nationalities resident in Aleppo, England is only represented by the Consul and his family, and the widow and daughter of a late Consul. Most of the Europeans reside in the Azizia suburb, though there is no distinct Frankish quarter.

Mr. Jago took me the first day to call upon an Italian gentleman named Stano, now employed in the Government tobacco regie. Mr. Stano knew well most of the routes between Aleppo and Bagdad, and at once entered into my plans, in the kindest way. He informed me there were three ways of approaching Bagdad :

1. The Euphrates valley route, which is to travel caravan to the river, and then follow the course of the valley down to a point opposite Bagdad, whence that place is reached by a short cut across Al-Jezirah. This route would occupy nineteen to twenty-five days.

2. The route by Birejik, Urfa, Mardin, to Mosul, and thence by kellek (raft) to Bagdad on the Tigris.

---

* In this I do not think he meant to include Europeans connected with Aleppo or the district, such as consuls, merchants, or missionaries.

3. By Birejik to Diarbekr, and thence by kellek to Mosul and Bagdad.

The objections to the two latter routes were, that I should probably experience considerable cold, and in the case of No. 3 there was a mountain pass which might still be snow blocked. This was a serious objection in my case, as I had hardly regained my strength from my severe attack of influenza. There was also the fact that Turkish and Armenian is a good deal spoken on these routes, of neither of which language I knew a word; and it seemed highly improbable a trustworthy interpreter could be obtained in Aleppo. Route No. 1 would be sunshine all the way, and lay chiefly through the desert on the edge of the Euphrates. There would be of course less of interest on this road, and provisions were not too plentiful. There would be some risk of being plundered by the desert Arabs, but neither Mr. Jago nor Mr. Stano had ever heard of an English traveller being meddled with here. It would, however, be necessary to take one or two mounted police (zabtiehs) with me.

Armed with this preliminary information, I proceeded to make enquiries for a servant, and, if possible, for one who could speak English. The first

individual who presented himself was a dark, sharp-
looking Greek, dressed in European clothes, and
speaking English fluently. He told me that he had
been one of Cook's dragomans at Damascus, and
knew all the strings of Oriental travel. Asked if he
had any references, he said they were all at Damascus.
He complained of not having anything to do here, but
could not explain why he did not return to the dominions of "Cook-ery." He informed me that Mr. and
Mrs. Jago both knew him well, which I discovered
afterwards was a barefaced lie. He also said that
the Greek Consul would be willing to recommend
him. He said further that he would wire to Cook's
agent at Damascus to send him a recommendation,
and would call on me the following day. He did not
keep his appointment, and I learned that he had
arrived at Aleppo some time previously without any
papers, and had been thrown into prison by the
authorities. Of course, this might mean nothing in
Turkey, and indeed from this "durance vile" the
Greek Consul had rescued him. But the man could
not show a solitary reference, and in fact report was
against him. So that it seemed better to travel
servantless than with such an uncertain personage.
The next applicant was a young Armenian named

Boghos, with deep-set, cunning eyes. He acknowledged he could not cook at all (the only thing which
I really required a servant for), but could speak a few
words (about a dozen) of English, which he had
picked up in some American mission station. He
said " If you please, take me with you." Asked how
much he wanted for three weeks' journey, he answered,
" One napoleon." The Greek had named ten pounds,
which I had considered too much ; but one napoleon
staggered me. I afterwards learnt that he was a very
bad character, and in fact it would hardly be safe to
travel with him. After him came a professional cook
who spoke Arabic and Turkish only, and whose
countenance was so forbidding that I sent him away
without questioning him.

After this the Greek military doctor stopping at
the hotel told me he knew of an excellent man, who
could talk English perfectly, and had an excellent
character. He turned up on the 6th, and although
not particularly clever-looking, he had an honest
face. He knew a good smattering of English, and
said he could cook a little. I offered him a pound
a week for the journey, and two pounds for his ex-
penses home from Bagdad, if he wished to return.

He seemed quite inclined to accept this offer ; but unfortunately his patron entered the court at this minute, and called him to speak to him. After this he told me he could not take less than ten pounds, saying that his present occupation would be lost. I ascertained afterwards that this same occupation was about thirty shillings a month. At the same time it seemed there was a story to this young man. It appeared he was brought up in Constantinople as a student, and then this medical Effendi, being hard up, offered, in consideration for a bakhshish of about fifteen pounds, to obtain for him some good position. The young man then sold all his worldly possessions for this purpose, and his patron, for some reason, failed in his promise. The Effendi could not, or would not, pay back to him the money, and was therefore much in his debt. This story, if true, might have inclined me to offer him a better wage, but on the other hand, he did not know much about cooking, and in fact was not a servant at all. As it seemed hopeless to obtain a reliable man, I afterwards sent word to him that I would increase my offer ; and received a reply that his present employer had advanced his wages to three pounds a month, and he had decided not to go with me; so that, at any rate, I was the means of bettering the unfortunate youth's position somewhat.

Later on, after I had decided upon the Euphrates route, and was making active preparations for a start, I was one day making my way into the town, when I was accosted by a tall, handsome, good-natured-looking man, who said he wished to be my servant. He spoke very little French, and no English, but I felt sure from his face that he was an excellent man. I told him to accompany me to the Consulate, and on our way we met Mr. Jago, who, it turned out, knew the man well, and gave him an excellent character. He had, it seems, been cook at the French Consulate. It transpired that his idea was that I would take him to England with me, and he would become an English soldier. I am bound to confess that he would not have disgraced the uniform of a guardsman, but I had to inform him that I could not possibly retain his services after I left Bagdad. I offered him, however, a pound a week for so long as I retained him, and I promised to give him whatever was necessary for his return to Aleppo, the sum to be settled at the Consulate at Bagdad. Although much chopfallen at the fall of his " castle in the air," he expressed his willingness to come at these terms, and arranged to meet me at the Consulate to sign a contract the next day. I felt pleased at the turn matters had taken, as I felt that the man's physique and transparent honesty were worth more than all the English of the others. I was, however, doomed to disappointment. George, for such was his name, turned up punctually next day, and after the contract was read to him, he hummed and hawed, and began to make difficulties. When asked to sign, he said that the sum offered was insufficient. He, like the others, wanted ten pounds. This was intolerable. It was evident, as is often the case, that a ring had been formed against me, and no one was to go under this sum. George, honest as he was, had been got at, and so refused my offer, which was a very good wage—servants in these parts being very cheap. I was not going to be done in this way, so George was dismissed. The fact was, that it had got all over the town that the Englishman who had arrived, and was going to Bagdad, was not travelling for business, but for pleasure. I was accordingly set down as "immensely wealthy." If I had given out that I was an English merchant it would no doubt have been different. Live and learn.

One other individual turned up just before I left, and offered to go for six pounds. I had, however, by that time decided to travel without servants, and I refused to negotiate with him.

I have mentioned that I had decided upon the Euphrates route; many things led me to this decision. The finer climate, the fact that on this road Arabic, of which I knew a smattering, was the only language required, whereas, travelling without an interpreter as I was, I should find considerable difficulty among the Turkish and Armenian speaking peoples on the other roads. There was also the consideration that this was the quickest route, and a week or so delay might let me in for a dose of the monsoon in the Gulf and Indian Ocean on my way back to Europe. Lastly, I developed a painful boil on my side, which threatened to overthrow my plans altogether, as it rendered me quite unfit to undertake a long and arduous ride. In this difficulty Mr. Jago came to my rescue, by suggesting that I should travel in a takht-i-rawan, a sort of litter, chiefly used by Persians, which consists of a square wooden box with doors and windows on each side, and a pair of shafts before and behind, by means of which the "takht" is carried by two strong mules or horses. I could sit or lie in this, on a bed or mattress, at my ease, and I need feel fear neither of wet nor heat of the sun.

Mr. Stano had kindly undertaken to inquire for me about mules and muleteers for the road. The rate of hire of caravan animals depends on the current price of fodder in the country. Through Mr. Stano's agency I eventually hired six mules and a takht-i-rawan from Aleppo to Bagdad for ninety mejidies or Turkish dollars. The caravan was to have three attendants, the muleteer (Turkish, katterji; Arabic, mukari) and two grooms or akams. I eventually purchased the takht, and the hire was five mejidies less. On the 4th Mr. Stano informed me of these arrangements, and introduced me to a Greek, a doctor in the army who had been waiting some time at Aleppo in order to get mules for Bagdad; he informed me that a caravan, or caravans, were preparing to start on the 7th, 8th, or 9th, and suggested we should start together on that date. On the 7th I heard that a Pasha had arrived at the hotel from Constantinople, and the doctor sent me word that we should all start together on the 9th. I saw no signs of Pashas at the hotel, except a tent folded in the court, and the addition at our festive board of a strange gaunt young man in uniform (in appearance exactly

like Barnum's skeleton dude), who, report said, was
the Pasha's son-in-law and aide-de-camp. The following day I went into the bazaar with a Mr. Yusuf,
a Chaldæan Christian merchant of Aleppo, who had
been resident in Bagdad, and having been at one
time employed in one of the houses of the English
merchants there, knew a smattering of English. He
had a great deal to do with the Bagdad caravan
trade, and was of great use to me in my preparations.
He was a fine-looking man, dressed in European
fashion; and was singularly un-Oriental in appearance.
He took me to various shops, and I purchased a large
stock of necessaries for the journey, such as candles,
tinned meats, chocolate and coffee, rice, a sackful of
hard biscuits in the shape of rings called " kak,"
ghee or clarified butter, sugar, biscuits, brandy (in case
of illness), and a large stock of figs and dates; in addition to these I bought a lot of pots and pans for
cooking, a large leathern water-bottle called a "mattara," and an enormous saddle-bag for carrying all the
provisions. This last, which was furnished with lock
and key, I purchased from Mr. Yusuf himself.
When all these articles were piled in a stack in my
room I felt quite a man of property, and I realised
for the first time that I was going into the desert.

The same afternoon Jaleel came to me and said that
the Pasha did not start till Saturday, the 12th. On
hearing this I was at first inclined to order my mules
to make a start the following day, but on the advice
of Mr. Jago and Mr. Stano, I decided to ascertain if
they would really start on that date, and if so to wait.
I felt that in some ways it would be better travelling
alone, but, on the other hand, the escort of a Pasha
was not to be despised. The next day my mukari
and akams came and asked for a present, as they
were not starting on the appointed day. This was
simply a try on, and when I refused they departed
quite happy.

On the 10th my difficulties again increased, and
things assumed yet another phase. First I ascertained that the Pasha was really not starting that
week, so I at once sent word to my men to be
ready the following day. Immediately after arose a
trouble about my takht; I had seen and approved
one, a strongly-made and roomy construction, that
I had ascertained by experiment I could lie at full
length in. It now transpired that the one they were
going to send me in was a different one. I instantly
demanded to see it, and was shown into a yard,
where, leaning against a wall, was a wretched,

F

rickety old contrivance, with windows and doors loose, and much smaller than the one I had seen. I immediately denounced the affair as a swindle, and told Yusuf that unless they were prepared to send me with the one originally agreed on, I would not go at all, and the money I had paid in advance must be at once returned. The explanation seemed to be this. The good takht I had seen belonged to the Patriarch of one of the native Christian churches at Mosul. The worthy prelate had travelled in it to Aleppo, and it was left there for sale. When I had entered into negotiations with Yusuf he had found a muleteer who was willing to buy it, and when he had taken me to Bagdad, to try to dispose of it there, where he would probably make a profit, as they are much used on the pilgrim road to Kerbela. This muleteer, however, Yusuf knew to be a disreputable character, so he went to another man who owned the inferior takht, and omitted to inform me of the change. I then enquired if I could not buy the better one, and Yusuf succeeded in purchasing it for me for the sum of four napoleons, which the reader must admit was a cheap price to pay for a bishop's private carriage.

Through Mr. Jago I had obtained various documents necessary for travel. First the teskereh,* or Turkish passport, a formidable-looking paper, setting forth the route I proposed taking, and sealed with six different seals. Secondly, a buyuruldi, or general introduction, which no doubt would have been very useful in travelling through a thickly-populated country, but which down the Euphrates wasted its "sweetness on the desert air," as there was hardly anyone but the Anazeh Bedawis to be introduced to, and these sons of the desert neither cared about letters of introduction, nor indeed could have read them if produced ; and lastly a teskereh of smaller dimensions than the other, permitting me to carry a revolver. Armed with these I was ready for a start.

* Properly, " tethkireh."

SKEIKHU BEKR.

CHAPTER IV.

SOMETHING ABOUT ALEPPO.

History—The English Factory—Description—Dimensions—Walls and Gates—Interior of the City—Streets and Houses—Bazaars —Mosques—The Citadel—My visit to It—Khan el Wezir— Heraldry — Suburbs—Cemeteries — Wells — Sheikhu Bekr — Mixed Population of Aleppo—Politeness in Aleppo—Slumbering Fanaticism—Costume—Climate—The Aleppo Button— Street Life.

THE Aleppines have a tradition of their own about the origin of the name of their town. The story runs that Abraham on his way to Canaan remained some time at the hill, which is now their citadel. Within its walls still stand the fragments of a mosque sacred to his memory. It is said that at certain hours of the day the patriarch distributed milk to the assembled villagers of the neighbouring country. These people collected at the foot of the hill, and the word was passed about "Ibrahim halab," "Abraham has milked;" or "Ibrahim halab

as shahba," " Abraham has milked his dappled cow."
Hence came, they say, the name Haleb, which we
have long Anglicised into Aleppo.

Aleppo has been identified with ancient Berœa,
supposed to have been originated by Seleucus
Nicator, the founder of Antioch, and Seleucia near
Babylon. The apostate Emperor Julian in his fatal
campaign against the Persians in the fourth century
halted here on his way from Antioch. In 611 the
Sassanian Khosru II., marching from Hierapolis,
seized and burnt the town, although he failed
to reduce the citadel. In 636 the town was besieged by the Mohammedans under Abu Obeidah,
and Khalid " the sword of God." By some
accounts the resistance was brief. According to
others the garrison sustained a loss of three
thousand men, but still held out. At last, after a
siege of several months, it was taken by a curious
stratagem. An Arab giant called Dames supported
several of his comrades on his shoulders, and by this
means an entrance was forced into the citadel, the
guard slain, and the gates opened to the besiegers.
It afterwards became a capital of Hamdanide
Sultans. In the tenth century it fell into the
hands of the Byzantines, but it again showed its

strength, and was not taken. In 1114 it was destroyed by one of those fearful earthquakes which have repeatedly laid it in ruins. Ten years later it was besieged by the crusaders under Baldwin, but a sudden rise in the river flooded the investing camp, and the besiegers had to retreat to Antioch. In 1139 and 1170 it was devastated by other terrible earthquakes, after the last of which it was rebuilt by Nur-ed-din. In 1183 it was captured by the enterprising Salah-ed-din (Saladin), who upon his death bequeathed it to his third son, Malik-ad-daher. In 1260 and 1280 the town was destroyed by the Mongols, and in the first case most of the inhabitants were massacred by their bloodthirsty leader, Hulagu. The first year of the fifteenth century saw the city ransacked by the troops of the victorious Tamerlane, In 1427 the fortifications were re-erected, and in 1516 Selim, Sultan of Turkey, became master of Aleppo and finally overthrew the Mamluk supremacy.

Van Egmont, who travelled in the middle of last century, says: "The city is likewise celebrated for being the birthplace of Tzevi, a poulterer's son, who in the last century pretended to be the true 'Messiah.'"

About the end of the sixteenth century the Levant Company of Turkey merchants opened a factory at Aleppo to trade overland with Persia and India. The French and Venetians had established similar houses at an earlier date. An English consul was then appointed and recognised by the Sultan, and the name of the first consul, who was appointed soon after 1583, was Barret.

During the existence of this factory there was of course a small resident English community at Aleppo. In 1605 they numbered three English families, including the consul, who was at that time a merchant. In 1738 Pococke informs us that the number of houses of English merchants was six or seven, and he remarks that the factory was by that time much decayed, owing to the cheapness and perfection of French manufactures. About 1740 the factory consisted of a consul, ten merchants, a chaplain, chancellor, and physician; and in 1753 the number of houses is given as eight, exclusive of that of the consul. Van Egmont (1759) says: "The English merchants have twenty houses. The consul's salary is £4,000, but he must not carry on any trade." He is probably very wrong as to the number of houses, as in 1772 they were

reduced to four.   The opening of the Cape of Good
Hope route for trade gave the factory its death-
blow.

The officers of the factory in Russell's time were
consul, chaplain, chancellor, and physician, and an
officer named the " chause," * who walked before
the consul, carrying a staff tipped with silver.   There
were also two dragomans and two janissaries.   " In
going to audience, or in similar processions of
form, the honorary druggomans walk two and two
immediately behind the janizaries, who are preceded
by the chause.   The officiating druggomans walk
next; and after them the consul, followed by all
the gentlemen under British protection."

Russell also states that in his own time the
Europeans resident in Aleppo consisted of English,
French, Venetians, and Dutch.   Italian was then
the Frank language.   In 1605 there were five

* Apropos of this title, I subjoin a cutting from the column
which the omniscient Mr. Sala contributes every week to the
Sunday Times: " ' Chouse ' has a very curious origin, of which the
writer in the *Daily News* does not seem to be aware.   It was
formerly spelled ' chiaus,' ' chiauz,' and 'chaous'; various corruptions
of the Turkish word for a messenger, agent, or interpreter.   It
happend that a Turkish commercial in London, in the reign of
James I., swindled some of the merchants trading with Turkey out
of large sums of money ; and from the notoriety of the circumstance
the word came to mean a cheat, and so gave rise to the verb 'to
chouse.'   Ben Jonson mentions a ' chiaus ' in the ' Alchemist.' "

French families and fourteen Venetian families, besides that of the consul. In 1753 the number of French houses in trade was nine, and in 1772 they were reduced to six or seven.*

Van Egmont (who is probably not very reliable) tells a story which is anything but creditable to the English, if it is true. A drunken janissary had murdered the Armenian servant of an English merchant. Van Egmont says the English bribed the judges with 1,000 sequins to hasten his execution, which was eventually carried out by his being strangled by the hand before the castle. "This affair cost the English some thousands of piasters." Van Egmont may or may not have believed this story, and not improbably a certain amount of national jealousy may have induced him to include it in his book; but my own experience has taught me that about one-third of the stories heard at Aleppo are true: and it is highly probable this story is perverted.

In 1822 Aleppo was again visited by a calamitous earthquake, which destroyed part of the city and buried thousands of inhabitants beneath the débris. It is said that one-third of the entire population

* Even as late as 1850 an English traveller reported that there were a few English merchants here.

and two-thirds of the houses were destroyed. Another, but less severe, visitation happened in 1830. In the ensuing year Ibrahim Pasha conquered Syria, and Aleppo remained under Egyptian rule till 1839, when by intervention of England, Syria again became part of the Ottoman Empire, and Aleppo a Turkish town.

Aleppo is placed in the middle of a sterile wilderness, which is, in fact, the northern corner of the great Syrian desert. The town itself is built on a number of small eminences which Russell gives as eight. To the west rise a series of stony undulating hills, through which the traveller from the coast passes before he descends to the town. At their base meanders the river of Aleppo, the Kuweik Su, which is identified with the Chalus of Xenophon, a somewhat sluggish stream wandering through orchards of ash, maple, poplar, and other trees. This stream is never very full, and is at the dry season of the year almost empty, as most of the water is taken for irrigation. Curiously enough, it has no outlet either to the sea or a larger river, but eventually loses itself in a morass some two hours south of Aleppo. The river, and certain small spongy marshes near it in the vicinity of Aleppo, abound with frogs, which in the evenings cause a din almost incredible for such small creatures. On the approach of anyone they cease croaking, and it is difficult to get a view of any of them. Such as I managed to get a sight of did not appear to be larger than the English species. From this noise Russell says the river is reported to have got its name of Kuweik, that word being similar to the frogs' cry. To support this he cites the chorus from "The Frogs" of Aristophanes. The river abounds in fish, and there is one species, which the Europeans at Aleppo told me is the lamprey, to which the natives give the name of "Sammak Inglize," or the English fish. Russell makes mention of this fact, and identifies the fish as *Ophidium mastacembelus*, which is a fish of the order *Apodes*, and quite distinct from the lamprey. Russell was so good a naturalist, and being physician at the English hospital there, had so many opportunities of verifying his work, that I have small doubt he is correct. The native name is very curious, and was no doubt given because the members of the English factory held it in particular esteem. Now, when our country is only represented by the British Consul, it strikes the traveller as curious to hear of a fish bearing such a name.*

* Since writing the above a Syrian resident in London has assured me that "Al hankliz " is good Arabic for eel, and does not refer to the English nation. The Aleppines slur their words, which has given rise to the error.

On the north and south lies the valley of the little
river, clothed in its orchards. But on the east side
lie a series of somewhat gentle undulations and up-
lands, which stretch far away, even to the Euphrates.
A good deal of this has been brought, in comparatively late years, into cultivation; and, in fact, from
Aleppo to Meskineh the traveller passes through
patchy cultivation almost the whole way. Emerging
into full sight of the city, the stranger coming from
the coast must be struck at once—if he is accustomed to Oriental cities—by the extraordinary
absence of minarets, that feature which lends such
beauty and dignity to most Mohammedan towns of
importance. If Aleppo showed but a proportion of
such beautiful structures as Cairo can boast, a bird's
eye view would have no inconsiderable beauty, in
spite of the barren and plain surroundings. As it
is, one solitary feature gives it nobility, and recalls
to the stranger that he is gazing on one of the
historical cities of the East. This is the precipitous
hill which rises in its midst, bearing the shattered
and crumbling fragments of the fortified citadel.
But these, seen at a distance even, can be recognised as ruins, a condition due to the repeated and
disastrous earthquakes, which have, of course, de-

stroyed the minarets, and by their frequency impressed upon the inhabitants the futility of building many such structures. To the same cause may be attributed the poverty of structural remains of all ages in Aleppo; and, taking into consideration the persistency and destructive character of these visitations, it seems almost a wonder that in Aleppo we find so flourishing and well-to-do a town as it is at the present day.

All authors "agree to differ," both in their accounts of the dimensions of Aleppo and in their statistics as to its population. Dr. Pococke, in 1738, states that, with the suburbs, the circuit cannot be much less than five miles. Dr. Russell declares that the same is about seven miles in circumference, but that the city (*i.e.*, the walled quarters) is only three and a half. Van Egmont, a little earlier, gives the complete circuit as three hours. "Murray's Guide" makes it a little less than Russell. As Van Egmont's three hours can hardly represent less than nine or ten miles, the town must be decreasing if that traveller's statistics are at all correct. But as he states that the population was then generally computed at 300,000, a figure which it probably never reached—and certainly not in his time—it is likely

that his statistics of dimensions are also exaggerated.
With a town that has often been overthrown by
earthquakes and as often rebuilt, it is very difficult
(as there are no ancient plans to consult) to know
what its dimensions may have been at different
periods. The plan given in Dr. Russell's book shows
a considerably smaller place than it is at the present
day, as the suburbs of Azizia, Kittab, and those on
the south had apparently no existence. Azizia is,
indeed, quite new. The plan in Bædeker's "Syria"
shows two suburbs on the south, which seem to me
to be considerably exaggerated. As, however, I only
visited that side of the town once I may easily be in
error here ; but I should be inclined to think that
some of the mounds on this side of the walls represent
suburbs destroyed by some earthquake and never
rebuilt. Although I made a complete circuit of the
town myself on foot, I omitted to note down the
exact time it took me ; but my belief is that the walk
was accomplished in less than three hours. We are
told that the fortifications were re-erected in 1427,
after the destruction of the city by Tamerlane, and
the present walls are probably partly of this date.
Being now both utterly ruinous and in a great
measure built up among the increasing suburbs, they

are not easy to trace; and it is consequently difficult to see the method of their construction. The condition they are in is doubtless due to the destructive earthquakes which have at various times devastated the city. Van Egmont records that in his time they were in a ruinous condition. The wall is strengthened at frequent intervals by towers, and outside has been protected with a ditch of considerable width. The following is a list of the gates mentioned by Russell:

Bab Kinasreen,* sometimes called the prison gate, supposed to have been built by Saif ed Daulah Ebn Hamdan about the end of the tenth century; rebuilt 1244 by Malik an Nasr. This gate is situated at the south-west corner of the walls, and takes its name from leading to the road to Kinisrin, sometimes called Old Aleppo. Kinisrin occupied the site of ancient Chalcis. The remains of this gate can still be examined, and, like the only two others I had an opportunity of seeing, consists of two strong towers with a recess between them, the peculiar feature being that the entrance does not pass through the centre of the building, but opens in the side of the right-hand tower.

* Russell's spelling of the gate names is preserved.

Bab al Makam, called the Damascus gate, begun by Malik Ad Daher and finished by his son Al Aziz. This is the southernmost gate of Aleppo, being a short distance east of the Kinisrin gate, and the wall being thrown forward between them. It is on the same plan as the last. Opposite this gate are large mounds, which seem to be, at any rate partly, artificial débris. On these stands a sheikh's tomb, Sheikh Ali, on which are several curious coats of arms, which will be re-verted to. These mounds block a singular natural ravine that leads directly towards the gate. If it was not for these mounds, which can hardly be all arti-ficial, it would seem that this ravine contained the road of approach, and dictated the position of this gate. It is possible they represent some extramural buildings destroyed by an earthquake. Within this ravine are numerous extraordinary limestone caverns or grottos, some of great length. Many of them are now occupied by silk-weavers. It is very difficult to guess their origin, as they are probably all more or less artificial; they may have been ancient quarries. Bab al Nereeb and Bab al Ahmar, both on the east side; Bab al Hadeed at the north east-corner; Bab al Naser, or the Victorious gate, on the north, re-built by Ad Daher.

Bab al Furruge (Faraj), also called Pharadeese or Al Abara, originally built by Ad Daher. This is on the north-west side, and the present building is a wretched construction. And on the west side the gates called Babs, Jinein (the gardens), and Antaki (or Antioch). On this side of the town there is the best section of wall remaining. There are some seven or eight strong square towers, the third or fourth of which from the north I noticed was sculptured with two lions passant.

All the towers seen here have apparently been much higher, and most of them have heavy machicolations. About the fifth, as far as I could see, for the wall is so built in with modern buildings that it is difficult to trace it, is the Bab Antaki of the same plan as Kinisrin, and having some sculpture and inscriptions. Against the front is built a bazaar, which makes it impossible to examine it in detail. Further south towards Bab Kinisrin the towers are weak and small. Russell also mentions two gates into the northern suburb, by the names of Al Jideida and Al Urbain.

The plan of the city within the walls is almost a square, but the suburbs which surround it give it a very irregular shape. Before proceeding to give some description, I reproduce an extract of Van Egmont's

G

statistics, which, like his other statements, are probably much exaggerated.   He states " that the city is divided into seventy-two wards, twenty-two in the city and fifty in the suburbs.   The whole is computed to contain two hundred and seventy-two mosques, sixty-eight khans, sixty-four bagnios, thirty-seven mills turned by mules, two convents of durweeshes, eight schools, three madhouses, a prison, four soap-houses, eight slaughter-houses, six dyeing-houses, five churches, seventy-seven bazaars, and above five thousand houses."

The general aspect of the interior of the town is extremely substantial for an Oriental city.   The streets are built of excellent freestone, well fashioned, and the masonry fairly well put together.   They are, however, with the exception of some of the bazaars, crooked, and of course narrow, although there are one or two by which a carriage can enter the bazaar.

The roads are mostly fairly well paved, and on the whole moderately clean.   The private houses, of course, present, except in some of the non-Muslim quarters, a plain and uninteresting expanse of wall to the road. A great proportion of them are only one-storied buildings, experience having taught the inhabitants the danger of tall edifices in a town where earth-

quakes seem to be " laid on." Some of them, however, have two stories. As a rule they surround a
somewhat pretty little courtyard, into which the windows of the establishment look. In the case of some of
the older houses, pretty little panels of arabesque are
to be seen over these windows, and over the entrance-
door. Sometimes windows themselves are cut into
geometrical or other tracery in stone, which has a
good effect. In the courtyard there is almost invariably a well.

The roofs are, of course, flat, and upon them the
inhabitants pass a great deal of their time. It is
said that a great part of the town can be passed
over without entering the street, by passing over the
roofs.

To the stranger making a call at a native house,
Muslim or Christian, the mode of procedure is somewhat embarrassing. The door is generally furnished
with a knocker, in many cases now a French importation in the shape of a lady's hand in iron or bronze.
Upon this being applied no one opens the door, as Europeans would expect, but instead a squeaky voice is
heard somewhere in the distance saying " Min "
(Who)—a somewhat awkward query to the traveller
whose Arabic is not of the best.

G 2

There is no European quarter in Aleppo, and consequently there are no European shops. There is, however, one street which is particularly occupied by shops selling Frankish wares, and these are mostly kept by Levantines. There is among them one shop where a good many useful things for a journey, such as tinned provisions, biscuits, and similar things can be obtained.

The bazaars themselves are extensive, and though, compared with Cairo, in every way inferior, yet they are superior to those seen at the present day at the more famous Bagdad. They are as a rule fairly wide, arched or covered over, and the shops (square niches in the wall, in which sits the merchant among his merchandise) are often larger, though less characteristic, than those of Cairo. Manchester cotton and prints are seen everywhere, which ugly, but cheap and serviceable, manufactures are cutting out the beautiful old silks of native make. Of course the silk manufacture is still carried on in Syria, at Aleppo and elsewhere, and beautiful things can be bought; but the industry is sadly on the wane. Separate bazaars or markets are devoted to separate wares; and the curious traveller can inspect markets teeming with wool, cotton, or hides, or tramp through long

alleys hung with festoons of red slippers or silk
kaffiehs. Under the friendly guidance of Mr. Jago,
I had many rambles through these picturesque scenes.
The size of the bazaars is shown by the fact that I
was as much at sea as to my whereabouts in them
at my last ramble as at my first; but whether Van
Egmont's seventy-seven bazaars exist now, or ever
did, I have no means of knowing.

A barber's shop in Aleppo is very characteristic.
A square room is surrounded by a wooden bench,
which is divided by arms into separate seats. This
bench is very high, so that the individual to be oper-
ated on has his feet about twelve inches above the
floor. His face is thus brought out the correct level
for operations. In the centre of the apartment is a
tank, from which the water is taken, which after use
is thrown on to the stone floor. The attendants of
the barber are boys, who are fitted with tall pattens
varying according to their own stature. A small boy
has pattens a foot high, so as to bring him on to the
right level.

Of the mosques of Aleppo I saw nothing but the
exteriors, as it is not customary to allow Europeans to
enter. The great mosque, situated in the west part
of the town, is called the Jamah Zakari, or Amawi,

and is supposed to contain the tomb of Zacharias,* and to replace a Christian church. Its chief feature is a handsome square minaret, divided externally into five stages by string courses; the upper two being enriched with cusped arcades. The remainder of the building is a square court surrounded by colonnades. The mosque is said to have been twice burned down and rebuilt, so that between this and earthquakes it is improbable that much early work remains. The tower, however, which is said to bear the date of 1290, is in fair preservation. Some travellers assert that it is the belfry of St. Zacharias' church itself, which has been incorporated with the Muslim mosque. The church is said to have been built by the Empress Helena. (See Plate.)

There is rather a pretty, though small, mosque on the south side of the citadel opposite the great gateway. It is called Sultanieh, or sometimes by Levantines and Franks, the Cruch or Crouche Mosque. It is now unused, and the doors are blocked up, so that I could not get inside. The front has a very tall pointed arch, in the recess of which is the doorway. To the spectator's left of the door are three tall square recesses, with stalactite work at the top. They are

* Father to John the Baptist.

almost as tall as the great arch, which is in fact the height of the building as it is at present. These recesses each contain a square opening near the ground, and a small pointed window above. On the right of the door are three other similar recesses, which are not, however, close together, like those to the left. An octagonal minaret and two small domes rise above the building.

Both upon the doorway described, and upon one on the north side of the building are coats of arms, which may be blazoned—On a fess a goblet, another in base.

The citadel is by far the most interesting and remarkable place in the town. It is placed rather towards the east of the centre of the walled city, upon the highest ground within the walls. The great mound upon which the ancient fortifications stand is roughly circular, and surrounded by a wide and deep ditch. The circumference, taken at the edge of the ditch, must be close on three-quarters of a mile. The hill or mound itself is about two hundred feet in height, and although continually stated to be artificial, is in all probability only partly so, as Russell states that live rock has been found near the summit. It is not improbable that the citadel occupies part, possibly the whole, of the site of ancient Berœa, and it may be compared to some of the large mounds which stud the great plains of Northern Syria and Mesopotamia. The old Arab authors record a tradition that the hill is supported by two thousand columns, which may be but Oriental romance, or possibly have its origin from the discovery of ancient columns and buildings at the time when it was fortified by the Mohammedan conquerors. Indeed, Dr. Pococke states that he was informed that marble columns were frequently found deep in the earth to the north-east of the citadel. Mr. Jago kindly obtained an order for me to view the place, and accompanied me himself on the occasion of my visit. We made our way to the great entrance on the south, which is by far the finest feature of the whole structure. I noticed that the slope of the mound was strongly faced with masonry, which proves that even if the hill is partly natural, it has been much improved and fashioned by art, as this masonry is no doubt meant to keep loose made earth from slipping down. The arrangement of the entrance is this: A massive square gate-house of great size has been built on the summit and slope of the hill, from which a stone bridge of six pointed

arches crosses the moat to a smaller gate-house, or
barbican, placed within, but near the outer edge of
the ditch. From this, again, a half-arch is thrown
into the counterscarp, completing the connexion
across. (See Plate of the gate-house.)

The barbican is a handsome construction, square
in plan, with the angles rounded. The doorway
is plain, with a flat segmental arch, and on either
side is a small window. Straight above is a triple
machicolation for the purposes of defence. The
summit is battlemented. The great gate-house is
a noble structure thrown out nearly a square from
the *enceinte* wall of the citadel. The entrance is
through a lofty pointed arch, above which, rising to
the present summit of the building, is a tall, right-
angled recess, ornate with variegated masonry, and
finished at the top with pendant or stalactite work.
On either side of the entrance, at the spring of the
arch, which is about half the total height of the
building, are three sets of machicolations, those at
the angles being sextuple and the others triple.
Below these is a long inscription in the Kufy
character, which is said to bear the name of Malik
ad Dahir, A.H. 605. On either side of the tall
square recess are small windows, and on the face of

the building are various circular medallions, some of
which are inscribed. The citadel is at present
unoccupied, except by a few soldiers, as the interior
is quite ruinous. The Pasha of Aleppo, however, is
a man who is particularly anxious to present a smart
and soldier-like appearance in things military to any
Europeans, and especially Englishmen, who visit the
town, and whose curiosity leads them to examine or
inquire in any way into such matters. The consequence of this was, that on our arrival at the great
gate we were received by a guard of four men under
the command of a junior officer, or captain over ten,
who all came smartly to the " present " as we
approached. The consular dragoman was in attendance, and the officer first drew our attention to a
great number of holes in the outer wall, which he
informed us were made by arrows and bolts, the
heads of many of which, he stated, were still im-
bedded in the stone. The holes are certainly
there, but it is difficult to believe that an arrow
launched from an ordinary hand-bow would have
sufficient strength and penetration to force its way
two inches or more into hard freestone. They are
more probably formed by bullets, but if, as is stated,
the arrow-heads are still within the holes, some very

powerful engine must have been used to launch them at the walls. Passing under the great arch we found ourselves within a lofty recess, all three sides of which were defended by machicolations, which were carried on at the same level, and were, in fact, the continuation of the line of machicolations observed outside.

The approach to the interior of the castle from here is by a long winding staircase of great breadth, and vaulted above at a great height. This stair turns first to the right, out of the arched recess, and afterwards makes several turns in either direction, before the level of the *enceinte* is reached. It is defended at intervals by strong iron doors. I believe, though here I speak from memory, that these are three in number. The outer one is plain, but the inner ones are decorated in a somewhat curious fashion, the surface of the metal being divided into small squares, each of which has in the centre a horse-shoe of wrought iron. On one of the gates there is also an inscription in the same metal. At the last turn before the *enceinte* is reached there are on the right the tombs of two holy men, whose names I was not able to ascertain. These are decorated with tattered flags.

Just inside the gate, a grating close to the ground, and giving light apparently to an underground chamber, was pointed out to us as a window of the old castle prison;* and close by, our attention was gravely drawn to a large tank of water, which tradition said was the identical vessel in which Abraham kept the milk of the self-same dappled cow who had the honour to giving a name to Aleppo. From here we were conducted through desolate ruins to the north side of the hill, where there still stands a square minaret, the solitary remnant of the citadel mosque. Here chairs were brought for us to sit, and another officer, of superior grade, appeared to point out the beauties of the scene, while coffee and glasses of the citadel water were brought us. The latter was drawn from a well, said to be one hundred and fifty yards deep, at the bottom of which is a roaring torrent, an assertion which we received with the utmost gravity, and tried to look as if we swallowed it with the same facility with which we swallowed the water. The view from the summit of the minaret is extremely fine. At one's feet lies the town, which in itself, however, is somewhat

---

* Described by Tyrwitt Drake in "Unexplored Syria" as an immense rock cut column-supported vault, probably originally a cistern.

uninteresting, as little besides the courts of the
mosques and the roof-tops is to be seen. One
notices but half-a-dozen minarets and a few domes.
How different from the gorgeous spectacle that
unrolls itself at the feet when one gazes from the
citadel of Cairo. At the same time one realises for
the first time the great size of Aleppo, and the buzz
rising from the city apprises one of the great population thronging it. To the north-west lay in the
distance the mountains about Beilan, which I had
but a few days before crossed ; due north at a great
distance another low blue mountain, which must be
somewhere close to Aintab ; in the same direction at
our feet was the Serai, while just outside the city
the domes of Skeikhu Bekr, a monastery of durwishes,
formed a striking object; and close to it an ugly
range of barracks. East, lay miles of moory desert,
stretching away towards the Euphrates ; south-east
could be discerned the depression in which lies the
great salt lake of Jibul ; while on the west and
south-west we saw the blue plain through which
the river winds in its orchards of fruit trees. Due
west rose against the sky the snow peaks about
Antioch.

Leaving the minaret, we were conducted to the

castle well, where the water is raised by means of a
horse and windlass. From the sound caused by
dropping a stone into it, it appears to be of very
great depth. All the while we were moving about,
soldiers rushed hither and thither with chairs, to
stick them down before us whenever we paused.
Having now seen the sights, a third officer, still more
mighty than his predecessors, appeared, having
apparently been kept hidden to the last as a special
treat and mark of honour. With him we proceeded
to a small room in the walls, which was furnished
with divans and was apparently used for the reception of superior officers when they visited the citadel.
We were no sooner seated than coffee was again
served, followed immediately by enormous glasses of
orange sherbet. Etiquette demanded that we should
drink them, which we did, all swelling visibly under
the operation. Some desultory conversation followed,
and we then departed with much bowing, salaming,
hat removing, and bakhshishing; the latter, of course,
being conveyed to the guard of honour of four men,
commanded by the captain of ten, who in their
exuberance came to the "present" with redoubled
violence as we left the building.

Mr. Jago informed me that such a display of fantasia was quite unusual on the occasion of the citadel being visited by Europeans. As a rule a solitary soldier conducts the stranger over the place.

The wall enclosing the citadel is strengthened at frequent intervals, but the whole is now in a state of utter ruin. There are also one or two outworks in the shape of towers, built out into the ditch, and connected with the main fortification by walls.

The citadel, of course, played an important part in the various vicissitudes which Aleppo passed through, and of which mention has already been made. In 1630 the Sultan Amurath IV. stripped it of such artillery as it then possessed, to make use of in besieging Bagdad. Van Egmont informs us that in his time the castle contained about two hundred and fifty houses; its inhabitants were usually twelve thousand, and its garrison three hundred and fifty; that the janissaries in garrison never took the field in any emergency, but when once in the castle lived and died in that service, and that it did "not seem to be answerably provided with cannon and other military stores." Some of the vaults are now said to contain a quantity of ancient bows, arrows, and other weapons.

Being now upon things military, I may mention

that the only troops I had an opportunity of seeing at Aleppo on parade were five batteries of artillery that passed one morning through the Azizia quarter, on their way to the plain outside the town, where they were going to exercise. The guns were Krupps in good order, and some of the horses excellent. But the men were dirty, and the harness and trappings very rotten-looking and not clean. The latter was, as I learnt afterwards, a job lot, bought cheap after the American Civil War.

There are many khans in Aleppo, in which, indeed, even at this day, much of the trade of Oriental towns is transacted, and the great courtyards of which are generally stored with vast piles of merchandise. Some among them are handsome structures, vividly recalling the romances of the " Thousand and One Nights." One, probably the finest in Aleppo, is called the Khan el Wezir, and is situated in the west of the town. It is entered by a fine gateway, the masonry of which on the side facing the street is in courses of black and white laid alternately. On the front are carved panels and bosses sculptured with lions. The inner side of the entrance has a pointed arch supported on columns, with stalactite caps. Passing through this gate I found myself in

a large square, in the centre of which was a fountain, so that the whole building had very much the
appearance of an early mosque. The quadrangle
buildings were of two stories, the lower plain, with
doorways entering from the court, while the front of
the upper was an open arcade on all sides, except
that on which was the entrance. This colonnade
was mostly of plain character, being simple arches
supported on square columns; but in two places—
namely, at the left end of the side to the left on
entering, and a section at the same end of the side
opposite the entrance—there was arcade work of
more ornate character, having slightly ogee arches
supported by Saracenic columns with stalactite,
or otherwise ornamented capitals. At first I was
inclined to think that this indicated a difference of
date, but as, where the two styles joined, there was a
bastard column consisting of a square support, with
a demi-column built to its side, it is possible the
whole building is of one date, and may, perhaps,
have been built a hundred and fifty years ago.
Many of the windows looking into the court had
very pretty arabesques over them. The fountain
was also supported by columns of the same character as the ornate part of the arcade.

H

I have mentioned that curious coats of arms occur on various ancient buildings. Such as I noticed were all very similar. The following is a list :—

1. On a fess a goblet or cup, in base another. On Jamah Sultanieh.

2. On a fess between two cornucopias (mouth downwards) a goblet, in chief a lozenge, in base another goblet. On a pretty old Saracenic fountain or watering place, on the north side of the town, close to Sheikhu Bekr. The arms, as usual, are on medallions. There is also in the centre a devotional inscription, and there are other medallions with inscriptions.

3. Arms as No. 2. These again occur on a tomb called Sheikh Ali, outside the Bab el Makam.

4. On a fess between a hieroglyphic formula ▯ on dexter, and ◁ in sinister, a goblet, in chief a lozenge, in base another goblet.—This curious variety I observed on a piece of wall, in the west side of the town.

Similar coats of arms to these occur on Egyptian mosques, and sometimes on small objects, such as glass lamps for mosques, in Cairene work of the fourteenth and fifteenth centuries, under the Mamluk dynasties. A memoir on this subject was written by the late E. T. Rogers Bey, and is published in the "Bulletin d l'Institut Egyptien," 1880. This I have not had an opportunity of consulting, but there are some interesting remarks on the same subject in the South Kensington Art handbook on Saracenic Art in Egypt, by Mr. Stanley Lane Poole. From this I learn that the coat No. 1 was a common combination, and that No. 2 was actually used by Sultan Kait Bey in Egypt, and also by one of his officers, Amir Janbalat, who afterwards became Sultan. It is conjectured that the use of the goblet indicated that the bearer had held the office of cup-bearer to the Sultan, and in Cairo other charges of a similar nature are found, such as a pair of polo sticks, indicating the office of "jokendar" or polo master, and keys, that of chamberlain.

No. 4 is a remarkable coat, as the hieroglyphic formula ▯▯▷▭ is also found, though in different combinations, upon shields of Egyptian Mamluk rulers of the fourteenth century. The hieroglyphic formula in question is a common one on ancient Egyptian monuments, and signifies " Lord of the Upper and Lower Country." It is the opinion of Rogers Bey that the Mamluks using this charge must have understood its meaning ; but Mr. Lane Poole suggests that this particular title may have been preserved by the Copts ; or that the Mamluks, without understanding it, may have inferred, from its frequency, that it was a title of honour. The occurrence of it in Northern Syria is still more remarkable.

There are few miscellaneous antiquities to be seen in Aleppo. The wall at the Antioch gate is built as a sort of revetment, the level within being at a much higher level than outside. At a point here inside, but on a level with the top of the wall, I noticed a curious building, with many fragments of ancient basalt and granite columns. There is also built into its wall a curious stone, sculptured with what may be an inscription. It is much worn, and appears to be upside down. The work is divided into two rows, and appears to consist of human figures and trees. I should doubt if it could be deciphered.*

The suburbs of Aleppo consist of Jedeida on the north, Azizia on the west, Kittab on the south-west, and Ferdus on the south. There are also considerable suburbs on the east, to which I could not ascertain that any special name was given. They are probably the oldest extramural portions of Aleppo.

Jedeida and Azizia are principally inhabited by Christians. The former suburb existed in Russell's day, but is increasing in size at the present day. Azizia is quite new, and is separated from the town

---

* I fancy this stone must be the subject of the engraving in Burton and Drake's " Unexplored Syria," Vol. II., p. 185.

by the belt of cemeteries which surround the town. It is built of excellent masonry, with wide streets. The houses are all built in two stories, and are in no case European in style. Like the town houses, they surround a court, but being nearly all built for Christians they have also large windows facing on to the streets. These are generally large projections, like the *mushrabiehs* of Cairo, but of course without the elegance. Many of the windows have a good deal of rather pretty wrought-iron work about them. This is all done in Aleppo. The doors are generally studded with iron nails, many, indeed, being plated with sheets of that metal.

Although so much of the bazaars and streets in the town is covered over, this mode of building has now been made illegal. Close to the hotel was a new street, all of which belonged to one owner. He, wishing to vault it over in the old style, bakhshished the authorities handsomely, and having got every-thing in readiness, ran up the scaffolding in a night, and when morning broke two hundred men were just getting to work to set the arches. Unfortu-nately for the enterprise, it came to the ears of some superior authority, I think the Waly, who dropped on the proceedings in a trice, and put an end to them. The walls all stand unfinished, with the corbels fixed, on which the arches were to rest.

Aleppo, as I have said, is completely surrounded by cemeteries. The majority are of course Moslem, but on the north are to be found the European, Armenian, and Jewish burying-grounds. The former is close to the Azizia quarter, and contains many inscriptions in remembrance of English and other European merchants, who were members of the factories during the last two hundred years. I should have liked, if I had had time, to have transscribed the English ones. They are mostly very simple as,

Charles Robert Thompson, Esq., of Whitehaven, in England Died at Aleppo on the 20th of December, 1865.

Some, probably foreign, are embellished with florid coats of arms, and nearly all are unfortunately in a sad state of disrepair.

Mention has already been made of the river, and the pretty orchards on its edge. Aleppo is, of course, too far north for date palms, although one or two stunted specimens exist in private gardens as curiosities. Neither are oranges to be seen here, as the climate is too cold. Ashes, poplars, and walnuts, however, grow well, and there are a variety

of fruit trees.   Considerable fig and olive groves are
also to be seen, but these are mostly found on slopes
south-west of the city.   To the east of Aleppo there
are also large plantations of pistachio trees.   Indeed,
the Aleppo pistachio nuts are said to be the best in
the world.   The irrigation is chiefly by the Persian
water-wheel or nahura, which is in use on the
Euphrates down to its junction with the Tigris.
There is also an ancient aqueduct bringing water
from near a place called Heilan some distance to the
north.   Russell states that this conduit was supposed
to be as old as the city, and to have been repaired
by the Empress Helena.   There are in places on the
outskirts of Aleppo little wells and sanctuaries,
which have no doubt been charitable foundations of
princes or other wealthy individuals.   One of these
has already been mentioned, situated north of the
town, near the durwish monastery of Sheikhu Bekr,
as having a sculptured heraldic device upon it.
Another I noticed near the river in the same
direction.   It consisted only of a small building with
two arched recesses, one containing a well or tank
for ablution, and the other a *mihrab* or niche for
prayer in the direction of Mecca.   It thus formed
a well for the weary traveller to halt by, and a

complete *masjid*, or place of worship, for the devout.

The durwish monastery on the north of Aleppo, called Sheikhu Bekr, forms a somewhat striking feature, as it is situated on high ground. It has externally but few architectural features of beauty, but its five domes and one minaret have a very pleasing, and truly Oriental effect. Some very tall trees growing about it also add to its appearance. The durwishes are not, I believe, of the whirling or dancing kind. One of the pleasantest walks I took in the vicinity was across the river and on to the summit of high ground lying to the south-west. The road lay part of the way through beautiful olive orchards, after which we passed two large buildings situated under a cliff to the right. These I was variously informed were mosques and durwish monasteries, the former account being, I believe, correct, although the places seemed almost unused. From here we wound out into the high ground, where a very fine distant view of Aleppo was obtained.

The population of Aleppo are a very mixed breed: the chief proportion are of course Syrians, but there are many Armenians, Jews, and Turks, and a considerable smattering of semi-settled Bedawis, who reside on the south side of the town, partly in wretched hovels and partly in huts and tents. There is also the European element, consisting chiefly of Greeks and Italians, with a few French, Russians, and English, some of which nations are, however, represented chiefly by the consular representatives; these latter mostly reside in the Azizia quarter. The languages in use are Arabic, Turkish, and Armenian, the former being used not only by the Syrian Mohammedans, but also by the Syrian Christians; Turkish is a good deal spoken in the bazaars. The number of the population has been, and still is, given in very various figures; the old Arab authors computed it at 250,000; M. D'Arvieux in 1683 at 205,000; Van Egmont in 1759 says it was generally computed at 300,000; Dr. Russell in 1794 tells us 235,000, out of which 35,000 were Christians and 5,000 Jews; the Editor of "Murray's Guide to Palestine" remarks that all these are probably exaggerated, and that the population probably never exceeded 150,000. There is no census now to go by, but the present population is variously computed at 70,000 to 90,000, of whom 16,000 or 18,000 may be Christians, and 3,500 or

4,500 Jews ;* and it is improbable that the city ever covered more space of ground, if, indeed, as much as it does at the present day. Van Egmont, who gives some curious statistics about the number of houses, which are reproduced elsewhere, remarks : "It is said that six hundred sheep are killed for meat every day."

The Halebis, or inhabitants of Aleppo, have always prided themselves on their courtesy of demeanour and good breeding. Among the upper classes of Mohammedans this may be so, but it is hard to believe it to be more than skin-deep where society is in such a corrupt condition as it is said to be in all classes throughout Aleppo. Among the lower classes met with in the bazaars and streets, the ordinary traveller may be excused from entirely agreeing with this adage. The native people of all races in Aleppo appeared to me, as far as from my passing experience I could judge, rude, ill-mannered, and false. Coming out of Egypt one misses the smiling civility of the fellahin. In both places, indeed, one may be followed about and stared at, but in Aleppo there is an offensiveness in the way of doing it which is never met with in Egypt. Of course the explanation

---

* In the time of Benjamin of Tudela (twelfth century), there were 1,500 Jews.

of this is partly, that the sight of a European is so much more unusual. But there is undoubtedly still a slumbering fanaticism left, a hatred of Frankish dress and customs, which, although not much shown, is nevertheless there. An Englishman cannot pass through many of the Eastern streets of Aleppo without being assailed with the cry of " Frenghi " from the children ; and on one occasion when I had sat down on the north side of the town among some tombs to make a sketch, I was suddenly pelted with stones by a lot of boys who had noticed my arrival, and now assailed me from an ambush of tombstones ; of course the minute I sallied out with a good oak stick they dispersed : but these small matters show the latent disposition of the people.

The Mohammedans of Aleppo have always borne a character for fanaticism and intolerance ; even at the present day it is commonly said that a European cannot enter the mosques with impunity. But this is of course a common state of things in most Turkish towns which are off the track of the tourist.*

* Of course nothing more than annoyance might result from entering many of the ordinary mosques, if the traveller was careful. Mr. Tyrwitt Drake walked into the great mosque and some others at Aleppo, rather, it would seem, because he was told Christians could not enter ; but it does not follow that a less experienced traveller could have done so without trouble.

It is equally impossible in Bagdad, where I was even hindered from ascending a solitary minaret, the mosque of which had disappeared. Van Egmont, on the subject of intolerance in Aleppo, tells the following :

"There is a story current here that a Turk of considerable fortune having read something in the Alcoran which he could not well understand, and being desirous of information, went to the Cadi to ask the meaning of it, to which the Cadi answered, 'Follow me, and I will explain it to you,' and leading him into another chamber, he suddenly drew his sabre and struck off his head." Again: "That two Turks playing at chess, the one pausing a long time at a move, the other said, 'Do play, for Abubekr's sake.' The former musing on his game, and not willing to be interrupted in his thought, dropt scme hasty abusive word on Abubekr, which the latter, being on the losing side, reported to the Cadi; and on this bare deposition the antagonist was sentenced to lose his head, and was accordingly executed the next day."

The native Christians of all sects impress one with the general idea that they are "too sharp to be honest." Among the Armenians, however, of whom there are some 2,000, some good faces are to be seen. The majority of the Christians are Greeks, but there are also a good many Maronites and some Syrian Catholics. The American missionaries have managed to form a small Protestant community.

Costume as seen in Aleppo is very various. Among the townspeople, the tarbush (or fez) is perhaps the most usual. These are made a variety of shapes. The stiff felt sort is sometimes an absurd height, giving the wearer a ridiculous appearance. Sometimes, instead of the usual red, they are made in black. The soft tarbush, fitting more close to the head, has generally wrapped round it a small pocket-handkerchief, thus making an attempt at a turban. The proper and more dignified turban is also seen, but it has greatly given way to the tarbush. The Arabs of the desert, and indeed the villagers and country people throughout Northern Syria, wear the kaffieh, not the gorgeous silk kaffieh, resplendent with gold thread, but a Manchester pocket-handkerchief of a simple but not ugly pattern, which never deviates from the Syrian coast to the Persian Gulf. It is worn thrown loosely over the head (on which and under the handkerchief is worn a white skull-cap), and is secured by a double band of camel's

TTA-E

hair or wool. These bands vary greatly. Some are a stiff thick roll, like a German sausage, three feet long; others are made of loose yarn, neatly gathered in with gay coloured silks at intervals. I bought a variety in the bazaar at Bagdad at various prices and of various patterns. The colours are black, brown, and white, the latter being very effective.

A great many Aleppines now disfigure the dignified Oriental costume by wearing a long, ugly black coat, cut in European style instead of the *jubbeh* or *abbah* which ought to form the outer garment of the Turk or Arab. This, together with the tall tarbush, a combination one continually sees at Aleppo among the townspeople, is a sad falling off from the dignified turban and jubbeh of the Turk of the old school. Some of the Effendis who lodged at the Azizia wore Frankish dress altogether, excepting only the tarbush.

The Aleppo climate is fine, dry and bracing. The summer heat is said to be never excessive, and the winter, although fairly rigorous, is not trying; snow is known, but does not remain long. The European residents have, of course, stoves and fire-places, but I believe the natives entirely depend on the charcoal brazier for warmth. Like most

of the towns in this part of Asia, it has its occasional
bad turns of cholera, as, in spite of its appearing
cleaner than other towns in this part of Turkey,
the sanitation is probably equally ineffective.   The
Aleppo button or boil, the " Hebbet es Sinah," or
" botch of a year " of the residents, is no doubt one
of the causes why so few tourists visit the capital
of Northern Syria.   This disease is, however, not
confined to Aleppo: it is found all down the valleys
of the Tigris and Euphrates, and is very prevalent at
Bagdad, where it is called the "date mark."   A
great deal has been written on the subject, but no
one understands either the cause or nature of the
complaint, which is certainly a scourge on the
country.   It consists of one or more painful and
disfiguring sores, which at Aleppo make their appearance in the winter months, and remain for a full
year.   Nothing will heal it, although some doctors
have made the truly useful discovery that it can be
driven from one part of the body to another.   In
the case of children, who are most liable to it, it
generally appears on the face and legs.   I have seen
European children of six or seven, with three or
four disfiguring scars on the face and a similar
number on the calves of the legs.   I do not think

it is too much to say that half of the children of
five to ten in the streets of Aleppo show scabs or
scars on the faces. European adults who come to
Aleppo may escape or live years without it, but if it
attacks them it is more generally on the forearm.
There is no rule for this, however, and I have seen
English ladies, who have resided but a comparatively short time near the Persian Gulf, with bad
" date marks " on their faces. Travellers passing
through this district may develop it on their return
to Europe. Various conjectures have of course been
made as to the origin. The idea that it is due to
bad water might have merited consideration had
the ailment been confined to Aleppo ; but as it is
equally prevalent in the valleys of the sweet-watered
Tigris and Euphrates, the theory may be dismissed.
More credit may be given to the supposition that it
is caused by a fly. Mr. Jago, indeed, informed me
that there was a certain insect which appeared, I
think in December, and that the cases generally appeared a short time later. The disease is neither
infectious nor dangerous, but it is of a sufficiently
troublesome nature to deserve a careful investiga-
tion.

Van Egmont says: " It is a common saying that if anyone comes to Aleppo in a state of health, he will not soon fall sick; on the other hand, if he have any latent illness, it will soon declare itself."

The characteristic but not always pleasant traits of Oriental custom and life are perhaps not as common in Aleppo as in some other Oriental towns. Yet in this nineteenth century, in this populous city but seventy miles from the Mediterranean, I saw a mad durwish standing shivering stark naked against the wall of a mosque, in the heart of the bazaar, in the full light of day, and unnoticed by the enlightened Turkish authorities. Long black locks hung dishevelled on his shoulders, and he demanded, in a quavering voice, alms from the passers by. There are, or were till recently, several individuals of this character to be seen in the bazaars. Curiously enough, one of the gala days in Aleppo seems to be Sunday. It is, of course, the Christians' holiday, and Muslims take the opportunity to meet their Christian friends for a chat. On Sunday the coffee-houses near the entrance to the town are crowded with narjileh smokers, and the roads are crowded with all sorts of people. Amongst the medley crowd, one is sorry to notice how few Turks

I

of the old school are to be seen. Effendis, Greeks, Armenians, and Jews, all jostle each other in confusion, and in the side-roads young men are galloping about furiously on horseback, their only idea of good horsemanship. Here and there a showy Arab is to be seen, but most are fearful screws.

ANAZEH CAMELS AT MESKINEH.

CHAPTER V.

ON THE ROAD.

Make a Start—Bakhshish—Jebrin, a Beehive Village—Cruelty to Caravan Animals—Sabbakh, a Salt Lake—Arrive at Deir Hafr—The Khan—My Zabtieh's Yarns—Fleas—My Takht-i-rawan—Order of March—My Attendants—A Ferocious Lizard—Bedawi Sheep-stealers—First Sight of the Euphrates—The Anazeh Camp —Meskineh—Balis—Sheikh Ghana—Abu Hureira and Kalah Jaber—We meet my Men's Uncle—Turkish Police—Leben Butter and Dates.

On the morning of the 11th of March I rose with the lark, hoping to make an early start. As it was Friday, I had told the muleteers, in response to a request that I would not start till after the morning prayer, that I had no wish to interfere with their religious arrangements, and should be quite satisfied if everything was in readiness at noon. Haji Mohammed, the chief akam, with whom I had arranged that he should do the little cooking I should require, turned up early and informed me that all would be in readi-

I 2

ness at that time. But immediately after my lunch,
the katterji appeared and professed complete ignorance as to my intention to start that day at all. One
of the consular cawasses, however, having come to
inquire when I started, volunteered to go with the
katterji and see that the takht and mules were
instantly forthcoming. I then walked down to the
Consulate, and at about two o'clock word was sent
down that all was ready. Mr. Jago walked up to the
hotel to see me start, where we found the narrow
street filled with my mules and baggage. At a little
distance stood my "takht," gorgeous in blue and red
paint, and mounted on the backs of two strong and
active looking mules. At half-past two my traps were
all secured, somehow or other, on the backs of the
animals, and as they filed down to where the takht
was, the clanging of the great mule bells brought
everyone to the street-doors to see the Englishman's
caravan take its departure. My zabtieh, who had sat
under a wall opposite the hotel since eight o'clock,
smoking cigarettes and talking to his fat little horse,
climbed laboriously, rifle, jackboots, and revolver, on
to his animal, and moved to the front: a chair was
brought and put for me to climb into my conveyance,
and after a hearty handshake with the kind Consul, I

scrambled in and was off. A few townspeople joined the procession till we got to the suburbs, and then returned to their homes. No sooner were we quite clear of the houses before the muleteers appeared at the door and demanded bakhshish for the " katterji bashi," or head muleteer. I did not understand at first that this was for the head muleman, who was resident in Aleppo, and after, so to speak, seeing us off the premises, was now about to return. Probably it is a custom to give this individual something on this occasion, but of this I knew nothing, and absolutely refused, saying that not a penny of bakhshish would be forthcoming until we arrived at Bagdad. Thereupon the katterji bashi departed in great dudgeon, and looking out of the window, I perceived Haji Mohammed produce a shilling from his pocket and offer it him; the katterji bashi on his part only cursed, and knocked the shilling into the mud. Whereupon Mohammed picked it up, and we resumed the even tenor of our ways.

It was a glorious breezy day, and the route lay over a similar wide plain to that over which we approached Aleppo from the west. Here, however, it was much less stony, and was partly under cultivation. In an hour's time we passed on the right a

TTA-E*

village called Deir, which being built of conical huts, looked at a distance like a collection of beehives. In another hour we came to an exactly similar village, which was to be our resting-place, the first stage on journeys of this description being always a nominal one. In this village, which my men called Jebrin, I was glad to find that there was no oda nor khan, so that we encamped in a square covered with green turf in the centre of the village. This square was surrounded on three sides with conical huts, and the fourth side was open except for a small building with a courtyard and a bell, which had the appearance of a khan, but which Haji Mohammed said was a mosque. Although there were, I should think, several hundred of these huts, hardly a soul was to be seen, and no one evinced the slightest interest in my arrival. A little well in the square afforded water for the use of caravans.

A line was pegged to the earth forming three sides of a square, and to this my mules were tethered for the night, having their huge pack-saddles left on them. This ignorant and cruel custom is rendered worse by the fact that all caravan animals in the East suffer grievously from sore backs consequent, of course, on the heavy loads and hard work, and

especially on these villainously heavy saddles, which
are invariably badly stuffed. It is impossible to make
a muleteer remove these at night, as, from time immemorial, it has been the custom to leave them on,
and it is impossible to convince him that any other
arrangement is preferable. The answer is that the
animals have sore backs, and will catch cold. So
they have; but it is due to the saddles, and if, at the
commencement of a journey, these were removed
every night, the backs would get harder, and the
sores slower in forming. Towards the end of the
journey some of my unfortunate mules' backs were
so sore that I felt like a demon of cruelty to use
them. But there was no help for it. There were no
new animals to be obtained, and I could not camp
for a fortnight in the desert till they got well.

The caravan-men themselves think nothing of it.
They are so accustomed to the sight that I believe
if they saw a mule or ass without a sore back, they
would think it a new species of animal.

My tent was then pitched near the mules, and
after my frugal meal of cold fowl, bread and dates, I
went to bed, and, in spite of the ceaseless clanging of
the mule bells, and the barking of the village dogs,
I obtained some sleep.

At half-past five o'clock the next morning, just as I was preparing to make myself a brew of coffee, I heard a hoarse voice outside my tent door saying, " Yallah, sahib." This was Haji Mohammed's signal for departure, and immediately after I heard them loosing the lines preparatory to striking the tent. I accordingly rolled up my bed, while the men struck and packed the tent, and then swallowed my coffee while the men packed the animals and lifted the heavy takht on to the mules. At half-past six all was ready, and off we went. There had been a heavy shower of rain in the night, and the morning was overcast and cloudy, but everything smelt sweet and pleasant as we got out into the plain. The country we first passed over was similar to that of the preceding day, and in the distance we discerned low brown hills. Artificial tells or hillocks, marking ancient sites here and there, villages of similar character to Jebrin, some with a herd of cows or flock of piebald sheep, an occasional caravan of camels wending its way to Aleppo, and a few big birds which looked like gigantic herons, were the only objects that broke the monotony of the road. One of the tells of very considerable size, apparently not much inferior to that of the citadel hill at

Aleppo, we passed close to the base of, about ten o'clock, and at eleven and half-past twelve we crossed two small streams running south. A few miles to our right lay a depression, in which lies the salt lake (or *malih*), called Sabbakh, or Subkhet el Jebool of Russell, Jebool or Jebul being the name of a village on the edge of it. This curious place Henry Maundrell, who was chaplain of the Aleppo factory at the end of the seventeenth century, gives an account of, in an appendix to one of his books of travel. He states that " it is of two or three hours' extent . . . and is of an exact level, and appears at a distance like a lake of water. . . . In the heat of summer the water is dried off; and when the sun has scorched the ground, there is found remaining the crust of salt, which they gather and separate into several heaps, according to the degrees of fineness, some being exquisitely white, others alloyed with dirt. . . Along on one side of the valley, viz., that towards Gibul, there is a small precipice, about two men's lengths, occasioned by the continuous taking away of the salt. . . . At Gibul are kept the magazines of salt, where you find great mountains, as I may say, of that mineral ready for sale. The valley is farmed of the Grand Signor at twelve hundred dollars per annum." From Jebul I believe all the salt for Aleppo comes at the present day.

At a quarter past two we arrived at Deir Hafr, a village situated at the foot of an ancient tell, and in the midst of a plain covered with soft green turf. A little west of the village is a good-looking house with a few willow-like trees near it. This is the residence of some rich inhabitant of Aleppo. Half-a-dozen colts were grazing in front of the village.

We put up at a miserable-looking khan, where a room—certainly with a lock and key, but in other respects much inferior to an English cow-house—was allotted to me. There were spaces for windows, but all the fittings were gone, and the filthy and ruinous ceiling was tenanted by a large colony of swallows. The people about, however, seemed civil and obliging, and when I inquired for some milk, a pleasant-faced young villager brought me a refreshing draught, for which he refused to accept any payment. I then, with an eye to the next day's breakfast, purchased for a piastre (twopence) nine eggs, which I made Mohammed boil hard in my presence, in a little hovel, which acted for kitchen to the khan.

After I had eaten, I set out for a short stroll with

my zabtieh, with whom I had yet had little conversation. He was a funny fuzzy-faced man, more in
features like a Cossack than an Arab, and was
dressed, as most of these men are, half in shabby
uniform and half in mufti. On his head, of course,
the everlasting kaffieh. I found him a simple,
goodnatured sort of chap, but could make little
of his Arabic, which shattered all my preconceived
notions of that tongue. He pronounced keteer (big)
" chiteer," and kelb (dog) " chellib." I found him,
however, very handy at making himself understood
by signs. He told me that he had accompanied an
Englishman and his dragoman over this country
several years ago. The Englishman was of course a
sportsman, and a wonderful one, for he bagged
four wild pig with one shot, the bullet passing
clean through the head of each animal. The zabtieh
added that he had a dog—a black retriever, who
immediately retrieved the lot. To make this story
intelligible, he illustrated it by placing four little
stones in line, to represent the pigs, and knocking
them all over with his stick suddenly to represent
their simultaneous death at the hands of the sportsman.

On my return, as there was nothing more to be

done, I sat with my pipe, watching the proceedings
in the khan courtyard.   My six mules were busy
in tether at their chopped fodder, and rough-looking
peasants were engaged in grooming their sorry sore-
backed nags.   From the hovel kitchen, where the
simple fare of my men was preparing, poured a thick
black smoke, which made the air in the court even
more unpleasant, though I was in hopes that it
would act as a soporific on some of the insects
which I expected were in my room.   When I
turned in for the night I found that my conjectures
on the subject were correct, and I had not lain down
for more than ten minutes, when I had to rise and
distribute Keating's insect powder wholesale.   I did
not find it very efficacious, and had a lively night.
As a matter of fact, I did not get my bedding clear
of these pests for about a week, and excepting two
nights at the town of Deir, I slept in my tent all the
remainder of the route to Bagdad.

Before continuing the narrative of my journey, it
may be of some interest to give some description
of my takht-i-rawan, and the order of travelling I
observed.   The takht-i-rawan is a square-built box
about six feet long by three feet nine inches wide.
It is painted blue, except the roof, which is red.

There are glass windows all round, protected on the
outside by thin iron bars, very necessary in making
one's way through the tamarisk scrub on the edge
of the river, and a pair of doors on each side.
Inside, at the end next to the leading mule, is a
shelf, on which tobacco, refreshments, and a book
or two could be placed; and below this was suffi·
cient space for a bag or basket. At each end,
outside, are a pair of shafts, terminated by big rings.
The mules to carry the takht are provided with
immense saddles, on each side of which is a big
hook. To place it upon the animals, the takht is
raised by two men, and the animals being placed
between the shafts, the rings are caught on the
hooks, and it is so suspended. It is further steadied
by a rope attached to one of the shafts, which is
passed over the saddle, and secured to the opposite
shaft.

The takht is very strongly built, of ridiculous
solidity, and cruel weight for the poor mules. The
plan is not bad, but a similar and strong enough
conveyance might be made of half the weight.

The order of the day was this. At the first
glimmer of dawn Haji Mohammed roused me, and
while I brewed my coffee or cocoa, the tent was

struck, bedding rolled, and everything was packed on
to the mules. The takht was then slung, Haji gave
me a "knee," I scrambled in, and off we went,
generally just as the sun rose. Inside I settled
myself for the day as comfortably as possible. A
quilt was placed on the floor to be more easy, and at
my back was my roll of bedding. I had my Gladstone bag in alongside of me with notebooks and
some literature. It was of course necessary to trim
the takht, so that it did not bear unevenly on one
side of the animals. Settled down, I finished my
breakfast with bread, hard-boiled eggs, and perhaps
dates, and then I snuggled down at nearly full
length, with my pipe and my notebook, and between
reading, writing, and perhaps a doze, I got on very
well till ten or eleven o'clock, when I got out for a
couple of hours' walk. When I returned I opened
my basket and made my lunch of bread, cold chicken
(if I possessed any), and more dates. Some time in
the afternoon, generally about one or two, we arrived
at our camping place, "outspanned," the tent was
pitched, and after I had had a luxurious wash in the
turbid Euphrates, I set off for a walk before my
dinner, which I had about five o'clock. My dinner,
cooked by my trusty Haji, consisted of rice or vermi-

celli, bread, dates, and, when I had it, chicken. The last luxury could only be obtained some five or six times during the journey, on which occasions I generally bought two or three, and had them all cooked at once. After dinner I had one pipe, and then to bed about half-past seven or eight.

The motion of the takht is not so bad as might be imagined. It certainly rolled a great deal (Europeans first trying them are sometimes sea-sick), but except on rough ground there was none of the jolt of a wheeled conveyance, and as one can sit or lie at full length, it is much easier. In spite of its weight the mules never fell, but crossing streams or ascending steep inclines the jolting was very bad. If the weather was hot, I opened the doors and windows and drew the curtains; if cold, as it sometimes was in the early mornings, I pulled a rug over me and shut up. The order of march was as follows : The four mules not in the takht, and carrying my heavy baggage and sacks of provender, led the way, their headstalls gaily decked with cowrie shells sewn on in patterns. There was one game little grey mule who during the first week would always be a hundred yards in front of everyone. If the others passed him, he broke into a trot to regain his precedence. Poor

little grey : he soon found out the folly of these proceedings, and in ten days' time he was as sober as the
rest of them. These baggage mules kept no sort of
order, and would often stray off some distance to the
right or left, when they saw a nice bit of grass to
pick at. It was then the business of the muleteer to
stir them up. This worthy is generally seated on
a diminutive donkey, the speed and direction of
which he regulates by means of a large packing
needle, which he carries slung to his belt. This
packing needle goad is very usual among muleteers
and others in Turkey, and its use for this purpose
may seem somewhat barbarous to us at first sight.
It certainly is not more so than the spur, and I cannot say that I have ever seen it used to excess.
Something of the sort is undoubtedly necessary to
keep tired animals up to caravan pace.

After the mules and muleteer came my " state
coach " in all its dignity, the two akams or grooms
walking by the mules' heads, and finishing up the
procession was generally my zabtieh, puffing a
cigarette, and muffled up in cloaks and shawls, as if
he was in the Arctic regions.

The character and costume of my men may be of
some interest. Bukhit, the muleteer, was a wiry,

handsome man of pure Arab type, whose ancestors had
probably not abandoned the nomadic life of the
desert for long. On the whole, he was a very good
man, and well up to his profession of caravan
katterji ; but, as is often the case in travelling with
Arab attendants, he, the head man, was the one who
gave all the trouble. He wore a kaffieh formed of
a pink and white Manchester handkerchief, secured
to the head by a dark brown *akal* or band. A blue
shirt, open in front at the bosom, was girded at the
waist, from which hung a knife and the packing-
needle. The shirt had sleeves extending to the
wrist, and beneath it was worn a brown undershirt.
Over the blue shirt Bukhit had a handsome red coat,
open full length in front, and reaching to the knees.
The sleeves of this garment were short, coming only
to the elbow, and embroidered handsomely in yellow,
white, blue, and green, in stripes. On the under
side, next to the body, they were white. Similar
embroidery was on the back of this garment, coming
down to a point ; also on the bosom, and in stripes
down the front. A pair of wide red shoes completed
this very effective costume.

The name Bukhit or Bukheit is a diminutive of
" bakht," and therefore means " little luck." I can

K

hardly say that I consider the sobriquet quite applicable to my muleteer.

Haji Mohammed, chief akam, and my special attendant, was an excellent fellow. He had a great open, child-like countenance which bespoke honesty, *i.e.*, the honesty of an Oriental, in every line. He had the courage of a lion, and the endurance of one of his own mules. He was very proud of having been to Mecca, and was indeed a great traveller, knowing well all the caravan routes in Turkey in Asia. He served me faithfully all the three weeks, and never swindled me more than by mixing my rice of best quality with their own of worst quality, into a great pilaf, and giving me my portion out of the proceeds. The acts of Haji Mohammed and all that he did, will they not be written in the ensuing chapters, telling of my journey to Bagdad? The dress of Haji Mohammed consisted of under garments similar to those of Bukhit. His coat was brown with embroidered sleeves, having white stripes and red trimmings. The embroidery was more profuse than on the muleteer's. In front of each shoulder were three small red, yellow, and blue rosettes, and there were three more very similar lower down. He wore also long blue drawers, tucked into embroidered blue stockings, over which were the usual red slippers. Kaffieh blue, and a white *akal*.

Hamadi, the under akam, was a simple, inoffensive young Arab, whose merit, if merit it was, was his continuous light-heartedness, which caused him everlastingly to "burst into voluntary song." This voluntary song, inspiring as it doubtless was to all who understood its deep and tender pathos, was sometimes rather annoying to myself, as it was equally distributed over the hours of day and night. Hamadi would think nothing of walking in the blazing sun through the desert for eight or nine hours, and then of sitting up all night in front of the camp fire and amusing his companions by joyous and tremulous melodies, which seemed to me to last from sunset till sunrise. His coat was dark brown, lined green at the collar, and with a strip of blue down the seam at the shoulder. There were also white stripes down the front, in front of the shoulders, and under the arms. He wore a black shirt, white drawers, and kaffieh like that of Bukhit.

The morning I left Deir Hafr was perfect. The plain was bright with buttercups, larks were singing, and lively lizards were darting in all directions over the turf. As soon as we cleared the village we crossed a small stream, and after two hours emerged on to the plain, which here has cultivation only in small patches. Shortly after this we passed close to considerable mounds, which my zabtieh called Madum. Cultivation got scarcer and scarcer, until we left it altogether, and were passing over a gently undulating turfy plain, which is in reality the northern corner of what is generally called the Syrian Desert.

While I was taking my morning's walk I prodded with my stick a small grey reptile, which from its attitude I thought was dead. It was a small lizard about six inches in length, with a rat-like tail, rather long legs, and a mouth of great width for the size of the animal.* To my astonishment, instead of running into its hole it turned and attacked my walking-stick with the utmost fury. It took flying jumps of six inches, each time snapping at the ferrule, and pausing hardly a second between the jumps. If I held the ferrule too far for it to reach it, it would crouch, glaring vindictively, waiting until I advanced the stick nearer, in order to spring. Finding it made no impression on the stick, it went for my boots. The

---

* Apparently a species of Gecko.

pluck of the little animal was really remarkable, and
I made an attempt to photograph it with a hand
camera I had with me. The result, however, was a
failure.

Later on three Bedawis suddenly appeared over
the top of a hill, running as hard as they could and
in a great state of excitement. They said something
to my men and passed on. Immediately after we
saw a black object lying on the plain, and Haji
Mohammed, running up to it, soon returned with a
fine lamb, whose throat had just been cut. The
men who had just passed us were sheep-stealers
surprised in the act. My zabtieh and muleteer
immediately went in pursuit, and shortly after returned, bringing with them the culprit who had done
the deed. He was a handsome young Arab of about
eighteen, whose ragged white shirt and plaited locks
showed that he was a member of some small plundering Bedawi tribe. His face, hands, and clothes
were bespattered with the blood of the lamb. When
brought to my takht he burst into a flood of tears,
apparently thinking I should order his instant execution. Further on we came on the peasant whose
flock had thus been raided, and delivered the culprit
and his booty into his hands. This was the first

example I saw of the manners and customs of the desert.

Exactly at noon we caught our first glimpse of the great Euphrates, and after rising and passing over some downs, we came, half an hour later, in full sight of the great valley. The line of demarcation here between the desert we had been crossing and the river-valley we approached was marked by a line of chalk cliffs, which are not, however, generally precipitous. The plain which lay at our feet seemed from two to two and a half miles broad from the cliffs to the river, and as far as the eye could reach it was covered with the black tents and the herds of sheep, camels, and horses of the great Anazeh tribe of Arabs, who were just arriving from their winter quarters in Arabia, to take up their summer pastures in the desert south and east of Aleppo. The scene was certainly very impressive, and calculated to recall vividly scenes and passages from the Old Testament. After descending into the plain, we skirted along it, keeping rather near the cliffs, and close to the great Anazeh camp. The zabtieh galloped off to one of the tents, and soon after returned with an enormous bowl of new milk, a refreshing drink for all my party. This was my welcome to the "great river" by the

Arabs. Of course no payment was asked, and if offered it would not have been taken by the Anazeh, who are by far the most powerful tribe between Mesopotamia and Syria, and very hospitable.* Many of them were galloping about on their mares, with lances of bamboo fifteen feet long : swarthy, wiry looking fellows, with black plaited locks. I noticed some large birds flying about, which seemed to me seagulls. Whether they came from the Mediterranean or up the river from "the gulf" is a curious question.

Soon after this, we turned a corner of the cliff, and found ourselves in sight of a few buildings, to which my men gave the name of Meskineh, and where, they said, there was a khan, and a small fort with a few soldiers or police. Meskineh is fairly close to the river, and is the proposed port for Aleppo, if ever a steamer line is put on the river. The old fort of Balis is a short distance further down stream. My men said I could either go to this khan, or camp close to the river. I chose the latter, and soon after

* For much interesting information about the Anazeh Arabs, and the other tribes of Turkish Arabia and Mesopotamia, see "The Bedouin Tribes of the Euphrates Valley," by Lady Anne Blunt. Mr. Blunt reckons the number of the Anazeh at thirty thousand tents, or one hundred and twenty thousand souls.

the tent was pitched within a quarter of a mile of the
Euphrates and near a couple of Arab tents, belonging to some pastoral tribe.   After a brew of coffee
and a wash, I walked down the river bank.   The
stream here seemed to me not more than half a mile
in width, the current very rapid, and the water extremely turbid.   This is the case with both the Tigris
and Euphrates throughout their course over the
great plain. I found the water very sweet, but to get it
clear it was necessary to allow it to stand for some
time before use.   A tumblerful will deposit, I should
think, close on an eighth of an inch of fine brown
mud.   A little below where I stood, a spit of land
reduced the breadth of the river to about half.   The
Mesopotamian side at this point has no cliffs, but is
flat near the river, and undulating further back.   A
long way due north a range of hills were discernible.
While I was standing gazing at the river, a young
shepherd came down to water his flock. He had no
dog, but walked in front of his charges, summoning
them to follow him, and directing their movements by
different cries which they seemed to understand.   I
tried to engage him in conversation, and found him
inquisitive to know what nation I belonged to, and
where I was bound for.   He also told me, as far as I

could understand, that he belonged to a fellah tribe
called Shohr, a name I do not find in Mr. Blunt's list.

I had bought some eggs and milk from a man belonging to one of the adjacent tents. In the evening
I was suddenly aroused by a tremendous row just outside my tent between my people and the man, his
wife, and boy. I rushed out and found Bukhit sitting
astride of the unfortunate youth, hammering him
like steam, while the man and woman gesticulated
and screamed and appealed to me for justice. Battle,
murder, and sudden death seemed imminent, and I
accordingly interfered. The dispute was about the
price of eggs, but I could not make head or tail of it,
and was glad when it slowly subsided, and the Arabs
took their departure.

The following day we passed, about half an hour
after starting, the ruins of Balis, or Kalah Balis,
standing out clear on the top of the cliff. A lofty
castle, and a noble octagonal Saracenic minaret were
all I could discern, as we were nearly a mile distant.
This Balis (the Barbarissus of Ptolemy and Barbalissus of the Theodosian tablets) was formerly a place
of importance and the port of Syria. The plain near
it is also said to have been the paradise or park of
the Persian Satrap Belesis, destroyed by Cyrus the

Younger.* Benjamin of Tudela identified it with
the Pethor or Pthora of Numbers and Deuteronomy,
and when he visited it (1163), it contained ten Jews.
The town was conquered by the Crusaders under
Tancred in 1111. The ruins of the present day are
a mixture of Saracenic and Roman work. The river
now flows several miles distant from the cliffs on
which the ruins are situated, but it is evident that at
one time the base of this high ground was washed
by the river, or more probably, as Ainsworth suggests,
by a branch of it, which rejoined the main stream at
a point further down. On this level ground I noticed
the remains of several ancient canals.

After passing Balis, we cruised along the plain, sometimes close under the chalk cliffs, and sometimes at a
considerable distance. At the summit of the cliffs I
noticed a bed of indurated gravel or breccia, and in
one or two places on the cliff face, excavations, which
had somewhat the appearance of ancient tombs.
Many birds—crows, big hawks, and one or two vul-
tures—were fluttering about, or were perched high up
near the summit. On the plain through which we
were passing was a good deal of scrub, the green
tamarisk jungle, of which I was to see so much

* Ainsworth: " Personal Narrative of Euphrates Valley Expedition."

BEILAN.

before I arrived at my destination. After about three and a half hours the cliffs disappeared, and were replaced by a gentle rise from the river plain to that of the desert. We here left the river, and, after crossing a piece of desert to save the bend of the river, we rejoined the valley and shortly after encamped for the night at a charming place under an ancient tell, called Sheikh Ghana, and opposite a scrub-covered island which divided the stream. On the top of the tell was one of the mud forts erected by the Turkish Government to contain a few police or soldiers, but these worthies were occupying a tent near the base of it. An old man who looked after the place pointed out to me from the summit of the tell, Kalah Jabar, a castle and a minaret crowning a precipitous headland on the opposite side of the river. This lay some distance east from Sheikh Ghana, the river here flowing in that direction; on the right bank, behind some cliffs, he told me lay Abu Hureira. From this old gentleman I purchased a lamb, which I presented to my men, and Haji Mohammed turned me out a very respectable dinner of lamb's head (a tit-bit in the opinion of Arabs) and rice. The climate was already changing, and the day had been warm, and now the evening was lovely. The moon as it rose was of a deep orange tint, and appeared strangely distorted in shape. As it slowly ascended throwing deep shadows over the desert hills, and lighting up the placid river, the scene was strangely beautiful and solemn. The only sound was the melancholy wail of hundreds of jackals on the island and opposite bank, and occasional plash of a big fish in the river. We had long since left the Anazeh camp, and the only signs of human life in sight, besides my little encampment, were the two tents near the foot of the tell.

The next morning, after an excellent night's sleep, we were off about six o'clock, making our way over a plain, cultivated here and there in patches. After an hour's journey we were again at the cliffs, now gypsum and marl, on the summit of which is to be seen a round tower, probably the sole remains of a ruined mosque, and a little higher up another ruin. This place is Abu Hureira, which I had seen the previous day from Sheikh Ghana. The cultivation I had seen was probably the work of the Wulda Arabs as mentioned by Ainsworth. But Lady Anne Blunt saw here the ruins of mud huts, which she explains as the result of an enterprising Pasha to induce some of

TTA-F

the Anazeh to settle here as fellahin. An experiment which seems to have been a failure.

In another half hour I was gratified by a good view of the fine castle called Kalah Jaber on the Mesopotamian side. This ruin has a very remarkable appearance, occupying as it does an isolated cliff, which, as far as I could see, was square, and the side facing the stream precipitous at the summit. The lofty minaret towered above the fortifications, and between the base of the cliff and the river lay a forest of scrub.

Kalah Jaber is mentioned by both Benjamin of Tudela (1163) and Abulfeda in the fourteenth century. It also seems to have passed at various dates by the names of Dauser, Dausara (Stephen of Byzantium), Dauses, and Dabanas. Various historical events are connected with the place, and, as Ainsworth remarks, this district, containing Kalah Jaber, Abu Jaber a ruin close to, and Deir Mahariz (the Sela Mid Bara of Benjamin of Tudela, who describes it as containing in his time 2,000 Jews), and Abu Hureira, may at one time have been the centre of a large population.

After winding about the base of these cliffs, we emerged into the desert, leaving the river by ascend-

ing a wide wady, which was evidently at times the
bed of a roaring torrent. Passing up here, I noticed
many circular and semi-circular piles of stones, such
as are to be met with on moorland countries in the
North of England, and are supposed to be of high
antiquity. Those near the Euphrates are not improbably of Arab origin, but their use and antiquity
are matters of speculation. We then passed across
a corner of the desert, which here is very stony and
rough, and having a slight scrub growing upon it;
and in an hour and a half we rejoined the river
plain, where we were again hospitably treated to
milk at an encampment of some people calling
themselves " Raih " Arabs. There were a great
many sheep about their tents, but I noticed no
horses.

During the day we passed a few peasants occasionally near the river. One man, accompanying a small
party with a few mules, apparently travellers for
Aleppo, was greeted warmly by my three attendants,
who in turn fell upon his neck and kissed him on
both cheeks, addressing him as uncle. He was, like
them, a caravan Arab, belonging to Bagdad. Near
this place I saw to the right upon some high ground
two figures who looked by their costumes Europeans.

I was, unfortunately, at such a bad part of the road, that I was unable to alight, or even stop the takht, and we soon left them behind. I must, however, have been mistaken, as I met no caravan upon the road.

The last part of this day's march lay over very rough and stony ground, the track leading over hummocks and hillocks which break up the desert platform at the edge of the river plain. Takht travelling on this sort of country is not pleasant, as at one minute the unfortunate occupant is jolted into the stern of the conveyance, only to toboggan wildly forward a minute later, as the mules top some little elevation, and descend a steep slope on the opposite side. Eating lunch inside a takht under these circumstances is not unlike the same perform- ance in the Bay of Biscay, with the exception that one cannot have the "fiddles on." At half-past one my tent was pitched at a charming place on the edge of the river, called Hammam (*i.e.*, the bath), although neither tent nor building of any kind was in view. The desert here rises in a regular platform, the edge of which is a low cliff, at a short distance from the river. In a walk I found many rudely- worked flints (relics perhaps of that wonderful stone

age which seems to have existed everywhere), and
the ground was covered with a very pretty blue
orchid-like flower. On my return, my zabtieh
Jameel, who had accompanied me from Aleppo,
came to say that he was going with me no further.
He brought me his successor, and a sergeant from
where I do not know, unless Turkish policemen
make their appearance in the desert like manna,
and I interested them all by showing them my maps
and revolver. The police themselves carried good
revolvers, all of which were, however, of American
make. The new man was a handsome old grey-
bearded Arab, without a vestige of uniform about
him, and whose appearance, barring the revolver,
was much more suggestive of Abraham or Aaron
than of a policeman. My larder was empty, but
nothing in the way of chickens or meat was to be
obtained here, so that I had to content myself with
a tinned kipper for dinner. No comestible in the
world is more truly beastly than a tinned kipper,
but I ate what I could, and then washed the taste
away with a draught of leben, a bowlful of which I
had fortunately been able to buy. Leben is a most
excellent and refreshing drink after a long and
hot day's march. My plan was always to buy a

L

bowlful when I could, and after putting aside enough for my immediate wants, to pour the remainder into a handkerchief, and to suspend it to a tent rope, to allow the water to drain off. The result was an excellent substitute for butter, which did much to render palatable stale dry bread that had been baked over a week before. Dates and leben butter made a rich confection fit for a king.

ANAZEH ARABS ON THE MARCH.

CHAPTER VI.

CONTINUATION OF JOURNEY.

Anazeh Arabs on the March—The Haudaj—Costume and Arms—We
Sight Rakka—Arabs on Inflated Skins—A Mudir Effendi—A
Howling Durwish—Unwelcome Visitors—Bathe in a Backwater
of the River, with bad Results—Camp in Robber-infested District
—Reach Deir—The Khan—Description of the Town—Its
Poverty—Its Agriculture—"Cherrids"—Arab Population—Its
Political Importance—An "Englishman" turns up—His Account
of Himself, and his Peculiarities—Woodfuel Fishing—Altone Again
—The Terrible Desert—Visitors—Arrival of the Pasha—Haji
Mohammed's "Stiff Stomach"—Hardihood of Muleteers.

As the next day's march was a long one, we struck
camp, and started in the dark at half-past four. I
attempted to make myself a cup of coffee, but being
half asleep, I upset it in the dark, all over my bed.
As soon as we were off, I snuggled into my great
coat and rug, and was soon fast asleep again, and on
waking an hour later I found that we were in a
level and tufty part of the desert. We rejoined the
valley again in another hour's time. For five hours
we kept across a very wide and barren plain, having
some distance away on our right the limestone cliffs.

L 2

It was, however, anything but dull, as the whole plain
was alive with the Anazeh on the march.   Groups of
horsemen mounted on their active Arab mares, many
with their foals running at their heels, carrying their
lances on their shoulders, and driving in front of them

THE HAUDAJ.

great droves of unloaded camels, were continually
passing us.   Then would come two or three large
camels carrying the " haudaj," a sort of howdah fitted
with an enormous superstructure like the yards of a

ship, on which can be set an awning in hot weather. In these haudajes were the women and children. The women, some of whom are very pretty, wear nose-rings, and have their under lips painted a dark blue or black. They are all unveiled, and I was much flattered by the great interest they seemed to take in my proceedings. They are under no restraint what-ever, and although they live a hard working life among the herds and flocks, they are happy, contented, and in almost all cases modest. The men are all built in a small mould, but are as active as cats, and have great powers of endurance. In colour they are some-times almost black, but their features are lit up by teeth of the most dazzling whiteness. As they use none of the dentifrices of civilisation, and their diet is largely farinaceous, it is hard to know how they are kept in such beautiful order. Many of them have long plaited locks hanging on either side of the face, and they all wear the Manchester kaffieh. Their costume is various. Many are dressed only in a few black rags, while others sport the striped Bag-dad abbah. Long flint lock guns, ornate silver-mounted pistols, and cross-handled swords are borne by many. Others carry a curious little axe with a hooked spike on the opposite side to the blade, or a

mace formed of a straight stick, with a heavy knob
of bitumen attached to the " business " end.   Either
of these are formidable weapons.   The lance is, however, the attribute of the noble Arab tribe, and the
gun is much less usual among them than among the
smaller tribes on the banks of the Euphrates.

Although I was unaware of it, I had passed some
time this morning the ruins of Surieh, the ancient
Thipsach or Thapsachus, "the fatal pass," as Ainsworth
styles it.   As my camping-place was twenty miles
east of Kalah Jaber, I fancy that in consequence of
our early start we must have got past them before it
became light.   There is said to be little left of the
ancient town, of the history of which Mr. Ainsworth
gives an admirable summary.   A causeway marked
in the Theodosian and Augustan tablets led from
Auranitis, by Palmyra, to this place, and on the other
side of the ford it was carried on to Edessa (Urfa) by
Carrhae (Haran).   Mr. Ainsworth points out the
strange series of calamities that followed the crossing
of this ford by various expeditions ; those, to wit, of
Xerxes, of Cyrus the younger, of Darius Codoman,
of the great Alexander himself, who founded Nicephorium (the present Rakka) a short distance further
down stream. Crassus, Julian, Galerius, and Gor-

dianus all followed in their wake, and in every case the passage of the ford was followed sooner or later by great disaster. It was a strange fatality that after the Euphrates Valley Expedition had passed this spot, the steamer *Tigris* was struck by a hurricane and sank, nineteen lives being lost in the disaster.

At nine o'clock we got a sight of Rakka, on the Mesopotamian side of the river. It is situated near the mouth of the tributary of the Euphrates called the Nahr Balik, and was founded by Alexander the Great under the name of Nicephorium. It became Callinicus under the Romans, and Rakka "the illustrious" under the Mohammedans. It was a stronghold of Harun al Rashid, who erected there a citadel, palace, and other buildings. The place is a ruin now, and a few years since, the only inhabitants were a few Arabs dwelling in tents. There are, however, a few fragments of Saracenic architecture still remaining.

As we jogged along over the plain, I noticed the remains of an ancient canal, and shortly after seeing Rakka, we sighted straight in front of us a curious isolated hill, to which my men gave the name of Munkhir. This is the hill marked on Kiepert's map as "Tel el Menakhir," and is situated on the opposite side of the stream. As it is quite isolated, and indeed has but little high ground in the vicinity, it forms a prominent landmark to travellers for miles. The general course of the Euphrates from some miles west of Kalah Jaber to Rakka is east, after which it takes a south-eastern course, which is preserved for about one hundred and fifty miles, measuring as the crow flies, when it turns east again until it reaches the town of Anah. The afternoon was spent in passing rough, hummocky ground and numberless small wadies, similar to the latter part of the preceding day's journey. I attempted to lunch off tinned kippers, and succeeded in spilling the oil in the tin all over my clothes, creating a fishy and oily smell, which nearly made me sick. At three o'clock, after a long and tiring stage of ten-and-a-half hours, we stopped for the night at a place called Sabbakh, close to a police fort of larger dimensions than any I had yet seen. My men attempted to pitch the tent without my supervision, and made a hopeless mess of it, putting down the pegs at the wrong place and bending the spikes at the tops of the poles. Arabs are extraordinarily clumsy at any sort of work new to them.

The current of the river at this place is very rapid,

and for the first time I saw men paddling down stream on inflated sheep skins, in the same manner as represented on ancient Assyrian sculptures. In consequence of the swift current, these navigators whirled down stream at a most astonishing speed, and it was difficult to see how, under these circumstances, they could retain much power of steering. The Mudir Effendi, or chief of the police here, called on me soon after I arrived ; he was a pleasant-looking old Turk. I found conversation with him anything but easy in consequence of my lack of knowledge of the language, but interested him by showing him some photographs of English steamers I had with me. After dinner I returned his call. His quarters were a wretched hovel in the mud fort, which we should consider not good enough for a favourite horse. But the old gentleman did the honours and entertained me with the well-bred courtesy of a Turk of the old school. He carefully prepared coffee for me with his own hands, and when I departed he accompanied me back to the tent, and I found he had sent me a welcome present of half-a-dozen new laid eggs. His pleasant kindness was an exception among the Turkish police officials whom I came into contact with along the road.

Just before dinner my attention was attracted by a

curious noise a little distance behind my tent. On looking out to ascertain the reason, I found two men kneeling in the direction of Mecca. One of them, a wretched, ragged scarecrow, was a howling or barking durwish, and with his whole body swaying wildly from side to side, he was repeating the name of Allah in a sort of hoarse gasp with every swing of his body. He had wrought himself to such a pitch, that at every repetition the violence convulsed his whole frame. The gasp gradually rose to a sound like the barking of a dog, and then slowly declined into a sort of agonised grunt, when, apparently utterly exhausted, he staggered to his feet, and, though now scarcely able to stand, disappeared, supported by his companion and still gasping the sacred name, into the darkness of the desert.

In the night I had several unwelcome visitors in the form of cats. The first awoke me by perambulating my recumbent form in order to inspect my basket, which contained some cold chicken, my lunch for the following day. On seeing me rise in my bed, it prudently departed. The second, a very large one, immediately it entered gave vent to a loud "yaou" of pleasure on perceiving the smell of food. I immediately seized my stick, which was fortunately handy, and smote it a shrewd blow on the head ; whereupon it left hurriedly, apologising for having called at such an inopportune moment. No. 3 I suddenly discovered standing on its hind legs, with its head in another basket, licking the handkerchief which contained my leben butter. I strongly protested, and though the force of my arguments did not strike home with the same accuracy as in the last instance, yet the marauder left, to appear no more.

There had been one or two heavy showers in the night, and when we got away at a quarter to six the morning was cloudy. My men were for some unknown reason very larky, and continued bear-fighting and singing and playing tricks on each other like a party of great babies. The road throughout the day was exceedingly monotonous, being all the time in the plain, the part passed through in the early morning being scrubby, and that later on, clear. In the former we encountered more large parties of Anazeh on the march. When I was walking, three wild Bedawi girls came from some tents we were passing, and inquisitively peeped through the window of the takht, whence they were pushed giggling away by Mohammed. They thought that there was a European lady within. These desert

damsels had not the least shyness, nor any of the
mock modesty of the townswomen. They were as
free, or freer, than English girls.

We stopped at one o'clock, near what I thought
was the Euphrates, but which I afterwards found
to be a backwater. I had a row with the men, who
insisted on pitching the tent on the top of a
hill, near a mud fort. The place was dirty with
the refuse of other caravans, and when I ordered
the men to move the camp to the edge of the
water they refused, and with good reason, as the
water being stagnant, to sleep on the edge of it
would incur risk of malaria; but this I did not
then know, and accordingly swore at the men for
their disobedience. I then, still thinking it was a
slow part of the river, went and bathed in the
water. This brought on, the ensuing morning, a
preliminary attack of dysentery, from which I was
destined to suffer seriously before reaching Bagdad.
After the bath I walked on to an eminence on the
hummocky desert behind. Here I noticed immediately that the water was not part of the
Euphrates, but a large semi-circular backwater unconnected at that time with the river, but
probably, when the latter was at its greatest height,

joined to it. It is, I fancy, marked in Kiepert as Lake Mogla, and would seem to be artificial in origin. In my walk I saw for the first time close, a brace of beautiful sandgrouse. I regretted not having a gun with me, as in spite of the assertions that plenty of provisions were obtainable on the road, I had been able to purchase but one solitary chicken in the first six days. Looking exactly north-west from here, Jebel Munkhir still formed a conspicuous object; and to the left of it I saw heavy smoke rising from the plain, which I could not imagine the cause of.

During the night I had to rise to get Mohammed to remove the bells from the mules, as their incessant noise prevented my obtaining any rest. When we left our camp at daybreak I found myself anything but well, with great internal pain, and totally unable to eat. My men attributed it to bathing, which I did not then believe, as they maintained it was good water to drink. As the very serious and prolonged attack, which seized me a few days later, also followed a bath in the Euphrates, I am inclined to believe that it may have been so, and would caution travellers against bathing in the cold waters of the Euphrates before nightfall and after a long and hot

day's journey. About nine o'clock I got out to
attempt a short walk, and found that we were in
a sterile but pretty part of the desert, with some
higher hills than I had yet seen to the left, and
broken ground with low cliffs to the right. Amongst

MY CAMP.

the very scanty vegetation were many beautiful red
poppies, which had a charming effect on the desert.
Soon after we were again on the scrubby plain, with
low sandstone cliffs on our right. The sandstone here

rests on a sort of gravelly mudstone, and is itself
in places very soft. Feeling a little better in the
afternoon, I ventured on another little walk. While
I was out the plucky little grey mule, overcome by
the heat and its heavy load, came heavily down, and
we had to unload him before he could again be got
on his legs. I again flushed a lot of sandgrouse,
but having no gun was unable to replenish my now
absolutely empty larder. At about one we arrived
at our camping ground, a most romantic place on a
bend in the river, and close under a headland of grey
desert cliffs. Through these cliffs to the river ran
several rocky scrub-grown wadies, one opening out
close to my tent. There was no sign of any sort of
human habitation in sight, but the district was full
of Arabs; and my men would not allow me to go
for a short walk on to the cliffs behind until I had
promised not to go far and had shown them that I
carried my revolver. From the summit I found there
was a beautiful prospect. The portion of the river
which I gazed over has a general direction of due
south, but in its course makes several huge bends;
in one almost completing a circle, so that the curves
at the commencement and end of the loop nearly
join. Far beyond the river, in noble white clouds,

lay a range of Mesopotamian mountains, over which, as the night drew on, flickered almost incessant lightning. Behind me, on the Arabian side, lay another range at some distance. The whole scene was desolate and rugged in the extreme. On my return I found several wild-looking and fully-armed Arabs questioning my men, who, however, were very anxious to get rid of them. Haji Mohammed also told me next day that he had not dared to sleep, but had prowled round the encampment all night on the look-out—a statement I received *cum grano*. They also said that as Deir was to be reached next day it was absolutely necessary to make a very early start. As I had no idea of the distance, and they told me it was a ten hours' stage, I of course acquiesced ; and after about four hours' sleep the tent was struck, and we left soon after midnight. I found out, however, that it was really only six hours, and that this was simply a trick to get the full day in Deir. This was a lesson to me to refuse all ridiculously early starts in the future. This is, of course, the great drawback to getting a muleteer to contract to take you from one place to another in the East. Unless he is bound down by an agreement he considers that he can dictate the hours and pace of travelling, and in fact is rather apt to treat his "fare" as a bale of merchandise. By acting with decision and determination he will certainly "knuckle under" to some extent; but by buying or hiring animals by the day or week the traveller will find himself much more his own master, and free to choose his own hours and pace, and to stay when, where, and how long he pleases.

The journey to Deir was, therefore, chiefly made in the dark, but by the rough ground that I felt we were passing over I knew we were most of the while in the desert. When it became light I found that one of my poor mules was dead lame, and was going without any other load than the khurj or saddle-bag. About six o'clock we entered the narrow, wretched-looking streets of Deir, and I "took up my inn" in a khan near the centre of the town, a respectable enough looking little place of two stories surrounding a courtyard. In this khan there was no accommodation for animals, and my mules and men went to another establishment on the opposite side of the way. Great curiosity was evinced at my arrival, and the courtyard was full of people to see the Englishman. The khanji gave me the best room in the building, but it was so

M

filthy that I had a good sweep up done before I went into residence. This, however, did not dispel the ants which swarmed on the floor, nor the flies which infested my room in myriads. Under these circumstances, one of the first things I did was to

KHAN AT DEIR.

rig up my " Levinge " bed in order to secure a good night's sleep. The other two features about the khan were the immense size of the sparrows on the house-top, and the primitive character of its sanitary arrangements, the "adab khanah" or privy being the flat roof of the building, which, if it had not been put to this purpose, would have been a pleasant evening lounge.

Deir is built on a slight eminence, said to be the débris of an earlier edition of the same town. Why a "later edition" should have ever been produced is hard to understand, as a more wretched hole it has never been my ill-luck to see. It is built on the edge of the Euphates, here divided by an island, and in the middle of a desolate clay waste, upon which there is not a solitary feature of beauty. No tamarisk jungle, no cliffs near the river, and this last, not the noble Euphrates, but a poor insignificant branch of it. The town itself consists of a long street running parallel with the river, from which numerous side streets lead either to the water on the east side, or to the cemeteries which enclose the town to the west. The houses are built of mud, and are mean in the extreme. The bazaars are also squalid and ill supplied.

To give an idea of the wretchedness of this town of 2,500 inhabitants, on the banks of a noble river, I may state that I was unable to

Change a napoleon,

Buy fish of any sort,

Buy a basket or small tin box.

Nor could I obtain any sort of tinned or preserved provisions. Perhaps the latter ought not to be expected, but that the other articles were unobtainable certainly seems absurd. Dates and oranges can, however, be bought here, the former coming from Bagdad, the latter from Birejik. For the first time, however, since leaving Aleppo, I found myself again in the midst of agricultural industry. A few date palms are to be seen, but they are wretched, stunted specimens. The island, which is connected with the town by a shaky wooden bridge, is in a high state of cultivation. Maize, rice, and other grain are produced here, and there is a sprinkling of fruit trees, chiefly apple and pomegranate. The method of irrigation used on the island is entirely the "cherrid," a rude apparatus much used also at Bagdad. It consists of an overhanging framework of wood on the river edge. In this framework are two rollers, and working on these are ropes, to which are hung two big water skins, with leathern tubes or hose attached. An inclined plain is dug sloping down from the bank, and in this work two horses or mules. By walking down the slope, the animals set the gear to work which raises the skins from the water. When they get to a certain height, the water runs from the skins down the tubes into a dyke or watercourse, which carries it on to the land. The animals are then turned round, walk up hill, and the skins return to the water for a new supply. The cherrid is perhaps more primitive than the shadoof of Egypt, as it requires a horse and man to do the same work that is performed in that country by a man alone; a somewhat greater quantity of water is, however, raised each time.

The population of Deir is not, like most towns in Asiatic Turkey, a medley. The residents are almost entirely Arab. The Syrian costume is hardly ever seen here, and the kaffieh of the men, and nose-rings and painted underlips of the women, show the traveller that the people of the town are in reality but Arabs of the desert, who have been induced, by the advantages of commerce, to settle down to a more sedentary existence. There are besides, a few Christians, and of course the Turkish officials at the Serai, and a few Turkish troops. Deir has been well called the centre of desert politics. It is in fact the point on the Upper Euphrates which the Turkish Government has chosen to keep in hand the tribal Arabs on both sides of the river. The method by which their policy is carried on has been well described in Lady Anne Blunt's charming " Bedouin Tribes of the Euphrates," and although the morality of governing these wild spirits by incessantly setting them at loggerheads, and thus breaking their power, may well be questioned, it cannot be denied that it has been in a great measure successful. The comparative safety of the Euphrates valley road is a proof of this. It was only in 1862 that Deir was taken into military possession by the Turkish Government, and the Upper Euphrates again became part of the Ottoman Empire : and before that time it is more than doubtful if a solitary European could have passed, as I did, undisguised and practically unescorted, from Aleppo to Bagdad. That the road, considerably after that date, was not, however, safe for Europeans, and that the desert Arabs were not the only people to be feared, is proved by the fact that as late as 1874 two Germans were actually murdered for the sake of their horses, by the inhabitants of Deir themselves, and within two days' march of the town.* What the Ottoman authorities did on this occasion to punish the murderers I am unaware.

* " Bedouin Tribes of the Euphrates," vol. i., p. 102.

Of the history of Deir nothing much seems to be known. The usual meaning of the name is " convent" or " monastery," and accordingly it is chronicled by Idrisi that it was so called from Deir Abuna, the name of a monastery which formerly stood here; and that Noah (the Mih al Nabi, or Sheikh al Mūr īlīn of the Mussulmans) resided here after leaving the Ark, and here was buried.*

As soon as I had taken possession of my quarters, someone among the crowd who were busily engaged in watching my proceedings, told me that there was a man in the town who spoke English. Thinking he might be of use, I sent word to him to come to see me. In about ten minutes a blear - eyed fellow dressed in tarbush, English coat and boots, appeared, and greeted me warmly with " My dear fellow, how do you do ? " There was a debauched look about the man which at once made me suspect he was a drunkard, and although he interlarded his bad English with frequent callings upon the mercy of the Almighty, and denounced all his fellow-townsmen as Arab robbers, I saw that he was a shady character, with whom it would be advisable to have little to do. He told me his name was Altone ; that he was a

* Ainsworth : " Personal Narrative of Euphrates Expedition."

Christian, and that he had served in some capacity in the engine-room on board an English steamer. He also said that he had brothers at Bombay, Bagdad, and Liverpool. He had been to the latter place, *but not to England,* and wanted to know what was the distance between them. He was particularly anxious to go with me to Bombay or Suez as dragoman and general protector, asserting that the country through which I was about to travel was dangerous, and in fact impossible to an Englishman without the protection of an honest man like himself. He also hospitably invited me to share his board at his house, or at least to allow his wife to cook and send me my dinner. These offers I refused, and for my humble dinner sent Mohammed to the bazaar to buy me kabobs. I, however, told the man if he cared to accompany me into the town in the capacity of interpreter I should be glad of his services. In the afternoon I visited this worthy at his home, in order to get him to explain to Mohammed certain things, which, through my imperfect knowledge of the language, I had been unable to do. I found him seated in a small room in the bosom of his family. To these he introduced me, waving his hand airily at his wife, whom he termed variously " my woman " or " my lady "; an ancient crone squatting in the corner was his mother-in-law, or, as he delicately put it, "the old woman." There were several children, fat, black-eyed little bodies, who, to do him justice, he seemed very fond of. His son-in-law, who seemed a very respectable young man, was also in the room. Altone verified my suspicions about his character by immediately producing a bottle of arak and glasses, and begging me, "his dear brother," to partake. I refused, telling him I never drank intoxicating liquors on a journey, which indeed was in my present case a fact, as I carried nothing but a bottle of brandy with me, which I kept in case of illness. Mr. Altone, however, seemed to take my refusal very much to heart. I got him to tell Mohammed that in future I would permit no starts before daybreak, except in cases of absolute necessity, as the ridiculous early start of the preceding night was only a trick to get more time in Deir.* Haji Mohammed swore that the place we had encamped in was infested by robbers, and that he did not sleep at all, but was walking round my tent all night guarding me. According to him it

* The Prophet, however, said, "Choose early darkness for your wayfarings. The calamities of the earth appear not at night." —Burton, Mecca and Medinah, Chap. X.

was unwise to stop there for more time than was absolutely necessary for a rest. Although sounding very plausible, the desire to get among their gossips was doubtless the true cause.

When I left Altone, the son-in-law offered to accompany me for a walk onto the island. We passed over the rickety bridge, which my guide informed me would, later on in the month, be carried away by the river, which, as the snows in Armenia melt, rises some thirty feet. The bridge was crowded with boys, engaged in catching floating fragments of wood, which are brought down the river from the jungle on the banks, as the river rises. To do this they have a long line, and an instrument formed of a piece of wood with four barbs, or prongs of wood projecting backwards from the point. When a piece of wood comes floating down, this hook is thrown in front of it with great dexterity, and being drawn back, catches it in the barb, and is drawn up. This is, I fancy, the only fuel the Deirites have, and boys seem to be continually at work.

Passing through fields of waving corn, a welcome sight after the barren country I had been travelling in, I came to a place where several cherrids were at work, which I watched with much interest. My companion was an intelligent young Christian of Mosul, but I found he hated the Arabs and the town of Deir, which he styled "beled khanzir," a swinish village. Unfortunately for my pleasure, Altone himself had followed us, and now appeared armed with his bottle of arak and glass, and accompanied by his little girl. He immediately began a long anecdote about his brother, " the English sea captain," and yarned in such an idiotic and offensive manner that I left him, forbidding him or his son-in-law to accompany me, and refusing his repeated invitation to supper. On my return I found that it was impossible to start the next day, as the animals were tired and the unfortunate mule still dead lame. I was not sorry to have another day's rest myself. The pleasure of being able to undress and have an extra night in comfort between the (comparatively) clean sheets of my Levinge bed, was a luxury not to be disdained. These were the only two nights during the three weeks' journey that I did not sleep in my clothes. In spite of the discomfort, it is always unadvisable to undress at night in an overland journey in Turkey, as at any moment one may have to leave the tent, either to see to the tent ropes, frighten away dogs, or possibly even to interview the wily Bedawi. The nights are also, in spring, cold enough to render every precaution against catching a chill a matter of necessity.

The dread with which the "berrieh" or desert round the town is regarded by the townsfolk and authorities denotes either that the tribes in this part are peculiarly predatory and unmanageable, which (considering that I travelled altogether three weeks on the banks of the Euphrates, without experiencing any trouble worth mentioning from the Arabs) I see no reason to believe, or else bespeaks an amount of cowardice on their part which is remarkable. The second morning of my stay at Deir I went out for a short walk on the desert side of the town, and about a mile distant from the town I sat down. Scarcely had I done so, when a soldier or policeman who had followed me, came fussing up to tell me it was unsafe for me to stop there, and that I must return at once to the town or river side. I laughed at him, but he insisted he had orders from the authorities that I should return, and there was no alternative for me. If there was really any danger so close to a populous town, in which a garrison is maintained, it does not say much for the good government of the place. The dread, however, with which all settled Arabs, and even Turkish officials, regard the desert, is well known and seems utterly absurd, considering how in Turkish Arabia they are continually face to face with it. A short desert route seems to be regarded by the town Arab with absolute horror. And such as live in unhealthy and crowded towns like Deir, or Hillah, never think of taking a walk into the sweet and bracing air of the desert which comes up to their very walls. Their idea of pleasure would be to make " kaif " (or have an outing) by repairing to some damp orchard on the river edge, to spend eight or ten hours in smoking, drinking coffee, and sleeping.

On my return, I found the trusty Mohammed in a great state of apprehension lest I should have been kidnapped. " El hamdu lillah," said he; " You are safe : what made you go walking out into the desert like that, without a guard ? "

I saw nothing more of my friend Altone, but I was honoured by a visit from his son-in-law. An Armenian doctor who spoke English fairly well, and had spent some time in America, came next. He had heard that an Englishman had arrived at Deir : there were two reports, one, that I was the " Balios," or English Consul, on his way to Bagdad ; the other, that I was a doctor. The Armenian wished to know which was the case, and if the latter, if I had any works with me on " diseases of the eyes." I gently broke it to him that I was only an " or'nery " tourist, and wielded neither the consular baton nor the staff of Æsculapius. He told me that now and then an Anglo-Indian would return to Europe by the Euphrates route, but English travellers were very rare. The advent of one was indeed an event that set the tongues of all the town wagging for some time to come. After him came the head of the Christians in Deir, a dignified Chaldæan who spoke French. These calls of ceremony over, I heard a clatter of horses and jangling of bells in the street below, and looking out of the window I saw a large caravan filing down the street. It was that of the Pasha and Greek doctor with whom I had partly arranged to leave Aleppo. The Pasha, a fine-looking man, came clanking up the stairs spurs and all, and while the rooms were being dusted out for the reception of the new comers, I ushered them into my room. The Pasha, however, spoke nothing but Turkish. From the Greek doctor I ascertained that they had left two days after me, so that they had taken about the same time *en route.* Their caravan was accompanied by a considerable military escort, and Pasha, his son-in-law, and doctor were all crammed as full as they could stick with swords and pistols, as if it was a military expedition into a hostile land, instead of a peaceable journey through their own dominions. On the whole I felt glad I was travelling alone instead of with this formidable cavalcade.

Haji Mohammed came to me in the evening, his face wearing a smile of satisfaction, and, patting his abdomen, informed me that for the first time since he had left Aleppo his stomach was " mashdud " (*i.e.,* stiff). I congratulated him on this state of things, as I could well believe his statement. It is astonishing how the muleteers perform the amount of work they do on such poor fare. As a matter of fact, they hardly ever seemed to require food. They had never anything to eat before starting, but on an empty stomach would " shrub " vigorously in turn the great water pipe they carried with them. About ten o'clock Bukhit would produce three dirty crusts of bread, which formed their breakfast and lunch. And in the evening they had a small mess of rice among them. In spite of this ridiculous diet they walked most of the route, having only one donkey

among them, and never went to sleep till after I did.
If I woke in the night they were generally busy
doing something among the mules, and they were
nearly always up before me. I had been eating
heartily (*i.e.*, as heartily as my larder would admit)
three times a day, and yet felt three-quarters starved.
I conclude the British stomach exceeds in magnitude
that of the Arab.

ANAZEH HORSEMAN.

CHAPTER VII.

DEIR TO ANAH.

Leave Deir—Mirage—The Castle of Rahaba—" Rehoboth on the River "—Mayedin—More Cats—Pass Salahieh—A Sand Storm —The Mules Cry—Cold Weather—Wandering Durwishes—A Bedawi Escort—Abu Kemal—An Ingenious Beetle—An Extensive Ruin—El Geim—An Anazeh Ghazu—I am Asked if I would like my Throat Cut—Danger on the Road—Fall ill—Desert Wadys—Wild Pig—Pass Rhowa—And reach Anah.

I LEFT Deir early on the morning of the 21st, much refreshed by the two days' rest. The poor lame mule was as bad as ever, and it seemed to me extremely doubtful if it would ever reach Bagdad. Bukhit had refused to replace it in Deir by another; I had to get to Bagdad, and could not sit down in the desert to wait till it recovered. Our caravan numbered about twenty animals, as several individuals had taken the opportunity to start at the same time. Among these were three " sharifs," or descendants of the Prophet, with bright green turbans; and a

N

couple of mounted Arabs with their long spears closed the procession.

Immediately south of Deir, just beyond the houses, are large mounds, which are apparently the remains of an ancient canal. Beyond this we got clear of cultivation altogether, and entered upon a very wide plain of light clay with very little vegetation. The hills of the desert proper lay several miles away to the right. Although the morning was cloudy, and by no means hot, there was a good deal of mirage, known as " sarab " to the Arabs; this strange phenomenon has been considered by some to be due to the slats in the earth. As a rule it is best seen in the middle of the day when the sun is high, but that it is not dependent on sunlight is shown by the fact that on this, a cloudy morning, it was unusually plentiful. The appearance of wide stagnant lakes near the horizon is the most usual. At other times a hillock or ancient mound is completely cut off from the rest of the desert, and appears above the horizon completely detached. Again a caravan cf camels in the distance are so dwarfed that they look like sheep, while further on a flock of sheep are stretched into camels. A low line of dwarfish scrub in an arid plain will present the appearance of a forest on the edge of a

big lake, every tree being distinctly reflected in the
apparent water. A mound or building will sometimes be so raised up and magnified as to appear
quite close, when really at a great distance. On one
occasion, riding to Bagdad from Babylon, a ruined
well, about two hundred yards distant, was so distorted in appearance that both I and a native of
Bagdad who was with me, simultaneously pointed it
out as the great ruin Akarkuf, near Bagdad, which is
about one hundred and thirty feet high, and distant,
from where we then were, some twenty or more
miles.

From three to four hours south of Deir we passed
over quantities of broken pottery; blue, green, and a
rough red ware like our flower pots were the commonest,
and there were also fragments of common glass. These
potsherds covered a great area, but there were no
mounds, and I have no idea to what date the site might
belong. Worked flints were also lying about in the
vicinity. I noticed also that the lizards here, though
grey and spotty over the legs, head, and body, like
those seen further north, had a red tinge about the
body which I had not previously seen. A beautiful
white falcon was also observed. No Anazeh were
seen, but a camel caravan was passed in the morning,

and shortly after a large one of mules and horses, which with two takht-i-rawans, was conveying some Pasha, his harem, and effects to Aleppo. One of the takhts contained two, if not three, fair fat forms. After I had lunched I espied in the distance a black object, which, as we approached, we found to be a dead black mule, which had probably dropped out of the Pasha's caravan. My animals inspected the carcase with an indifference which proved that they had received a proper Muslim fatalistic education, seeing that almost certainly their own ultimate fate would be identical sooner or later.

It is at this point of the river, on the opposite side, that the river Khabur joins the Euphrates.

At noon we were well in sight of a fine castle, called by my men Rahaba, and as the village of Mayedin, where we were to sleep, lay some distance away to the left, I sent my people straight on, while I with my policeman walked on to the castle.

After about an hour's walk across a level and grassy plain covered with flocks of sheep with their shepherds, we found ourselves close to the base of the remarkable rock on which the castle is placed. This rock is quite close to the cliff of the desert platform, from which, however, it is quite separated by a deep chasm. Near the base were ruined bits of wall, and lying about were fragments of bricks that were apparently older than the castle itself, which is of Saracenic date.

The plan of the castle is an irregular oblong square, running north and south, and consists of strong outer walls, built on the edge of the rock, which surround a large internal keep of the same shape.

The northern outer wall, which is one of the short sides of the oblong, faces the plain, and is of poor masonry, probably a restoration of somewhat later date than some of the other portions. At the north-west corner there are remains of a tower. The west wall is of massive square stones, and is partly ruinous. Some portions are, however, fairly well preserved. It is pierced with loop-holes, and above there are small arched windows. The lower half of the wall here is partly brick built, and there is a pattern formed of bricks set in a sort of key pattern. The south end is strengthened by two towers, that at the south-west corner being set diagonally to the angle, and the other one square.

Below this wall the rock face has been streng-thened by a revetment of masonry, of which there are also traces on the other sides. The east side

TTA-G*

is irregular and very ruinous, and appears to have had a double wall.

As I could find no signs of a proper entrance into the castle, I scrambled up the rock, and through an aperture in this side, and succeeded in making my way into the keep. This I found to be an oblong parallelogram with one corner (the north-east) cut off, thus making it a pentagon, and the walls of which were pierced by curious little circular apertures, apparently for light. On the east side was a well lined with brick. The interior of this keep, as well as the spaces between it and the outer walls, were filled with the remains of brick-built chambers in a very ruinous condition. Outside the keep near the north-west angle were the remains of vaults.

A fragment of the north outer wall was somewhat peculiar in construction. It showed three tiers of windows. The uppermost small, with pointed arches set close together. Below these were similar windows of greater size, and set much farther apart; and under these were wide pointed arches, with comparatively small pointed apertures within them.

From the ruins there is a fine view of the green plain, with the river and village of Mayedin in the distance. The bricks of which the castle is partly built, and perhaps the stones also, seem to have been gathered from a more ancient site. The Arabs attribute its construction, like other ruins on the Lower Euphrates, to Nimrod. Ainsworth identifies it with " Rehoboth" on the river (Genesis xxxvi. 37), and calls attention to the fact that it must not be confused with Rehoboth Ir or Ur, which is on the Tigris. There is also, at a short distance further down the Euphrates, Rahaba Al Malik ben Tauk, now called Salahieh.

The Elizabethan traveller Rauwolf describes it as a " pretty large town"; but Balbi, a Venetian, in 1579 only found the vestiges of an ancient town, having but a few inhabitants dispersed among the ruins. It was also at one time a Christian episcopacy ; but at the present day the site is quite deserted.

A smart walk of three-quarters of an hour brought me to the small town of Mayedin. There is a good large tract of cultivation round this place, the general style of which is very similar to a Nile village. Although not big enough for a bazaar, Mayedin boasts several shops, a mosque, with slightly leaning minaret, and a large police-station, opposite which I found my tent already pitched.

The cats at this place were a great nuisance, as

they were continually climbing over me in bed to get at my provision-basket; at last, in despair, I slung it to the ridge-pole of the tent. Even this did not quite stop the nuisance, as they then came in to look at it, and other adventurous spirits tried to swarm the outside of the tent. On account of this, and the mule-bells, which Bukhit refused to remove, I put in a very poor night's sleep. We left about sunrise, and a bitterly cold morning it was. The river, close to which we were, soon after leaving, runs here under a clry bank, like the Nile. In about three hours we passed mounds to the left, which my men called Ushareh, said to be an old uninhabited village. It was, perhaps, an hour distant from the road. This is probably identical with El Ashar mentioned by Ainsworth, about this place. About an hour before noon, after having been for some time in an unfertile plain similar to that we had passed over the previous morning, we found ourselves close to the cliffs,—in this place of considerable height and formed of limestone, with thick beds of a sort of spar.* I calculated they were about 200 feet in height. Numbers of birds were to be seen on the cliff-face, chiefly

* Ainsworth ("Researches in Assyria, Babylonia, and Chaldæa,") gives the formations here as gypsum and marls, capped by red clay and limestone breccia.

blue pigeons, crows, and different sorts of hawks.
Soon after, we left the river, and struck into the open
desert behind the cliffs. The desert here is a stony
plain, covered with a tufty plant of a peculiar frosty-
green colour. For about three and a half hours we
pursued our course over this stony wilderness, the
last part of the time being under the somewhat
questionable escort of four mounted Anazeh, with
their long spears. I tried to talk with these fellows,
and they seemed to me extremely simple and child-
like. At the same time we passed on the left an
extensive ruin, which looked like the walls of a town,
with a tower or gateway in the centre opposite us.
This was Salahieh, a ruined town and stronghold of
Salah-ed-din, known also at one time as Rahaba al
Malik ben Tauk. I much regret that I did not visit
this place, as my men, who, like all Orientals, continually told lies from the mere pleasure of doing so,
told me that our camping-ground was several hours
off, and it would not do to stay. As a matter of fact,
it was only about an hour distant, and I might very
well have gone to the ruins and followed later
on foot to the camp.

Soon after, we descended by a steep road into a

wady of considerable size, and were shortly again on
the plain, dotted about on which were numerous
tents. Here we turned back to reach our camping-
place, also called Salahieh, where was a police fort.
Happening to look out at the cliffs we had just left, I
was astonished to see that they were hidden in
a dense blackness. Where we were at that time it
was a dead calm, but in a minute the storm was on us.
A fearful squall of wind and rain, carrying before
it an enormous cloud of dust, caught us up, blinded
all the party (except myself, who, dry and comfortable, smoked placidly within my takht), and passed
on, completely hiding from my sight the front mules
about eighty yards ahead, before it cleared them.
The wind when it caught our party was of sufficient
strength to make the takht rock so that I dreaded
the mules being carried off their legs. Other squalls
of similar character succeeded, but none of the same
violence, and looking out I could count four or
five separate sandstorms passing over the plain.
When we arrived at our camping-place, having
made a stage of over nine hours, it was blowing
and raining hard, although, as soon as my tent was
with difficulty pitched, it was bright and sunny.

Other squalls recurred during the night, but fortunately the rain had laid the dust.*

I insisted on having my tent pitched at a distance from the mules, and by this means succeeded in obtaining a good night's rest, in spite of the jackals, which were yelling on both sides of the river, and of the mules, which seemed to be made restive and exceptionally noisy by the storm. The cry of the mule, by-the-bye, is very peculiar. It is a mixture between the horse's neigh and the ass's bray. As a rule it commences with a shrill scream—an attempt at the former, anything but pleasant. This is sometimes followed by grunts similar to those with which a horse ends his neigh. And then follows an abortive hee-haw. The effect of this combination is uncanny and disagreeable in the extreme.

The next morning, the 23rd of March, was bitterly cold, as we struck the tent to start. I could not help congratulating myself on having abandoned the Diarbekr route, for if this cold wave included the high country on that road, it would have been a return to the rigour of an English winter. As

---

* It is only a day's march south of this place where the steamer *Tigris* was sunk by an exceptionally bad storm of this character, in the Euphrates expedition in 1836.

it was, here on the Euphrates, and nearly half way to Bagdad, a heavy riding coat was indispensable for the early hours of the morning. After an hour's journey we came to a small stream flowing through the scrub towards the river. We did not cross it, but turned west, and as we saw it no more, I conclude it ran out of some small marsh. It was the only stream I saw, however, on the whole route running over the plain towards the Euphrates. Many tents were scattered about in this jungle, but to what tribe they belonged I could not ascertain. About ten o'clock we passed, about a mile away to the right, a remarkable hillock or "tell," in shape like a volcanic cone. From its absolutely isolated position, I suspected that it was artificial, although, at the distance, it had a great appearance of being a natural formation.

Soon after, we met a strange group of about twelve ragged-looking devils, with wild elf-locks, and a general scarecrow "devil-may-care" look, that was totally different from the appearance either of the haughty Bedawi or the caravan Arabs we had met on the road. Travel-stained and ragged, they tramped along, with no pack animals of any sort; their only luggage a few pots and pans hung over

their shoulders, or round their necks. They were
a party of wandering durwishes, making their way
from Bagdad to Aleppo. Turkish Arabia and Persia
abounds with these singular vagabonds. They are
something between our tramps and gipsies, and in
many cases are half daft. Often they are mere
humbugs, trading on the charity or folly of their
betters in fortune ; yet I cannot help feeling a sort
of sneaking kindness towards the wandering durwish, for, whether humbug, fool, or fanatic, his
wretched, homeless mode of existence is about as
hard a lot as can be imagined.

Four of our long-speared friends were again
accompanying us, this time mounted on camels
instead of mares. One lithe rascal, with teeth
like pearls, asked me for some tobacco, which I
immediately gave him. A few minutes later he
appeared by my side with an apron full of dates.
Of course I accepted, and munched them with a
great show of satisfaction, which, in fact, I did not
feel, as they had just come out of a greasy old camel
saddle-bag, and were, in fact, anything but clean.
I would not have hurt my dusky friend's feelings
for the world, and he nodded with pleasure and
smiled, and showed his magnificent teeth, when I

told him that they were excellent, and that dates were my favourite diet.

In spite of the transparent honesty of this man's face, and his evident friendliness, Haji Mohammed came soon afterwards to me with a yarn that he had been inquiring if I carried much gold with me; and asserted that if an opportunity was given he would rob me. This was only part of the absurd cowardice and distrust with which every town Arab regards the Bedawi, and it is most improbable that, after the interchange of presents (small though they had been), any true Anazeh would have harboured thoughts of treachery. I told Mohammed he was a fool, but in spite of this, he kept a very careful look out for any further appearances of Arabs.

About noon we arrived at a police fort, and a crowd of hurdle-built cottages called Abu Kemal. There is also here a considerable patch of waving corn, irrigated by numerous cherrids. My teskerehs were immediately demanded and carefully examined by an official, probably more with an idea of getting bakhshish out of me than anything else; but if so, without any success.

Heated with the blazing sun, which during the day was now becoming very powerful, I foolishly

bathed again in the river. The water was icy, and
the evening was also cold and blustery, and to this
bath I am inclined to attribute the attack of dysentery that seized me two days later, and which was
destined to enfeeble my health sufficiently to make
the remainder of my journey an arduous toil instead
of a pleasure. As I was dressing I noticed several
troops of Anazeh riding past the village, and it then
struck me that there was an air of excitement in the
action of these groups that had not been noticeable
in those we met nearer Aleppo. As a matter of fact,
they were all making their way to a rendezvous for a
" ghazu," or plundering expedition against their
hereditary foes, the Shammar of Mesopotamia. Of
this " ghazu " I was destined to have a closer
glimpse the ensuing day.

Abu Kemal, my muleteers informed me, was the
half-way house between Aleppo and Bagdad, a piece
of news I was not altogether sorry to receive. Before
I went to bed, my zabtieh, a Nubian from above the
cataracts, came to me for his certificate and the usual
bakhshish, stating that he had performed his duty
properly. While I was writing it I asked him if he
belonged to Misr (Egypt). " El hamdu l'illah," he
replied, and every tooth in his sable countenance

gleamed as he thought of his home. "Do you know
Aswan?" "Wallah."

The night was very cold, and we were off the next
morning at our usual time—sunrise. I was glad to
notice as we left our resting place that the poor
lame mule was really going stronger, and was evidently
getting well. Soon after leaving I had a row with
stupid Mohammed because he insisted on trimming
the takht all wrong by hanging the heavy " mattara,"
or water-bottle, on the wrong side. When I pointed
out we were all askew, and bade him take it to the
other side, he obeyed; but about ten minutes later
I caught him secretly replacing it. The reason of
this nonsense was solely that the " mattara " on
the near side interfered with the usual position of
their great lumbering narjileh. In the morning,
while out for my walk, I witnessed a curious
performance on the part of a big black beetle.
This ingenious insect was engaged, for purposes
only known to himself, in removing a piece of
mule or horse dung to some place unknown.
His method was as follows : he walked up to it
backwards, and then, placing two pair of his hind-
most feet against it, he rolled it rapidly away, pro-
pelling himself backward by means of his fore legs,

his head being thus on the ground. The performance
was, therefore, precisely similar to the familiar one
of the brewer and the beer-barrel, except that the
position of the roller was reversed. The ball of
dung was perfectly round, made so by the rotatory
motion imparted to it by the beetle, as I ascertained
by prodding it out of shape with my stick and letting
him go to work again, when he had it round again
in a "jiffy." The speed at which the little animal
propelled it was remarkable.

The country passed through in the morning had
no mountain on the west bank, but on the Jezirah
side there was a fine range in places close to the
river. This was the first time I had seen high
ground near to the river on the opposite side. The
road crossed first a gravelly plain covered with flints,
amongst which were many flakes, probably caused by
the manufacture of flint weapons in early times. At
about nine o'clock we came to and crossed a wide
but shallow wady, evidently a water-course in wet
seasons. This, a mullah of Bagdad who had been
travelling with us since Deir, called Wady Sheikh
Jebur, from a big tell at the mouth of it, close to
the river, which is Sheikh Jebur. Immediately after,
we passed, at about three-quarters of a mile distant

o

on the left, some extensive ruins, to which my informant gave the name of Sur.* As far as I could see, there appeared to be ruined masonry of six towers, and the ruins of a city wall on the desert side, and there seemed, also, to be considerable mounds. I had no opportunity of seeing these ruins without making a considerable detour and stopping the whole caravan, which was now nearly double my own party; but I regret very much I did not do so, as I am quite unable to find the barest mention of this place in such books as I have access to. Ainsworth, usually so careful and complete on the subject of ancient sites, was, apparently, ignorant of its existence. He mentions, indeed, a village called Jabaryah (or Jaburieh), but this is on the opposite side of the river, and some distance further down. As it was close to this point that the unfortunate *Tigris* was sunk, it is easy to understand how the place escaped his observation.

Shortly after this, another wady, and after about half an hour over a higher tract of desert we were again in the scrub of the valley; and at about half-past eleven we halted at a mud fort close to a water-course,

---

* " Sur " means in Arabic "walls," and in this sense only, the mullah may have used it.

known as El Geim or Keim, supposed by Ainsworth
to be the site of Ptolemy's Agamna: and the first
place where the old caravan routes from Southern
and Central Syria struck the Euphrates. At this
point the river, which for about one hundred and
twenty miles has been maintaining a south-easterly
course, turns east, or rather a point north of east,
which general direction, although with many bends,
it holds until the town of Anah is reached.

As we passed the mud fort I became aware that
something extraordinary was in progress. About
and in front of the "konak" stood several knots of
police and soldiers, who, instead of their usual list-
less air, carried their rifles, and were evidently in
considerable excitement. On the top of the building
stood a sentry, with bayonet fixed and his belt full
of cartridges, while on the river bank below an
exciting scene was in progress. A large crowd of
gesticulating, shouting Anazeh were engaged in
forcing struggling camels and horses into great
barges, in order to ferry them across. Some naked,
up to their waists in the river, were pulling, while
others on the shore endeavoured to push or drag the
frightened animals into the barges. The camels,
terrified out of their minds, flung themselves down,

o 2

roaring and gurgling with fear; while other boats, having been filled with horses, were shoved off to make the crossing, sometimes with the horses struggling and fighting, so as to make it appear that every moment a capsize would occur. Above and below were quantities of both animals tethered or hobbled, waiting for their turn. Besides the men engaged in the transport many other Anazeh were standing about, or were arriving or leaving on their mares, while

AN ARAB "GHAZU."

all about were their long lances stuck upright in the ground. At first I did not take in what this animated scene meant, and I walked down to the crowd and proceeded to "kodak" groups in the interesting spectacle in front of me. I then found out that a great ghazu was out against the Shammar of Mesopotamia, the hereditary foes of the Anazeh. The Arabs were all too excited to take much notice

of me and my kodak, although, I suppose, if it had
not been for the presence of the police my traps,
kodak and all, would have been confiscated to grace
the tent of some autocrat of the desert. As it was,
I attempted to get into conversation with a handsome
lad, who, from his dignified and authoritative air, I
concluded to be a young sheikh. He evinced a good
deal of interest as to my nationality and proceedings,
wanted to know what arms I carried, and inspected
with great curiosity my revolver; and, lastly, asked
me, with a somewhat defiant scowl, how I would like
to have my throat cut on the following day. As he
illustrated his query by drawing his finger across his
weasand there was no mistaking his meaning. So I
smiled—smiled, I say—as affably and serenely as I
could, and said that my English education had
always impressed upon me that the noble tribe of
Anazeh never descended to such unpleasant and
degrading behaviour, which was only fit for butchers,
Kurds, and similar offal. This confiding trustfulness
did not seem altogether to turn away his wrath, and
when I left him he still scowled defiantly at me,
although he returned my salutation fairly civilly.

Things, however, seemed really somewhat unpleasant, when, just as I was finishing my dinner a

deputation, consisting of my own men, the mullah, a green turban, and half-a-dozen soldiers, suddenly arrived outside my tent, to say that it would be totally unsafe to travel the following day, as the road would be filled with the ghazu, which, it seemed, was of large dimensions, and would be crossing the river for several miles. They said that even that day the soldiers had had a fight with the Arabs, who, being on the war-path, were turbulent and ungovernable; and that several of their mules had been killed and two soldiers wounded. In proof of this they produced an unfortunate zabtieh bandaged and bleeding, suffering from a bad lance wound in the head, but puffing away at the sempiternal narjileh. They represented that if I stopped here a day all would have crossed the river, and the road be safe I asked for an escort. They replied that they could only spare two men, and a hundred would be powerless against the crowd of Arabs if they turned nasty. I then asked my fellow-travellers what they said. They answered that they had nothing to lose, and if I went they would go, but that I had a lot of baggage and should run a great risk of having it all plundered by the Arabs in their present excited state. Bukhit and Mohammed said the same, so that, although I had doubts whether the Anazeh would attack the caravan of an Englishman, as they are decidedly well-disposed towards our nation, yet I felt it would be folly to run the risk of losing all my things when all danger might be easily avoided. I therefore consented to stay one day. Not half-an-hour later Bukhit came to say that he had discovered that there was no fodder for the mules to be got there, and we should have to travel to-morrow as usual : to which I at once gave my assent. In the night I was seized with excruciating pains in the abdomen, which I was quite unable to check, and when we left at five o'clock I was still suffering intensely, and completely exhausted by the terrible pain I had gone through in the night. Although the caravan numbered alto-gether about fourteen men, I and the solitary zabtieh were the only ones who carried arms, and if the ghazu had been troublesome, we should have been in sorry plight. The evening before, on arrival, two of the police had entered my tent, and in the coolest manner demanded drink. I at once sent them to the "right about," and told Mohammed not to allow any of the police to enter my tent. I have little doubt that it was in consequence of this that they refused to allow me more than one policeman as escort, although, according to their account, the road was about as dangerous as it well could be. I reflected, not altogether comfortably about this as we left, as nothing could be more easy for them, if they bore malice for their rebuff, than to put up a party of Arabs to attack me. We struck straight into the desert, probably because it would be the safest place if the Anazeh were all down at the river. We soon passed through two or three miniature passes, with great rocks and crags on either side, most handy places for an ambuscade. One of our party walked a long way ahead in order to keep a bright look out, but all was as silent as the grave.

After crossing a wide shallow wady, we were passing over the usual plain, when Haji Mohammed came to me to ask if my revolver was ready, as Arabs were behind. I was in such a state of drowsy exhaustion, partly caused by pain and partly, I fancy, by the opium contained in Dover's powder, of which I had taken a somewhat large quantity in the endeavour to alleviate my sufferings, that I could scarcely raise myself to look. When I did, I saw two solitary Arabs pricking over the plain after us, and our zabtieh, rifle unslung, firmly planted in their path. What the parley consisted of, I do not know,

but the Arabs retired. These, and another solitary
individual we met later on, were the only Arabs we
saw during the day, as the terrible ghazu had all
passed over early. The desert we were now upon was
very similar in character to that of northern Egypt.
About nine o'clock we passed a spur of mountain
projecting towards the river, terminated by two remarkable conical hillocks. At half-past eight, half-
past nine, a quarter-past ten, and half-past ten, we
crossed dry wadys, the last two being called respectively Wady Sofra and Wady Zella. The former is
a very fine example, broken up into many channels,
and bordered with jutting cliffs and rugged hillocks ;
where it opens out into the river there are the remains of an old nahura, now unused and partly
ruinous.

These wadys are rather picturesque, although as
a rule they are of no great depth. There is, in most,
a good deal of scrub growing on either side, owing,
no doubt, to the damp which remains in them after
the wet season. In March they are all dry, although
a few retain stagnant pools. I fancy, however, there
is no time of the year at which they all contain
water, either running or stagnant. They must therefore be caused by local storms of great violence. The

nahura, or irrigation water-mill, was the first I had seen since Aleppo, although at Anah, and villages further south, they line the river. At a quarter to one we were close to Nahia, another konak, where we were to spend the night. The cliffs here were again limestone, capped with a bed of gravel. Several nahuras were to be seen here, but only one in working order. Haji Mohammed informed me an early start was necessary the next day, as Anah was some eight hours distant, so I threw myself supperless, for I could not eat, and worn out, on my bed, on which, indeed, I hardly stirred till half-past two the following morning.

Soon after four we were again on the road, and as the sun had not risen it was very cold travelling. We sighted three wild pigs scuttling along the edge of the river; and the zabtieh rode on in great excitement to get a shot. This he effected at about two hundred and fifty yards, without, of course, touching them. Except lizards, these were the first and only wild quadrupeds I saw on the Euphrates road. Gazelle, of course, exist, but I never sighted any; and the Babylonian lion, which, until quite recently was found on both banks of the river, is seldom heard of now. I was pleased to find that the poor lame mule had got so much better that he could bear a heavier load.

Soon after five we crossed another wady of considerable size, and about two hours more brought us to Jebel Kushga, a mountain of a different type to those which we had hitherto seen. Instead of the level table-land bordered by an abrupt cliff at the river plain, we saw a range of which the contour was not dissimilar to a bit of Scottish moor. From the higher ground it descended in easy slopes, points, and gullies till the plain was reached. A ravine running from it to the river is called Wady Khushga. In the many nahuras on the edge of the river we saw that we were approaching a more populous district, and in the same reach I first saw human beings navigating the river. Two kelleks, or rafts, borne on inflated skins, were slowly floating down stream, guided in their course by men with big oars or poles. Shortly after a party of men and women on donkeys was met; almost the first life we had passed for two days. They were somewhat oddly dressed, and the akals, or bands with which the men's kaffiehs were secured, were of unusual width, and they were all armed with guns. I failed to ascertain who they were. A ruinous sheikh's tomb was then passed, more caravans, in one a native lady riding on a donkey, and then " El hamdu lillah," the village of Rhowa, on the opposite side of the river, came into view, standing in a palm grove; a truly refreshing sight to eyes of the traveller from Aleppo, weary with gazing for days on dreary desert and stunted scrub. Above the village of Rhowa is an enormous fort, built by Midhat Pasha, the good governor of Bagdad, for the protection of this route.

Rhowa is situated on a cliff side, round the end of which the river winds, forming a long reach at quite a different angle to that in which the river has been running. Passing over a wady we ascended slightly, and there at our feet we saw this reach, in which, embosomed in what seemed an almost endless palm grove, lay the town of Anah. Ill as I was, I could not but feel pleasure at the sight. The mules tossed their heads and rattled their bells. Haji Mohammed stepped out with redoubled pace, and Hamadi, in the exuberance of his spirits, burst into an ode in praise of Anah. Certainly the scene was lovely, and as we scrambled down the hill the place looked like an emerald set in gold, so green does it lie among the yellow hills of the desert. We made our way along a narrow lane, with a low precipice on the right and beautiful gardens, unfortunately much shut out by mud walls, on the left. This road, the chief and only approach to the town, was very narrow, and more than once we came to a dead stop, blocked by camels coming out. We then passed through a mud street, at whose doors women and children swarmed to see the arrival; and at last "outspanned" at an open space on the river edge, specially intended for caravans; for although Anah is a considerable place, it boasts no khan.

MY TAKHT-I-RAWAN.

CHAPTER VIII.

FROM ANAH TO BAGDAD.

Anah, an Arabian Sydenham—Illness—Wady Fahmin—A Dispute
—Haditha—Wady Bagdadi—A Thunderstorm—Arrive at Hit
—A Dirty Town—The Bitumen Springs—Ramazan—My Men
Catch Two Thieves—Kalah Ramadi—In Touch with Civilisa-
tion—Get Among Marshes—A Mule Sticks Fast—Accident to
the Takht—The Euphrates Ferry—Kofa Boats—Feluja—A
Night March—Lose Our Way—The Babylonian Canals—Akar
Kuf—Sight Bagdad—More Bogs and Difficulties—Arrive at
Bagdad.

THE town of Anah is quite unique among the
Euphrates towns, and is in every way a curious and
interesting spot. The river just above the town
winds round a limestone cliff, on which is placed
the village and castle of Rhowa, already mentioned,
and then forms a long island broken reach, on the
the west (or rather south, as the direction of the
stream is here easterly) bank of which lies the town.
The plan of Anah is remarkable; it occupies a narrow
strip of cultivatable ground, which must be at least six
miles long. My men told me it takes two hours to
pass through the town, and this I found to be true.
In spite of this the population is not great, as the

town is exceedingly narrow, bordered on one side by a low cliff and the desert, and on the other by the river. Unlike most Arab towns, the houses, instead of being crowded, are nearly all built in their own gardens of palms. It is, in fact, a sort of Arabian

A NAHURA AT ANAH.

Sydenham. The one interminable street that runs the whole length of the town is crossed at frequent intervals by the channels carrying the water from the nahuras to the gardens, and as each of these crosses at a much higher level than that of the road, a passage through Anah either by takht or on horse-back is anything but pleasant, as one is continually climbing over humpy aqueducts.

The people I noticed in Anah were remarkable for their healthy appearance and pleasant manners. The women and children mostly wear nose-rings in the desert fashion, and many have really rosy cheeks, a thing most unusual in Arabian countries. As at Deir, boys are to be seen all day long throwing for floating wood, which they do with great dexterity. Many of the Mussulmans of Anah claim descent from the Ommiade Caliphs, and in former times they were ruled by an independent sheikh of their own. Ibn Haukal states that in his time the name of this prince or emir was Abbas ben al Ummar al Ghani. Teixeira in the beginning of the seventeenth century found it governed by an emir called Abu Risha, " the father of feathers," whose power extended across the desert to Palmyra."* This name has been oddly corrupted by some travellers. Mr. Ralph Fitch, who travelled at the end of the six-teenth century, wrote : " In the river of Euphrates, from Birra to Felugia, there are places where you pay custom, ... which is for the sons of

* Ainsworth.

Arborise, who is lord of the Arabians, and all that great desert, and hath some villages upon the river." Again, Gasparo Balbi, who traversed the river in 1579, says " to Castle Anna, near to which in Diana, Arborise, an Arabian lord, liveth."

From the amount of green turbans and robes seen it is evident that there are many of the inhabitants who claim descent from the Prophet; but there are said to be also a considerable population of Christians and Jews.

The fortress of Anatha, or Anatho, from which Anah took its name, and which was conquered by the Emperor Julian, was on one of the islands in the river.

During the night I became very ill. Dysentery, consequent on my rashness in bathing in the Euphrates, had seized me, and the agony I endured was intense. Though racked with this, and fever, I was unable to get at my medicine, as the lock of the bag containing it had got out of order, and I had not been able to open it for two days. Some two hours before dawn my men, who, good fellows as they were, neither understood nor had any sympathy with my sufferings, came, and announcing it was time to start, proceeded to loosen the tent ropes. This I found was being done under the orders of Bukhit,

P

with whom I had had trouble before from the same cause, and who now thought I was too weak to resist his importunity, by which, as he was for some reason anxious to get to Bagdad very early, he hoped to make long stages. Prostrate as I was, I felt it would neither do for me to be travelling in the cold previous to sunrise, nor to give way in such a matter; I therefore rose, and it was not until I threatened the men with the tent mallet that they desisted.

At sunrise we left the camp and went bumping down the narrow road over the raised water-courses that intersect it. It was a full hour and a half before we really got clear of the last palm gardens and scattered houses. An hour later we came to a wady containing a long stagnant pool of water, to get round the head of which a considerable detour was necessary ; I was unable to ascertain the name of this, but it is about the same place where Lake Telbeis is marked in Kiepert's big map. At this place the mules were all carefully watered, and the mattara refilled, as we were to have a long day in the desert. Curiously enough, the Arabs prefer to drink the clear but stagnant, and probably unwholesome, water of these backwaters rather than the sweet turbid river water ; if I had been in the habit of doing this I should have attributed my ailment to it, but with the exception of once or twice tasting it, I was always careful to obtain the river water.

For another hour we passed over the fertile plain, for below Anah there is a great deal of cultivation, and we then struck up into the desert, a high and uninteresting plain, where we were for six hours. In the morning we sighted the tents of a few pastoral Arabs, but with this exception we saw no sign of life. At about noon we arrived on the edge of an exceedingly rough and dangerous wady called Fahmin. Although I had generally alighted at the rougher wadys to ease the mules in crossing, my men had always insisted that it was unnecessary : but here for the first time they came to request me to do so. The descent, when I looked down it, appeared to me about similar to the rocks and holes of the waterfall of Lodore in Cumberland, and it looked almost hopeless to attempt to bring the heavy litter with its mules over such a place ; however, they went pluckily at it, dropping themselves cleverly, in spite of the great weight they bore, off ledges of rock three feet high, and scrambling over and between immense rocks and boulders; it was, however, fearful work for the poor things, as being braced together, so

P 2

to speak, fore and aft with their heavy load, they could have no freedom of movement. At last they stood safe on the other side unhurt, though quivering in every muscle with the awful exertion and shaking they had had. The baggage mules managed very cleverly, picking their own way, and clambering about more like kittens than hoofed quadrupeds; other wadys similar, but less severe, followed. Soon after a furious altercation arose between the zabtieh and Bukhit as to which village we were to go to: at the nearest, which the former wanted, Bukhit affirmed no fodder was available; the other one, the zabtieh stated, was an unreasonably long distance from Anah, and he refused to go any further. Bukhit's statement I felt was not improbably a lie, as I knew he was in a great hurry to get on, but on the other hand it was equally important for me, ill as I now was, to lessen as much as possible the distance to my destination; I therefore gave the man the customary present and sent him about his business.

I noticed on the hill-tops about here huge piles of stones, which had the appearance of ancient sepulchral cairns; I cannot imagine what else they can be, although the Arabs deny this. We had now got sufficiently far south to begin to feel we were getting to another climate, and the heat and drought in this plain were very oppressive ; the sun was, and had been for some days, so strong that my light felt hat was insufficient head covering, even when accompanied by a pugaree, and I found it necessary to use an umbrella when walking.

We descended into the river plain at about three o'clock, but it was nearly three hours more before we arrived at Haditha. As we approached this pretty place we saw numerous sheikhs' tombs, some of which have the curious spire-like covering which often replaces the dome about Bagdad, but which is never seen in Egyptian work. We also passed quarries where many fine blocks of limestone had been detached, and were waiting to be transported down the river to Bagdad. Haditha is built partly on an island, and is supposed to be an old site, though it does not seem to have been satisfactorily identified. As soon as my tent was pitched, I forced the lock of my bag to obtain medicine, as my illness showed no signs of abatement, and I was unable to eat anything except one or two eggs and a little rice, which I had almost to force down my throat, so nauseous were they to me. We had made a double stage, having probably covered between forty and fifty miles. The

TTA-H*

medicine I took (a choleraic bolus) checked, but by no means stopped, my illness; but in spite of this, and also of dogs fighting among my tent lines, and a visit from a cat which I suddenly became aware of in the night, with its head in a milk bowl, I obtained some sleep. Later on I felt something stirring beneath my pillow, and having lit a candle to see what it was, the sweetest little mouse popped out from beneath my bag and looked at me, with hardly any fear; he was greyer and bigger than an English mouse, and had a pair of the most beautiful black eyes I ever beheld. He was exceedingly tame, and ran over me and darted under my bag, and behind my pillow and out again; and would almost let me take him up in my hand; he was a harmless little companion, so I let him stay, and blew out my candle; immediately afterwards I heard him negotiating a bit of biscuit.

In the morning, the 28th March, and the eighteenth day of my journey, we got away at about the usual time; in an hour we entered the desert, and soon after crossed a wady with a backwater in it. Nearly two hours later we came to another, which the men called Wady Sagreidan; and from that time till noon the road lay over a dull, monotonous plain, similar to that passed the day before. The air was heavy and oppressive, and there was some appearance of a storm brewing. A few showers were, however, all that we had during the day. About an hour later we were close to the river, under limestone cliffs, the outline of which was varied by a series of wadys, many of which were blocked by a sort of amphi-theatre of rock, which in wet times must be large waterfalls. The face of the cliff is here honeycombed with fissures, holes, and small caves, which seem to be due to the disintegration of the softer parts of the rock when the river was running at a higher level. Soon after we encamped at the mouth of a fine wady called Bagdadi, and, although not a house or tent of any description was in sight, I presume we were somewhere in the vicinity of the mosque and village of the same name, which Ainsworth mentions hereabouts. The place was lonely and desolate in the extreme, and had I been in health, and able to eat (which I was still quite unable to do), I should have fared badly, as I had nothing left except some rice and dates. I was so exhausted that I lay down and slept for nearly twelve hours on end, but on waking I found myself but little refreshed. At sun-rise we made our way a short distance up the wady, and then climbed out of it on the southern side. There had been no rain in the night, but when we got out on to the plain we found the sky inky black to the south, where there was also much lightning. Shortly after it thickened in rapidly, and after several flashes, and peals of thunder, which seemed to roll from one end of the plain to the other, the rain suddenly came down in bucketfuls. It only lasted, however, for a few minutes, but it freshened up the air considerably, and left all the ruts in the track filled with water, like an English lane in December. Small streams came gurgling down the stony slopes, forming tiny wadys of their own. When a spring shower has this effect, it is easy to understand how great storms will fill up the big water-courses. The men did not seem to mind the wet at all. This struck me as curious, in a country where rain is so infrequent. I suppose, in a hot climate like Turkish Arabia, it is considered a great luxury to get wet through now and then.

The desert, in gloomy weather, is about as ugly as anything can well be. In its normal state of glorious sunshine it has a beauty of its own ; but, without this, it is melancholy and uninteresting to a degree. Haji Mohammed came to me with a long face, saying that *he* had now got a bad stomach. Fortunately, his case proved to be anything but serious, and after I had given him a dose of Carlsbad salts he professed himself all right again.

After rejoining the river, we passed some cliffs, of which the strata was wavy or undulating, the first instance I had noticed since Aleppo, where the bedding of the rock was not horizontal. More wadys and backwaters were crossed, and we passed some curious examples of weathered limestones, where a layer of harder stone had protected the softer formation, and had left strange table-like excrescences dotted over the plain.

We soon came in sight of Hit, situated about a mile from the mountain, and on a black, spongy plain, the peculiar character of which is caused by the salt and bitumen, for which this singular place is noted. On the right hand we passed several sheikhs' tombs, among which was a large one in ruinous condition, which Haji Mohammed called " Mazarre."

The town itself is considerably elevated above the plain, being built on a large ditched hill, which appears to be more or less artificial, and similar to the citadel of Aleppo. It boasts only one minaret of any size, and there are, near the town, plantations of date palms, in which most of the trees are small and young.

About one o'clock we filed into an open space on the south side of the town, and close to the usual guard-house. The ground everywhere is covered with hard bitumen, exactly like asphalt, which made it very difficult to pitch the tent. In addition to this, the place was littered with filth of other caravans, and stank most abominably, so that I was in doubt whether I should not go to the khan close by, on the hilltop. Of the two, the smelly camping ground seemed the least of two evils, and with great difficulty my tent was pitched, the holes for the pegs having to be first made by driving big iron spikes into the asphalt. The fact that the place was just outside the town made it doubly uncomfortable, as a great crowd of boys and men insisted in wandering about the tent, prying into it, and tumbling over the ropes. After a short time, however, the Mudir sent a zabtieh to keep the people away, and to watch the tent during the night.

The town, which is of great antiquity, is, as already stated, built on what appears to be an

ancient mound.* The streets are about five feet
wide, with open sewers running down the centre,
and reeking with smell and filth. The wretched
hovels which compose the town are built of mud,
and, as far as I could see, were as filthy as the
streets. I took a walk through this paradise, and
although the townspeople did not actually insult
me, they appeared to resent my presence.

South of the town are extensive heaps of ruins,
apparently the remains of the ancient Is of Herodotus,
to which the mound of Hit must have formed the
citadel. On these are scattered about many beehive-
built kilns, in which lime-burning goes on, and the
lime from which is exported to Bagdad.

I afterwards walked to the bitumen springs
situated on the level to the west of the town, from
which they are distant about half a mile. It was
this remarkable phenomenon which gained for Hit
formerly the name of the " Mouth of hell." The
naphtha boils from the earth, and after being exposed to the air, becomes bitumen and petroleum.
The water is carried into pans or small square ponds,
where a great quantity of salt is formed by evaporation. The water in these pans is tepid, and in some

* It was taken by Omar's general in 637.

cases bright yellow. The salt in some is on the surface, in others beneath the water, or on the edges only. It has much the appearance of frosted ice ; the water is unpalatable to the taste, and the place itself emits an offensive sulphureous smell.

These bitumen springs were celebrated in antiquity, and were seen by Alexander the Great, Trajan, Severus, and Julian. Herodotus says that the bitumen of Is was used as cement in the walls of Babylon. At the present day it is used as fuel, and to cover the kofas or circular coracles used on the river, as well as other sort of crafts, and even, it is said, to line the water-courses formed for irrigating arable land and gardens. Both it and petroleum are exported in considerable quantities to Bagdad, but neither this, nor the salt and lime trade, seem to have given the town any appearance of success or prosperity.* On the river at Hit I

---

* Further information about the naphtha springs of Hit may be read in Ainsworth, "Researches in Assyria," &c., p. 85; "Personal Narrative of Euphrates Valley Expedition," vol. i., p. 143; Gratton Geary, "Through Asiatic Turkey," 1878, vol. ii., p. 17.

The accounts of early travellers are always of interest. Gasparo Balbi says: "to Eit, near to which is a boiling fountain of pitch, wherewith the inhabitants build their houses, daubing it on boughs cut from trees, so that they may seem rather of pitch than wood, everyone taking what pleaseth him freely : and if the overflowing Euphrates should not carry away the pitch thrown into the field where it ariseth, they say there would be hills raised by it."

Ralph Fitch, who travelled in 1583, writes: "By the river

saw several clumsy square-ended barges, constructed and used to transport cargos of bitumen to Busrah.

The nahuras here are more elaborate than those I had already seen, some of them having three or four water wheels.

The following day was the first of Ramazan, the great fast of Al-Islam; and when I went to bed the people were firing off guns all over the town to celebrate the event. In consequence of this, my men thought fit to make rather a night of it; Hamadi singing like a lark till goodness knows what small hour of the morning. Between these interruptions, and dog fights, and men driving donkeys over my tent ropes, and my policeman hawking and spitting outside the doorway, and thunder and lightning and tempest, I made but a poor night's sleep. At about one o'clock I was out

---

Euphrates, two days' journey from Babilon, at a place called Ait, in a field near unto it, is a strange thing to see : a mouth that doth continually throw forth against the air boiling pitch with a filthy smoke ; which pitch doth run abroad into a great field, which is always full thereof. The Moors say that it is the mouth of hell. By reason of the great quantity of it, the men of that country pitch their boats two or three inches thick on the outside, so that no water doth enter into them. Their boats are called danec."

It appears also from the *Tarikh Mirkond* (Teixeira) that pots full of burning naphtha and bitumen were used in the days of the Caliphate in battle ; an unsatisfactory weapon it was, for if the wind was in the wrong direction, the throwers instead of the enemy were burnt.

and saw the big mud brick minaret all lit up, and distinctly heard the chanting chorus of the faithful, which in the silence of the night was singularly impressive and beautiful.

We were off early, and for some time traversed low gravelly hills near the river. At one place we came to a recurrence of tamarisk scrub, a feature that for some days had been absent. After this we crossed a high piece of desert, covered with glistening fragments of some sort of spar. There was no sort of herbage growing here. Soon after we descended into a dreary salt marsh, the ground dark and quite spongy to tread on, although not wet. Through part of this ran the embankments of an ancient canal, the first we had seen of the great Babylonian network of canals. It consisted solely of two great banks or ramparts running parallel across the plain.

About eleven I was suddenly roused by the takht stopping, and, looking out, I beheld Bukhit, Haji Mohammed, and Hamadi, with their big sticks in their hands setting off at full speed across country after three flying figures. I had no idea at first what was up; but I saw them come up with the flying scarecrows, and strike at them

furiously. The scarecrows separated, but Mohammed tackled one and threw him, and the others
coming up, they set to and beat him lustily. As
I ran towards what looked like becoming a case of
murder with violence, the men desisted, and Haji
Mohammed fell on the unfortunate in a heap, and
pummelled him to a jelly. They then secured and
brought him back—a poor wretched-looking lad
with a cunning face. It seems that the three scarecrows had suddenly appeared, and had attempted
to steal something off one of the mules. The
zabtieh, who was behind, went flying after one of
the others when they separated, and he was now
brought up as wretched a looking creature as
number one. There was nothing to be done with
them; in fact, the first fellow had already been
punished very severely for his attempted theft, so
I dismissed them with a caution, after having
frightened them horribly by "kodaking" them.

In consequence of this little delay, a party who
was travelling behind us now came up. It consisted
of a man with two wives and children, the whole
being mounted on donkeys. The women, one of
whom was very handsome, would get in front of my
window, and have a good stare in. This, the man,

who kept the whole party in front of him like a
flock of sheep, soon noticed, and his big stick was
immediately brought into use to keep his good
ladies' mounts well to the front.

By and bye we came to a "wali"* or sheikh's tomb,
called Sheikh Waiss, which seems to be regarded
with peculiar local sanctity. An old man who took
care of the place came and requested a gift, a sort
of toll, which is levied on all travellers. At about
two o'clock we met a solitary Anazeh horseman, the
first we had seen for some days. The plain here is
in places richly cultivated, but in many places it is
a dull salty mud flat, here and there relieved by
sand hillocks.

After a long stage of ten and a half hours we
arrived at Ramadi, or Kalah Ramadi, a considerable
place situated among palms. We encamped in a
large square, having an enormous barrack on one
side and an even more imposing edifice, which I
believe was the Serai, on the other. Both of these
were built by Midhat, when Pasha of Bagdad. The
whole town as usual turned out to see my arrival,
and the crowd were unpleasantly inquisitive, and

* "Wali" really means the "beloved" or "favoured" (of God),
but is continually applied to the tombs of holy men.

some not altogether civil. I heard Hamadi explaining to these folks that I was a consul, which accounted for the rumour I had already found current to that effect. One individual asked me in French if I could speak that language, and although I replied in the affirmative, the ensuing conversation was not very brilliant, as those were the only words my questioner knew. A police official came and examined my papers and departed, having asked if my innocent basket of bottles, which only contained two bottles of purgative mineral water and one of brandy for medicinal use, were for my "kaif" or enjoyment. The inhabitants of Kalah Ramadi have the sallow complexions and manner of townsmen, very different to the bold swagger of the Bedawi I had seen so long, or even to the manner of the folks of Deir and Anah. The tarbush, however, which was so common in Aleppo, is not usual here. Kalah Ramadi is not situated quite on the river bank, and the only water obtainable was at a well in a neighbouring garden, at a water-course in which I performed my usual ablution, much to the amazement of the worthy gardener. Although a considerable place, I was unable to obtain a drop of milk.

Q

To show the cupidity of Arabs, I may mention that I presented my men with the little rice I had left (as we were but two days from Bagdad) and bought for them two chickens as a present. I had hardly done this, when Mohammed coolly came to my tent, and asked for money to buy fuel to cook with. I told him he ought to think shame of himself, and he left me looking crestfallen.

In the night, at the sixth hour, a gun was fired, and going out, I could see the white-robed form of the mueddin illuminated by torches or lamps, standing on a small minaret or roof of a tall house; and through the still night air came again the sweet chant. The night-calls of this functionary during Ramazan differ from those at other times of the year.

Next morning, as we left Ramadi, I felt we were regaining civilisation, as we were following the line of telegraph-poles connecting this place with Bagdad. Mohammed came to me with a yarn that he had heard that the British Consul had left Bagdad, and that I should meet him that evening at Feluja. This report proved untrue. He also said that during the day we should have to pass through mud up to our chests, a pleasant prospect to look forward to in our day's march.

The character of the country passed during the morning's march differed from what I had hitherto seen. The chief feature was mud-hills rising somewhat abruptly from the plain. These had the appearance of being alluvial, but of this I am not certain, as I noticed spar glistening on their slopes. About two hours after leaving, we passed the remains of another old canal, which must be that mentioned by Ainsworth as existing at Sura, four miles south of Ramadi, and which was known to the Romans as Nahr Sares, and called by Ptolemy the Maar Sares. After joining and leaving the river, we coursed along for some two hours between cultivated plain and more mud-hills, until at about ten, we again approached the river, here bordered by mud swamps. In spite of the bad ground, we kept going at a much quicker pace than usual, a proceeding very hard on the mules after such a long journey.

I was very disgusted with Bukhit's behaviour during the course of the morning. There was an old man following the caravan, who had with him a strong young unbroken mule colt. The poor old fellow had a heavy saddlebag with him, but his animal would not carry it, and indeed would hardly go itself. Every time he tried to place the saddlebag on its back, the beast plunged and threw it off, and it was piteous to see the old man with his load on his shoulder, dragging the unwilling mule, which hung back, thus adding tenfold to its master's work. I asked Bukhit to relieve him, by placing the saddle-bag on one of my animals for a bit, but the brute absolutely refused, saying that the man had his own animal, and that he (Bukhit) had only been hired to convey me and my appurtenances. A more churlish action I rarely witnessed amongst Arabs, who are generally charitable and kind towards the old or infirm.

About ten o'clock we entered a wretched quagmire of swamp, mud, and dykes full of stagnant water; and after floundering about for about half an hour in this slough of despond, we lost our way, which, however, we fortunately found again soon. The poor little grey mule came to grief in a pond, and had to be unloaded and pulled out, amidst much screaming and gesticulation. Getting quit of this in about half an hour, we entered a plain, partly under cultivation, and partly inhabited by pastoral Arabs, whose tents and herds of sheep and cows were to be seen in various directions. On the arable land I noticed in use a rude wooden plough, drawn

[*See p*. 86.] MOSQUE OF ZACHARIAS, ALEPPO.

by two horses.   About noon, while crossing over a
small earth bridge spanning an irrigation water-
course, I felt a sudden jolt, and the takht began to
roll over sideways.   I scrambled out anyhow, and
found the hinder mule deep in the water with its
head just sticking out over the bridge.   The poor
animal had its leg crushed up under it, and it was
necessary to unharness, and lift the takht clear before
it could be extricated.   The screams and yells of the
katterji and akams at this juncture were awful.
Fortunately, the mule was not hurt, and we resumed
our journey, no worse for the accident.   After this
we got into more swamp, the green of which, after
three weeks in the desert, was most refreshing to
the eye.   In one place we had to ford a big stagnant
pond, the water almost coming into the takht.   After
wading about in more marsh of this sort, we
arrived at the point where the ferry crossed the river
to Feluja.   A bridge of rotten boats crosses the river
here when the stream is of moderate dimensions, but
the floods, occasioned by the melting of the snows in
Armenia, were rising, the bridge was cut, and its
two halves secured to either side.   We scrambled
along a narrow dyke, formed apparently to keep back
the Euphrates water (with what success may be

judged by the swamps we had just emerged from), and halloo'd for the ferry-boat. While we were waiting, I found lying in the edge of the swamp an enormous dead turtle, or tortoise, about two-and-a-half feet in length, with a softish shell. I noticed here one or two of the curious kofa boats, which are so common at Bagdad on the Tigris. They are constructed of strong wicker-work, and are thickly daubed on the outside with bitumen. In shape they are perfectly circular, and are from six to nine feet in diameter. A large kofa will hold ten or more passengers, and it is said they never upset. They are " manned " by a solitary individual with a paddle, who propels, or rather guides, them on the current down stream. The return journey is made by pulling them along the bank. They are only used for transport across the rivers, and the type, as has often been noticed, is of extreme antiquity, as they are represented on the ancient Assyrian reliefs.*

After shouting for some time in vain, a square ferry-boat arrived, commanded by a fine, white-bearded, stout old Arab, who proved to be Mohammed's uncle. All the mules and myself were packed therein, the mules

---

* Herodotus describes similar boats in use on the Euphrates. He says they were covered with skins, and built in Armenia.

taking their places with a steadiness of demeanour that argued they had made passages in ferry-boats often before. My baggage was all put in a kofa, and a safe crossing was effected. The stream here is so strong that the ferrymen have to pull hard up stream till more than half-way across, when they abandon the oars, and the boat drifts rapidly down stream to a point of the east bank opposite where we started. I noticed that the current here, which is very strong, forms at intervals of a few minutes a large whirlpool in midstream, the gurgling of which is plainly heard on both banks. The ferry-boat, crossing to the west bank, makes a similar course, but reversed, as she is pulled and floated to a place south of the ferry point, and then pulled up under shelter of the bank. After arrival the boat made a second trip for the takht, which arrived not as much broken as might have been expected. The total fare for the crossing of takht, six mules, donkey, three men and self, was one mejidie and a bakhshish of a half mejidie to the ferrymen. Feluja is a wretched place, and my tent was pitched in a small open place opposite a coffee-house.

From Feluja on the Euphrates to Bagdad on the Tigris is a long stage. It is in reality two days'

journey, but is very often done in one. As I was
anxious to arrive at Bagdad, I consented to the double
stage, and after four or five hours' sleep, we left soon
after two o'clock. My men, although they had done
nearly ten hours' journey the day before, a great part
on foot, and with a fourteen hours' stage before them,
seemed to consider sleep of no importance, and talked
and sang most of the night. It was of course dark
for several hours after we started, and I could not see
much of the country we were traversing. When day
broke I found we were in a beautiful grassy plain,
totally free from the rough stony character of the
Arabian side. To our left lay a lake or large morass,
over the surface of which numerous flights of birds
were wheeling. In fact, the plain was alive with birds,
and far overhead were soaring large numbers of what
appeared to be wild geese. The zabtieh called them
" sakaklus."

From the uncertain way we were proceeding, and
the numerous stops we made, I felt sure that in the
darkness we had missed the road. There was indeed
no sign of a track on the grassy plain we were crossing. My men of course denied having lost their way,
but I resolved to watch our course with map and
compass. Fortunately we soon after met a man with

a gun, who directed us into the road, which we shortly struck, close to the cultivated plain which now we were close to on the right, and which was at a lower level than the uncultivated plain we were crossing. There was also a little scrub here, and the track was in a marshy condition, due to the recent rains, which had apparently been heavy here. Shortly after we sighted the mounds of an ancient canal traversing the plain, and during the hour and a half succeeding, we crossed over no less than five of these great double embankments, which seemed here to intersect the plain in every direction, crossing each other at all sorts of angles. Near the second of these I also noticed low mounds and fragmentary pottery. Everything betokened that we had entered that great network of ancient irrigation by which the ancient Babylonians raised their land to such power and affluence. The mounds of these canals are at the present day of such size that our view was limited as a rule in each direction by the nearest canal on that side. About the same time that we came to the first canal, we sighted straight ahead a curious looking object, which reminded me of the Westminster clock-tower as seen from Harrow Hill. This was the great mass of brickwork situated in the plain, some six or seven

miles west of Bagdad, and known to the Arabs as
Tell Nimrud, or Akar Kuf. This curious pile, which
is quite solid, and over one hundred feet high, has
been almost as great a crux to antiquaries and travellers as the Birris Nimrud. The earlier travellers
often took it for the Tower of Babel itself. Balbi
(1579) writes: "Before sunrise next day we traversed
again among those ruins, leaving them on the left
hand, seeing pieces of great walls ruined, and one
piece of the great tower of Babel, till coming to
Mascadon, they saw the towers of Bagdet or New
Babylon. From Felugia thither the soil seems
good, yet neither is there tree or green grass, house
or castle : but mushrooms so good that the Moors
eat them raw." And Ralph Fitch, who travelled
over the same route, a few years later, says: "The
tower of Babel is built on this side the river Tygris,
towards Arabia from the town" (*i.e.*, Bagdad, which
he distinctly describes, although he calls it Babylon),
"about seven or eight miles, which tower is ruinated
on all sides, and with the fall thereof hath made, as
it were, a little mountain, so that it hath no shape at
all; it was made of bricks dried in the sun, and
certain canes and leaves of the palm tree laid betwixt
the bricks. There is no entrance to be seen to go

into it. It doth stand upon a great plain betwixt the rivers of Euphrates and Tygris." It is probably the sole remaining vestige of some Babylonian city (perhaps Accad), of which all other traces have now disappeared, probably destroyed by the Caliphs for the construction of Bagdad. Gratton Geary* notices that the name of Akar Kuf is rather applied to the site than to the structure, which the natives invariably call Nimrud. Authorities are divided as to what the structure has actually been. A theory accepted by many is that it forms part of a temple of Belus. Buckingham, a traveller of great intelligence, thought it must be part of a structure something akin to the Egyptian pyramids; a likely enough idea, seeing that what remains is a vast solid mass of brickwork.

The morning was breezy and sunny, but not hot, and the ground we passed over was alive with large hopping insects of the grasshopper sort. Big yellow locusts were also fluttering about, flying against anything that got in their way, and settling on the ground with the extraordinary suddenness which is peculiar to this insect. Between the insects and the birds, we seemed to have got into quite a new

* "Through Asiatic Turkey," 1878.

country since we had crossed the Euphrates. The
Tell Nimrud, which we were now nearing, seemed to
alter continuously in outline, and several times it, and
the mound it rests on, seemed completely severed
from the ground,—the effect of mirage. The ruin
had such a very strange appearance rising, as it does,
in complete solitude out of the immense plain, that I
should not be surprised if it is not the original of
some of the very strange " efrits " or " jinns " we
read of in the Thousand and One Nights.

After passing this, and more canals, we came in
sight, at about noon, of a shining ball with four
needles standing round it. This was the gilded
dome and minarets of Iman Musa el Kazem, commonly called Kazemein, and ten minutes later rose
on the horizon a long low line of palm trees,
perfectly level and unbroken, but by a big smoky
chimney, such as we see at Warrington. This was
the first sight of Bagdad, the city of the Caliphs,
and " the abode of peace," over the marvels of which,
in Mr. Lane's " Alf Lailah," I had pored and
wondered for many an hour in the sunless north.
At these sights, the mules, who recognised the
" abode of peace " as soon as their human companions,
pricked up their ears, and put their best foot for-

ward. Hamadi tuned up, and we moved on with
renewed energy towards the city, which still lay some
four or five miles distant. But our difficulties were
not yet quite ended; in an hour's time we came to a
big backwater of the river, surrounded by marshes,
which it was no easy matter to cross. The first
mule that attempted the crossing stuck fast in the
middle, and had to be unloaded and led back to try
again. The takht then went in search of a shallow
and fairly hard place, which was at last found, and a
crossing effected. I was then carried across about a
hundred yards of boggy water, sitting on Hamadi's
shoulders with my legs on each side of his neck,
like an old man of the sea, but without the con-
fidence of that mystic old gentleman, as I felt every
moment I was going to fall into the mire. When
we reached the far side, and Hamadi, like Sinbad,
said, "Descend at thine ease," I did not pummel
him with my heels, as poor Sinbad was served, but
alighted promptly. Hamadi demanded "bakhshish"
on the score that he wished to treat his spouse to a
joint of mutton by way of a feast on his return.
To this I replied "Bukra" ("to-morrow"), as it would
not do to begin distributing presents before the
journey's end. After this another unfortunate mule

strayed on to a mud-bank and went in "up to its armpits," and had to be lightened and dug out like the other. All this was sufficiently annoying, within two miles of Kazemein, and it looked like getting to Babylon (or rather Bagdad) by candlelight, as the old rhyme has it. In addition to these discomforts, I had had no fresh water for some nine or ten hours, and dared not drink from the stagnant pools we passed. The palm groves increased in length, the chimney of the bread factory grew higher, and one or two long yellow buildings and a curious pointed structure, the tomb of Queen Zubeidah, came into view. Soon after we were at the outskirts of the western suburb of the town, and leaving the caravan, as my men said there would be some delay at the bridge, I followed Mohammed through an interminable maze of bazaars, markets, small mosques, and by-streets, all densely thronged with strangely-dressed people, until I arrived at the end of a bridge of boats similar to that at Feluja. Here we got into a kofa, and gaily paddled down stream to the British Residency. Near the landing-place a tiny fair-haired girl rushed into Mohammed's arms, and the great rough pipe-smoking caravan Arab melted in a moment. When the paternal embraces were over, the little thing kissed my hand and I bakhshished it. Colonel Mockler, the British Resident, received me kindly, and offered me his hospitality, and in a short time I was ensconced in a magnificent bedroom decorated in the Persian style, while Indian servants prepared my bath and unpacked my things. We had done no less than a fourteen hours' stage since our start that morning; so no wonder I fell wearily into a chair, the first I had sat on for three weeks.

CHAPTER IX.

Situation of the City—Advantages of the Site—Its Walls and Gates
now Destroyed—Old Guns at the Barracks—The Streets—
Houses—Architecture of the British Residency—Serdabs—
Coffee-houses—Bazaars—Shopping in Bagdad—Money—Mosques—The Tomb of Lady Zubeidah.

ALTHOUGH I arrived at Bagdad on April 2nd, and
did not finally leave for the Persian Gulf until the
19th, I was in Bagdad only ten days, as the trip to
Babylon and Kerbela occupied seven. During the
whole time I was in the town, my health remained so
bad, and I was so exhausted, that I was quite unable
to go about as I wished. On some days, in fact, I
was so prostrate, that I remained in my room at the
residency, totally unable to brace myself up to venture
out among the scenes and sights of Bagdad as I
desired. In consequence of this, the notes I was enabled to take were anything but copious, and the
reader must excuse the poverty of the following short
account of the city. To myself it was the greatest
possible disappointment to find myself thus incapaci-

R

tated at the culminating point (as it were) of my
whole journey.

Bagdad, the Baldach of Marco Polo, and the
Bagdat of other early travellers, is situated on the
river Tigris, some five hundred and seventy miles
from the Persian Gulf by the river, although a much
shorter distance by direct measurement. The situation has been well chosen, as it is placed on that part
of the river where it approaches to within some thirty
miles of the Euphrates, with which, indeed, it was
connected by a navigable canal called the Saklawieh
canal, the royal river of the Talmud. By means of
this it commanded the commerce of the two great
rivers of western Asia, which, although insignificant at
the present day, must at any rate in early times have
been very considerable, and the tradition of which
must, at least, have survived at the time of the foundation of Bagdad. From this point downwards the
rivers spread further apart, to close again at a point
some hundred miles from the sea, to which they then
flow in one undivided and magnificent stream.

The site of Bagdad had also other advantages; it
rose indeed from among, and was built from, the remains of a batch of ancient cities, whose decay had
made way for, and demanded the existence of, new

GATEWAY OF CITADEL, ALEPPO.

[See p. 89.]

R 2

great centres of population. Babylon, Selucia,
Ctesiphon, and Accad (of which the ruin of Akar Kuf
only is left), lay in vast ruins on the surrounding
plain, and the new comers had more than an ample
store of material at hand to raise their city.

The Bagdad of the present day extends on both
sides of the river (here one-eighth of a mile wide),
although that part upon the east side is considerably the greater, and is indeed Bagdad proper. These
two sections of the city are connected by a rickety
bridge of boats, which, to an eye accustomed to
Western engineering, looks indeed scarcely safe to
venture on. During the spring floods this bridge is
often cut, and then communication across the river is
by kofa boats, or by a small steam launch, which at
the time of my visit was run by an energetic Frenchman. At all times of the year there are certain hours
of the day when the bridge is opened to allow the
river traffic to pass.

The city, extending thus on both sides of the river,
was formerly surrounded by a brick wall, which, with
the exception of one or two towers, and a portion at
the north end enclosing the citadel and barracks,
was dismantled, or rather destroyed, by Midhat
Pasha, when he was governor—a governor whose rage

for European improvements did the city almost as much harm as good. Of this wall, descriptions remain to us in the writings of pre-Midhat travellers. Buckingham states that it was "built entirely of brick of different qualities, according to the age in which the work was done." It was defended " with large round towers at the principal angles, with smaller towers, at short distances from each other, in the intervals between the larger ones." On these larger towers were, in his time, some fifty brass cannons. At the present day Bagdad may be said to have no defences whatever. Hummocks of débris mark the sites of the towers. There were some six gates in all, but the majority of these have entirely or partly disappeared. There is indeed the remains of one on the south of the town, but it is a wretched affair; but one on the east side is said to exist in better preservation. The north-west gate was, however, the principal one. Ainsworth also mentions one called Bab el Talism, or the Gate of the Talisman, built by Khalif an Nasr, through which Amurath entered when he conquered the city; this, however, was built up and unused. Buckingham gives an engraving of a handsome structure flanked by two tall towers, each of which is ornamented by oblong

shields, in a similar style to which some of the old
gates of Cairo are treated, but to this he gives no
name.

Outside the walls was a broad and deep ditch, which
still remains to be seen, and which was apparently
never intended to hold water, although on the south
side it is now marshy and full of frogs in the spring
time, when the Tigris is full.   This, however, is only
the case at this time of year.

These defences surround an enormous area of
ground, which at the present day is by no means fully
occupied by buildings.   It is said, indeed, that more
than half of the enclosed space lies waste and unused,
or is, as at the south side, occupied by palm gardens.
This condition has caused Bagdad to be compared to
a walled province, such as Babylon is said to have
been, an incorrect simile, as the open spaces within
the walls of Bagdad are undoubtedly due to the decay
of trade, and to the lessening of the size of the city
consequent on the continued inroads of epidemics on
the number of the population, and were never part of
the original plan of the city.   Nothing, indeed, bears
witness more completely to the moribund condition of
the " Abode of Peace and the Tower of the Saints "
than these desolate wildernesses within her walls.

She has shrunk up like the dried and mouldy kernel of a nut.

The inhabited portion consists of the official quarter, Serai, and barracks, the bazaars or commercial portion, and the streets where there are no shops. All these, without exception, are built of brick, stone being unknown for building purposes in Bagdad. I walked one day to the barracks and citadel, which is still surrounded by an ancient wall, having several small and weak towers, and one very large one, thrown out clear from the wall itself as an outwork. Within, is a hospital, prison, and barracks, containing at that time several batteries (I believe three) of artillery. A curious collection of old guns and bronze mortars attracted my attention. One of very large size appeared to be old Persian, and was decorated on the flat-topped breech with a long inscription, while the parts technically known as the *reinforce* and the *chase* contained respectively representations of a man leading a horse and a lion hunt. These old pieces are said to have been taken from the Persians at the taking of the city by Murad or Amurath IV. in 1638.

The streets of the city are uninteresting to a degree. They are narrow, winding, unpaved, and filthy, and are closed in on either side by dead brick walls, unrelieved save by gloomy-looking doorways entering the houses. Although there are a few carriages in Bagdad, the roads are too narrow to drive in, and too smelly and foul to walk in, so that the temptation to explore is not great. In some of the more important thoroughfares, such as that approaching the bazaar from the south, they are a trifle less unpleasant, as they are wider, relieved at intervals by an occasional coffee-house, and as some of the houses belong to well-to-do Christians, or even Europeans, the walls are relieved by casemented windows. The majority are, however, without architecture and without interest. Passing along them, indeed, the eye may occasionally be caught by a little green and blue tiled minaret, but woe betide the wayfarer who should raise his eyes to solace them by gazing thereon, for in all probability he will trip over some dead or dying dog, or will be crushed to the wall by some donkey laden with not overclean water-skins.

Of the houses I, of course, as a stranger, saw but little. A great many of them are built in the Persian style, surrounding a courtyard. The British Residency, situated on the Tigris in the southern part of the town, is a fine example of the style. Its exterior is mean and uninteresting, and the entrance

is through a doorway opening straight on to the
narrow street. The visitor, entering, finds himself in
a fine courtyard, surrounded by buildings two stories
in height. The lower of these is occupied now by
servants' and different offices, and the British post-
office. The upper story has a sort of open balcony
all round, supported by pretty wooden columns with
stalactite heads. The rooms opening from this
balcony are the reception rooms and some bedrooms,
some of which have mural decoration of a sort
peculiar to Bagdad and Persia. The room I occupied
was the state bedroom of the place, and is worth a
little description. It was in plan a sort of T-shape,
and the walls for about half their height were white-
washed stone, above which was a stalactite dado.
Round the walls were stalactite-ornamented niches,
or recesses, between each of which was a small
mirror, the stone about which was gracefully carved
in a pattern. Above, in the cross part of the T, the
walls were entirely covered with mirrors of small
size arranged in panels and niches; while in the
limb of the T the wall above the dado was stone, on
which were picked out in mirror work, vases, stars,
and scrolls. The ceiling was entirely decorated in
mirror work, chiefly in diamond patterns, with a

mirror stalactite border, and the front part of the
room was supported next to the wall by two stone
columns with capitals of the same description. The
effect was striking and handsome, and had a
charmingly cool appearance, admirably adapted for
a climate like that of Bagdad. The house is, I
believe, of no very great antiquity, but this style of
decoration is very characteristic, and it would be
interesting to know at what date it was first adopted.
Two other features of Bagdad houses should be
noticed, and both are found at the Residency. They
are respectively the serdabs and the flat roofs. These
in this climate are both absolute necessities. The first
are living rooms built nearly underground, though they
generally have windows high up which admit light,
in a similar way to the area windows of a London
house. From May to September the heat in Bagdad
is so great that the inhabitants live by day in the
subterranean apartments, while at night they sleep on
the flat roof-tops. Of course, this necessitates early
rising, as the moment the sun gets above the horizon
it is too hot to remain there, and the sleepers have to
beat a hasty retreat into the serdabs. As the thermometer sometimes rises in the hot season to above 120°
Fahrenheit in the shade, it can easily be understood

that these arrangements are necessary, and that those who wish to venture out must do so either early in the morning or late in the evening. The sun of Bagdad has in it a sting which is perhaps hardly exceeded in any other part of the globe. Yet in winter both snow and ice are known.

At the southern end of the city, and overhanging the river, are some of the best houses in Bagdad. Some of these belong to rich European merchants, and though quite modern, are built in the old quadrangle style. Many of them have pretty gardens on the edge of the Tigris, and must indeed be pleasant places to live in, as no amount of Turkish misrule is capable of rendering squalid and ugly that noble stream. As a rule, these European houses can be distinguished by their greater smartness than the houses of natives, and by the fact that their doors and windows show evidences of the painter's art.

The coffee-houses of Bagdad form a characteristic feature. They answer in a sort of mild way to our London clubs, and are to be found everywhere. Many are pleasantly situated on the edge of the Tigris overlooking the river, while others are to be found in the bazaars, or more frequented thoroughfares. Others, patronised no doubt by such as seek

quiet, are placed more out of the town, and near
some quiet palm grove or garden in the outskirts of
Bagdad. They are mostly built on a similar plan.
Long rooms open to the front, where they are
supported by wooden pillars with the usual stalactite
capitals. Inside are generally benches or settles,
on which the faithful squat, and smoke their narjilehs,
and sip their coffee, and gravely discuss the affairs of
this life. In the month of Ramazan, when the said
believers must fast by day, these coffee-houses are all
ablaze with light by night, and groups may be seen
as the sun sinks all sitting ready, pipe in hand,
waiting for sundown to light up and commence their
mild revelry.

Although they are somewhat featureless, it is
necessary to say something about the bazaars.
These, on the east side, range north and south,
and in reality form the chief thoroughfares through
the town. They are, for an Arab-speaking town,
unusually long, wide, and straight. The majority
are covered with roofs formed of beams, cloth, and
straw in the usual manner, but a few are arched
over or vaulted in brick. In spite of their superior
width, they have somehow an air of squalor which
is not noticed at Aleppo or Cairo. They have, in

fact, an out-at-elbows appearance. As usual, certain
bazaars are given up to certain trades. There are
the invariable slipper and saddlery bazaars, and one
small street I noticed exhibited only the belts worn
by man, woman, and boy, which are, I think,
peculiar to Bagdad. Some of the finer of these
belts are very pretty; delicately woven in gold or
silver thread, and costing about seven or eight shillings apiece. The commoner sorts are inexpensive.
Another street is occupied by small warehouses,
containing nothing but the wooden columns with
stalactite capitals, which I have already noticed as
being used in the British Residency, and in many
coffee-houses. As Bagdad is in fairly good communication with the outer world, one finds a large
quantity of foreign productions in her market.
Indian goods make their way up " the Gulf " from
Bombay, and Manchester prints are, as at Aleppo,
very commonly seen in the bazaars. Mirrors, lamps,
and hardware are also imported, and great quantities
of loaf-sugar, which, I believe, all comes from France.
There is no proper European shop in Bagdad, which
is somewhat curious, as at Bushire, in Persia, on
the Gulf, there is an excellent one. I, however,
found a shop in a by-street, kept by a Levantine

who made a speciality of European goods, and who had quite a stock of wines and beer. There are a fair proportion of chemists' shops, but they do not abound as at Cairo, and all seem bad. Tobacco is all a government monopoly; but the price charged is higher than the original government price, as the good tobacco comes mostly from Samsun, and the cost of carriage has to be added. Fine Oriental fabrics are also to be had, but the purchaser must know where to go and what to pay before he ventures. They are mostly Persian.

Now that I am on the subject of bazaars and shopping, it is well to mention the difficulties which beset the uninitiated traveller who would " go a-shopping " in Bagdad. In the first place, there is a regular ring against all European travellers, and as soon as the hat of one of these victims appears at the entrance of the bazaar, up goes the price of everything, from a pound of butter to a Babylonian cylinder. The traveller who goes "mooning" down the bazaar in Bagdad thinking he will pick up bargains should be written down an ass—verily he will come forth as the sheep from the shearer. In fact, if any advice is to be given on the subject, it is that shopping in the "Abode of Peace and the Tower of the Saints" had better be left alone. If, however, the traveller wishes to buy, whether it be curiosities, carpets, or what not, the best way is to accompany some native, or, better still, send one alone to the bazaar to cursorily examine the things—which, however, should not be bought on the spot, but should be sent for again to one's lodging a day or two later. In this manner things can *occasionally* be got about their right value; but to appear and buy in person and on the spot is ruination, as throughout the town the shopkeepers have a regular high tariff for European travellers. There is only one regular dealer in antiques, one Ali Kurdi, whose shop and khan I visited several times, and made a few insignificant purchases. He had a varied and miscellaneous stock-in-trade of relics from the ruins of Babylon, Persian weapons and fabrics, and in fact all sorts of Eastern curiosities. Only one bargain did I make with this worthy, and that was a fine and beautifully engraved Persian astrolabe of the last century, which I only got cheap because Ali was ignorant as to what it was. As is usual among the dealers, he would not produce his best things for me to see, as he found I knew something—albeit very little—about their value. His prey was the wealthy

American tourist with the collector's eye and the millionaire's pocket.

The currency is the other cause of trouble to the new-comer who has to have dealings in the bazaars. In the first place, there are so many denominations, many of which are in base metal, that it is difficult to get hold of the subject. Then there are two rates of exchange—the bazaar rate, and the rate accepted at the government offices; and one never knows which is being asked. Lastly, the traveller from the north finds the very names of the coins transposed. A wretched little base coin, three and a-half of which, in Aleppo (if I recollect right) went to one "ghirsh" (piastre), and which was called " metalik," here becomes dignified by the name of ghirsh itself. Other coins in circulation in the north are refused altogether, and the value of all fluctuates daily! In consequence of all this, I do not suppose that the ordinary traveller comes out of any single transaction without being more or less swindled.

Most of the English residents, who are all more or less Anglo-Indian, do all their transactions in the Indian rupee, which is, of course, accepted everywhere. European gold is current, and there is also a good deal of Persian money in circulation.

The mosques of Bagdad are perhaps the most disappointing feature of all, for it is in these structures, if anywhere, that one would expect to find traces of the grandeur of the days of the Caliphs. It may be said at once, however, that in Bagdad there is scarcely a solitary building, mosque or otherwise, that is really worth study : a most remarkable fact when the great celebrity of the city in former times is considered. Neither is there here any such explanation as the continued earthquakes of Aleppo to account for the poverty of ancient structures. It is, no doubt, chiefly to the invariable use of destructible brick instead of indestructible stone that we owe this scarcity of ancient remains.

As to the number of mosques in the city, modern travellers give very varied accounts. No doubt at one time they were exceedingly numerous, but at the present day it is doubtful if there are more than twenty or thirty of any importance. There are besides these, no doubt, a number of smaller and unimportant sanctuaries, undistinguished in most cases by dome or minaret.

The external decoration of the mosques of Bagdad is in the Persian style. The domes and minarets are faced with coloured tiles, forming blue, green,

s

and white bands, diamonds or inscriptions. The
effect thus obtained is bright and pretty, but as the
dome and minarets thus adorned are in general
neither particularly elegant nor even well propor-
tioned, the art is more or less thrown away. Many
of the minarets are so much out of the perpendicular
as to strike the eye immediately : a feature anything
but improving to the appearance of a mosque, and
presumably due to bad workmanship.

Near the bazaar rises a heavy, but somewhat
curious, minaret, which is all that remains of the
" Jamah Suk el Ghasil," stated to have been, in
old times, the chief mosque of Bagdad. It is composed of brick, and is at present unadorned by tile
ornamentation of any sort; this having apparently
been all peeled off. Buckingham gives a somewhat
detailed description of this " minarah," and Niebuhr
had an inscription on it copied by a Mullah, which
recorded that it was built by Caliph Mostanser, A.H.
633. Europeans have often ascended this in order
to obtain a view, and one day passing it in company
with a young English officer, then staying in Bagdad,
a consular cawass, and my servant, I expressed a
wish to ascend it, which both of my attendants said
was quite feasible; and the cawass went to hunt up

the guardian and get the key. While this was taking place, a large crowd gathered round us, and in a great state of excitement, which at times almost verged on menaces, plainly intimated that we might not ascend. The cawass at last arrived, saying the guardian dare not admit us when the crowd was there: so that the ascent had to be abandoned. It is difficult to understand why the crowd should have thus opposed our ascent of this mosqueless minaret, to which access is usually accorded to Europeans.

In the Meidan or open space in the north part of the town is a fine and large mosque, called the Jamah el Meidan.

Among the others, the principal ones are Jamahs al Khassakeh, al Merjamieh, al Wezir (near the bridge), and Abbass el Kaddr, descriptions of some of which will be found in Buckingham's "Travels in Mesopotamia."

At the eastern end of the bridge of boats are the crumbling remains of the once renowned Medrassah or Educational College called el Mostansereh. Nothing now remains to be seen except portions of a long inscription in the Kufy character, recording that it was built by the Caliph Mostanser, A.H. 630. The

Medrassah would seem to have been a somewhat similar institution to the great Mosque College of El Azhar in Cairo.

I visited the so-called tomb of the Lady Zubeidah, the wife of the celebrated Caliph Harun al Rashid, the day after my arrival in Bagdad. In company with one of the Residency cawasses, I made my way across the river, and after passing through bazaars and streets almost as crowded and extensive as those upon the eastern side, we came in sight of this singular structure, situated in an open space, about which might be seen other tombs, most of which are, however, of a very humble character. The tomb consists of an octagonal structure of stucco-covered brickwork, each face of which is decorated with four square panels, the lower ones containing arched recesses, and ornamented with bricks set in geometrical patterns.

From the summit of this base rises a curious cone to a height of some seventy feet. The summit has fallen in, but the chief part which is standing is fashioned with a peculiar sort of stalactite work that I have not seen the exact counterpart of in other Saracenic work. The entrance to the structure is by a small external porch through an arched doorway. The interior is open to the apex of the cone, which is also

fashioned within with the stalactite work. On the
floor are three tombs of simple brickwork, one of
which is known by an inscription to contain the
remains of the wife of one Husein Pasha, who was
buried there A.H. 1131, at which time the tomb was
repaired by the said Husein. There are also two
small windows in the cone lighting the edifice.

A steep winding stair brought us out on the summit of the base, which seems about half the total
height. A sort of walk surrounds the dome here, but
it is now in a sad state of disrepair ; and from this we
obtained an extensive view of the surrounding country, including the pile of Akar Kuf, Kazemein, and
several of the domes and minarets of Bagdad.

If this is indeed the monument of Zubeidah, who
died about the year 830 of our era, it is of very great
interest indeed, but as we have seen, it has undergone
the process of restoration in modern times, and it is
not improbable that this has been repeated more than
once. It may be remarked that stalactite work,
which is so common in all Saracenic work of a later
date, does not seem to have been used in the earlier
structures. In the mosque of Ibn Tulun in Cairo,
which is a few years later in the same century, there
is no stalactite work, excepting over the Mihrab or

Mecca niche, and this is probably a later addition. Other tombs of a similar conical shape exist on this side of the river, and one much more pointed is the subject of an engraving in Gratton Geary's " Through Asiatic Turkey." * It can hardly be supposed that these slender, and not very strongly-built pinnacles, have survived unhurt for a thousand years, while all the more solid vestiges of ancient Bagdad have disappeared. On the whole it is more than likely that Zubeidah's tomb (if it does indeed cover the remains of that fair lady) dates in its present form from a considerably later period, and is hardly worthy of the attention that has been bestowed on it.

I returned to the Residency by a kofa boat. To pass beneath the bridge, it was necessary for us all to squat in the bottom of the boat, so as to avoid hitting our heads against the planking of the bridge, as the current bore us rapidly through.

* Compare also the tomb called Robein ibn Yakub or Rewah Ali, near the Karun river, an engraving of which is in the Hon. G. Curzon's "Persia," vol. II., p. 344. Buckingham ("Travels in Mesopotamia,") describes similar structures at Hillah.

CHAPTER X.

MORE ABOUT BAGDAD.

Kazemein—A Bagdad Tramway—The Mosque of Imam Musa El Kazem—Its Gilded Domes and Minarets—Population of Bagdad —The Plague—The Arabs—The Jews—Benjamin of Tudela's Account of the Jews—The Armenians—Christian Churches— Climate—Exports—Present Condition—Ramazan—A Bagdad Hotel—The Date Mark—Yusuf Antika—Preparations for a Journey to Babylon and Kerbela.

BUT undoubtedly the most interesting and beautiful place in the immediate vicinity of Bagdad is the village of Kazemein, with its magnificent mosque, one of the three sacred places of pilgrimage of the Sheite (Shiah) Mussulmans west of the Tigris. Here are said to repose the martyred bodies of Imam Musa el Kathem, or the patient, and Imam el Taki. El Kathem was the seventh Imam, put to death by the Caliph Harun al Rashid for supposed conspiracy (A.H. 185). The village which has grown up round the shrine is chiefly inhabited by Sheite Persians, and is connected by a tramway with Bagdad. This concern was one of Midhat Pasha's improvements, and except in their odd-looking loads of passengers and

strange surroundings, the cars are in every respect
like an English tram. The distance is nearly four
miles, so that it is a great boon to the inhabitants of
Kazemein. Although the solitary venture of the sort
in Bagdad, it is said to be a complete success. Kazemein, like Meshed Husein and Meshed Ali, has the
reputation of being very fanatical. As a matter of
fact, this feeling is in all three places on the decrease.
It is true that, even to the present day, Christians,
European or otherwise, are not permitted to enter the
sacred edifices, nor indeed is it advisable for any
Christian to gaze fixedly from without on their
beauties. The English or American tourist who would
take up his position in front of any of those mosques,
note-book or sketch-book in hand, would probably
receive anything but courteous treatment. Some
time ago, a European attempted to photograph
Meshed Husein at Kerbela, and got well drubbed for
his pains. In spite of this, the Englishman who
behaves with an ordinary degree of common sense
will meet with nothing but courtesy from the natives,
Sheite or otherwise. The fact of the matter is that
the old anti-Christian and anti-Frankish feelings are,
especially among the Sheites, slowly on the wane.
This is perhaps due to several causes. The British

rule over India where there are so many of the Sheite
sect; the increased intercourse between the East and
West; and especially to the shrewd insight of the
better-class Persians themselves, on whom the fact
has dawned that Christian Europe and not Mohammedan Asia is now the true fountain-head of civilisation, progress, and of commerce itself.

I visited Kazemein in company with Dr. Shaw, then
the physician attached to the British Residency at
Bagdad. We walked over the bridge of boats, and
took our seats on the summit of one of Midhat's tram-
cars, the iron seats of which we found unpleasantly
heated by the sun. The road led out by the river
bank, and after about half an hour we entered palm
groves. Soon after, we alighted and passed through
a crowded bazaar, in which many of the people were
evidently Persians. We were conducted by our
cawass to a private house belonging to a former
writer to the Residency, from the summit of which we
were to get a view of the mosque. Here we were
kindly received by the master of the house and a
Persian gentleman named Sayyid Hassan, to whom I
had been introduced at the Residency, and who had
most kindly offered me hospitality at his house at
Kerbela on my proposed visit there, which I was to

undertake shortly. We were conducted on to the flat roof of the house, where a most magnificent view was to meet our eyes.

The mosque of Imam Musa El Kazem, or Kathem, which lay before us, has a lofty and well-constructed containing wall, through which there are said to be seven entrances or gateways. The higher part of one of these (I think the principal one) faced us. As far as we could see, it was a fine and imposing structure, beautifully tiled with Koranic inscriptions and other ornamentation, and over the entrance itself was some decoration in mother-of-pearl.

Behind this rise two noble domes and four large minarets, besides which there are four smaller minarets at the same angles as the principal ones. The domes are of that form which increases above that point where it springs from the circular base which supports it. Both above and below this they are entirely covered with square plates of copper, heavily gilt, so that they shine in the gorgeous Eastern sunlight with a blaze which is most surprising. The minarets are similarly enriched. Below the mueddin's gallery they are tiled, but the balcony of this gallery, which is supported by stalactites, is gilt as well as the column above, and the fluted acorn which it supports. These minarets are much higher than the domes, and are of great elegance. One, however, like so many of those in Bagdad, has a distinct bend at the gallery. The whole combination forms a scene of surpassing splendour and beauty, which is only spoiled by two hideous clock-towers, erected recently, right in front and to the left of the domes, as we looked at them.

I was told, on this occasion by our host, and afterwards at Kerbela, that the plates of metal with which these mosques are decorated are made of pure gold. At the time I could not but feel sceptical on this matter, as the cost of thus plating in gold such enormous spaces would be simply fabulous. I noticed, indeed, that here and there were plates which were certainly not gold, and were, indeed, but wretchedly gilt, as they appeared quite brown in the surrounding blaze. This, however, might be the result of fraudulent workmen. C——, however, with whom I afterwards travelled to Kerbela, repeatedly discussed the matter with me, and he has since informed me that when pursuing his journey to Teheran, he often came across similar mosques. At that capital he inquired of some authorities regarding them, and was informed that all, without exception,

both in Persia and Arabia, were plated with sheets of
copper, gilt to the thickness of one-eighth of an inch
with pure gold.   Sheets of gold, he was told, would
be far too costly.   This is no doubt correct, and the
information I received was, perhaps, due to some
blunder between the Arab words for gold and gilt.*
After feasting our eyes, we left Kazemein, and
crossed the Tigris by a bridge of boats to the village
of Madaham, a suburb of Bagdad, and a summer
resort of its inhabitants.   This place is only about
half a mile from Bagdad, embosomed in palms, and
containing a fine Sunnite mosque — Jamah Abu
Hanefa.   Through the outer court of this our dragoman, who had formerly been gardener to the place,
led us unmolested ; and soon after we found ourselves
in a rickety carriage, rattling along a road—the only
one Bagdad may be said to possess—-towards the
town.

The population, which, owing to loss of trade, has
much diminished, is also very fluctuating, owing to
the terrible inroads of the plague, which, for the last

* The domes at Meshed, in Persia, are gilt, like the Arabian
shrines.   Chardin, in 1672, saw the plates being made at Isfahan.
He describes "plates of copper 10in. by 16in., and of the thickness
of two crown pieces."   On the inner side were two cross-bars to
secure them to the plaster.   Each tile was gilt, with " three ducates
and a quarter of gilding," and came to about ten crowns' value.
Curzon : " Persia, and the Persian Question."

hundred years has been particularly rife. In the days of its magnificence and opulence the numbers must have been very great, although the figures given by Arab writers are never to be depended on. I have already alluded to the great open spaces still existing within the walls. There has never been any sort of census, so that European writers, as well as natives, are only able to make guesses. In 1774 the plague attacked the cities of Bagdad and Busrah, and, according to records at the British Residency, the greater part of the population perished on that occasion.* The next visitation of importance was in 1804. Buckingham, who travelled in Mesopotamia 1816-17, estimates the then population at eighty thousand. Again in 1831 the scourge returned, destroying in Bagdad itself, according to one account, two-thirds of the population, and according to another one hundred thousand inhabitants. On these occasions the state of the city must have been terrible. Business was at an end, the bazaars shut up, and the very bodies of the miserable victims remained unburied. Mr. Southgate, an American missionary who was at Bagdad in 1837, found the city slowly recovering, and, according to his compu-

* Lady Anne Blunt : " Bedouin Tribes of Euphrates Valley."

tation, the population did not then exceed forty
thousand. In 1877 there was another outbreak, but
the *comparatively* small number of five thousand are
said to have perished on this occasion. At the
present day the population is variously given at
eighty to one hundred thousand, but the former is
probably nearer the mark.

In Bagdad the population is as great a mixture as
in the towns of the Levant. The Arabs, however,
constitute the principal part, and theirs is the tongue
chiefly spoken. After these in number come the
Jews, of whom there are said to be some twenty
thousand in Bagdad. Turks occupy, of course, the
official positions, but a Turk of the old school is
seldom seen. Persians and Hindus are a fluctuating
quantity, but besides the pilgrims, of whom the
number in Bagdad is at times very considerable, there
are also a few settled residents, who have taken up
their position here for religious, political, or commercial reasons. One-third of the entire Muslim
population are Sheite. The Christians are composed
of Armenians, Armenian Catholics, Chaldæans, and
Syrian Catholics. Upon the subject of them and
their churches I shall have a few words to say
further on. Besides these, one meets in the bazaar

Bedawis of various tribes and from different quarters
of the desert, Kurds from Kurdistan, pale Cairenes
from the Nile Delta, and strange-looking beings from
the wilds of Central Asia.

Among this medley, the Arabs naturally demand

A BAGDADI.

the most attention. Their numbers are, no doubt,
continually recruited from the ranks of the tribal
Arabs, who are occasionally attracted to town life,
lured by the hope of gain, or at any rate of a more
permanent income. In consequence of this, the

townsfolk vary considerably in type, the last comers,
of course, being Bedawi pure and simple, while those
whose families have for generations been inhabitants of the town, have a yellow complexion, and
a more unhealthy and unintelligent appearance. On
the whole, the Arabs of Bagdad compare very un-
favourably with the Cairene Egyptians, who have
never managed to get rid of the wonderful blood of
the pyramid and temple builders. The smiling courtesy of the Egyptians is not to be found among the
Bagdadis, although they, in their turn, compare
favourably with the Aleppines. Amongst the poorer
people, however, intelligent faces and active forms
are not uncommon, and some of these, as the caravan
Arabs, are hardy in the extreme, and capable of
undergoing the greatest hardship and fatigue without
murmuring. The white turban is worn by the upper
classes, but amongst the lower the kaffieh is very
common. The Bagdad *abbah*, or cloak, is worn by
all classes. The commoner sort is of wool, brown
with white stripes, and costs (at any rate to a European) about a napoleon. Others, made of finer
material and embroidered with lace, are very costly.
The languages spoken in Bagdad are chiefly Arabic
and Turkish. The former is the tongue of the

bazaars, and varies much from Syrian or Egyptian Arabic, and equally, I believe, from the tongue of Yemen or Mecca. It is considered very corrupt, and is unpleasant to the ear to a degree. Many words of Persian, and, I believe, also of Turkish, have been dragged into it, and the traveller conversant with the purer forms of the language would require considerable practice before he could freely hold communication in the language.

The Jews of Bagdad are an increasing community. Rabbi Benjamin of Tudela, the famous twelfth-century traveller, found but one thousand only, but, as he remarks, they enjoyed " peace, comfort, and much honour under the government of the great king." Buckingham* computed their numbers, nearly eighty years ago, at ten times that number, and about 1840 there were said to be fifteen thousand. At the present day they are variously reckoned at twenty to twenty-five thousand, which is a very high percentage of the total population. The remarkable account given by Benjamin of Tudela of their colleges, with their chiefs or presidents, and their principal officer, Daniel, son of Chisdai (or Hhasdai), whose title was Prince, or Conductor of the Captivity, and who

* " Travels in Mesopotamia," vol. II., p. 413, 423.

T

traced his descent from David, is of extreme interest, and has been often commented on. The po ition of this officer, whose authority was ratified and confirmed, under seal, by the "Lord of the Muslims." the Caliph himself, shows the Jews were no more a down trodden or oppressed race in Bagdad in the twelfth century than they are at the present day. It is especially to be remarked that not only Jews, but the Muslims of the City themselves, were expected to salute with due respect "The Lord of the Captivity" when he made his appearance in public. At the present day they are subjected to no sort of oppression, and form, indeed, a very important item in the population. Among them are many of considerable wealth, and most are engaged in trade and banking. The traveller will notice in the streets many Jews of noble and dignified aspect. They often wear yellow silk robes and flowery turbans.

The Armenians are the most important of the Christian communities. They are a go-ahead people, clever in trade and business, of all sorts and, according to report, not over-scrupulous or dependable. The ladies are supposed to be very beautiful, and it is well known that Europeans, settled in Bagdad for the purposes of trade, frequently contract marriages among their ranks. I visited the Armenian Catholic Church, and found it a simple oblong structure of modern date, extremely ugly, in considerable disrepair, and full of sparrows. On the walls were the usual quantity of pictures. I asked how many members there were of this church, and was told one hundred. On enquiring if the church possessed any old books or manuscripts, a lot of large volumes printed in Rome, in the Armenian character, were brought me to see. They were not more than a hundred years old, but contained some good old Italian engravings. The Chaldæans (or papal Nestorians) have also a church, but I was unable to obtain admission to it. I was informed that there were fifteen hundred members of this community, which I can hardly credit. The Syrian Catholics, of whom there are a hundred and thirty families, have a church, built some thirty years since, on the site of an older and smaller one. The present building is a large square room supported by eight green columns, and is decorated with the stalactitic ornamentation.

The Latin Church is a good brick structure, twenty-five years old. Internally it is an ugly cruciform building, with a central dome, and many glass chandeliers. Outside there is a serdab Church used for children.

Attached, there are two schools for boys, having at the time of my visit a hundred pupils in each. The school for girls is attended by four hundred pupils. There are a thousand members of the congregation, and five priests.

The climate of Bagdad has already been alluded to. The winter months, or, speaking more correctly, from October to April, it is all that can can be desired. In December and January frost and snow are not unknown, and overland travelling in these regions at that time has been found by some travellers unpleasantly wintry. April brings warmth, and sometimes, as I myself experienced, heat quite sufficient in intensity for the traveller straight from northern Europe. May is really hot, but is not, as at Bombay, the most trying month, as we are, at Bagdad, beyond the regions of the monsoon. June, July, and August are the summer months, a summer that to Europeans, and even to the natives is not without terrors. The serdabs and house-tops then come into use, and the house is more or less abandoned till September or even October. To give some idea of Bagdad at this time of the year, Buckingham records that when he was there in July, the thermometer was, at its minimum, at dawn 112° Fahrenheit, at noon 119°, at a little before two 122°, sunset 117°, and at midnight 114°. This heat, fearful as it was, was not exceptional, and even hotter weather sometimes occurs. For comparison, I may state that at Bombay in May, 1892, one of the hottest months in that broiling city, I never saw the thermometer above 99°, though of course considerably higher temperatures are registered at inland stations in India.

Wool, inferior cottons, gum, grain, and other products are exported from Bagdad. The dates sent to America and England come in some quantities from Bagdad, but in much larger amounts from Busrah.* Arab horses, but not of the purest Arab stocks, are to be bought here, and much more cheaply than in Indian markets. The horses mostly seen in Bagdad are handsome animals, of Persian or half Persian breed. The pure Arabs are only to be got by going among the horse-breeding tribes.† The characteristics of the Arab and Persian horses are quite distinct.

I will say nothing of the political or social conditions of Bagdad at the present day, because I had no opportunity of observing, and am not qualified to do so. Report says, and no doubt accurately, that it

---

* See Gratton Geary : " Through Asiatic Turkey," vol. I., p. 243.
† Lady Anne Blunt : " Beduin Tribes," etc., vol. I., p. 206.

is in as corrupt a condition as other Turkish towns.
The administration of its one pushing governor,
Midhat, has drawn from some writers unlimited
approbation, and from others as much censure.
Certain it is that traces of that administration remain
everywhere, but they are the witnesses of an energetic
and enthusiastic reformer, whose judgment was by
no means always sound, and whose reforms, where
they were so, came before their time.   In the un-
cleaned and often unlit oil lamps, and in the cast-
down walls of Bagdad, we see that, as one swallow
cannot make a summer, neither can one honest and
pushing Turkish Pasha make a civilised town. In the
untidy soldiers slouching about the streets ; in the
evil smelling bazaars and ruined mosques ; in the
rotten bridge of boats, and the mean dusty post-office,
one reads at every step that the curse of Turkish
inanition lies as heavily, or even more heavily, on this
once prosperous and magnificent city, than even on
many other Turkish towns. Pestilences have devoured
it ; trade has partly abandoned it ; the very Euphrates,
to which the country owes its history and former
opulence, has helped in the work by bursting its
banks, and by rendering the country to the west a
marsh, and so bringing fever and ill-health to the ill-

fated city. The glory of the city of the Caliphs has indeed departed. Will it return?

The morning after my arrival at Bagdad I summoned Bukhit, Haji Mohammed, and Hamadi before me, and settled up with them for the journey. To Mohammed, who had to the best of his ability served me faithfully during the three weeks, I gave two pounds, for although his services were not those of a trained body-servant and cook, I should have fared badly without him. To the other two I also gave a small present, and they all departed highly satisfied, and anxious that I should send for them if I wished for animals for the journey to Babylon. I then walked up to the post-office, whence I despatched telegrams to home and to Aleppo, with news of my safe arrival. The Turkish post-office, by-the-by, is not very much used by English people resident at Bagdad, especially for parcels, as tne Indian mail *via* Busrah and Bombay is found to be so much safer, although the time taken by this route is considerably more than by the Turkish mail *via* Constantinople. At Bagdad, Busrah, and the Persian Gulf ports, there are post-offices under the Indian Government, with English-speaking officials. From England letters or parcels may be transmitted to any of the stations at same rates as those for India. The British post-office at Bagdad is in the Residency, and on the arrival of a mail the crowd in the courtyard is a sight to see. Jews and native Christians are generally to be seen in great quantities, and Mussulman residents often prefer to receive their mails by this route.*

My stay in Bagdad was during the month of Ramazan, when street life in the East is scarcely in its normal condition. During the daytime the bazaars were quiet. Many of the shops were closed, or at any rate closed early in the day. A general air of inanition pervaded everything. The shopkeepers snoozed over their Korans, and from end to end of the long alleys not a solitary pipe or cigarette could be seen in operation. As the evening advanced, and the sun sank in the west, parties gathered at the coffee-houses and might be seen, pipe in hand, waiting for the welcome gun to light up, or to break their fast

---

* One of the results of the Euphrates Valley Expedition was a camel post between Bagdad and Damascus, which was worked from 1838 to 1881. It was kept up by the British Residency at Bagdad, and was subsidised to some extent by the Indian Government. The mails were carried by Ageil Arabs, who performed the distance, some five hundred miles, in ten to fourteen days.

with a cup of coffee, and the usual gossip. In the bazaars might be noticed great quantities of meat and bread, and other sorts of edibles, all destined to be consumed during the night.

Immediately after sunset the town seemed to spring into life. Music resounded on all sides, and bands of jugglers and conjurors paraded the streets to perform before the crowded coffee-houses. Later in the evening parties of revellers might be heard singing noisily as they passed along the streets on their way home. The bazaars, streets, and coffee-houses are, during the fast, illuminated at night, and the mosques are open and crowded.

An enterprising Levantine has recently opened on the edge of the river an establishment bearing the name (if I remember rightly) of Hôtel de l'Europe. I made inquiries concerning it after my arrival, but no one seemed to be able to recommend it, and no one had ever heard of any traveller putting up at this hostelry. I, however, with C——visited the place, which is a pleasant-looking little building built in the Italian style, and nicely situated close by the river. We sat in the garden, and indulged in the wild dissipation of a bottle of soda water and a bottle of "lager" beer, for which

" bust" we were charged two rupees. Nevertheless, this institution figures in Messrs. Cook & Son's list of " Oriental Hotel coupons." How it exists, unless it battens on the proceeds of drinking " Ramazaning" Muslims, I cannot conceive.

In Bagdad one does not, as at Cairo, see at every turn the lumbering camel, and one is not inconvenienced by being, as at that city, continually sandwiched up against the wall by the smelly pack of that useful, if somewhat ungainly creature. In fact, one may roam about the streets of Bagdad for a good long time without meeting a camel at all. I presume this is chiefly due to the caravans making always to certain centres of the town, where the caravanserais and khan accommodation are to be found. There are, however, to be seen in Bagdad a sprinkling of immense white asses saddled ready for hire, as in Cairo. In comparison, however, they are but few. These animals are large, even larger than those of Cairo, and are said to be very easy in their paces.

The unsightly sore known as the Bagdad " date mark " appears to be quite identical with the Aleppo " button" already described. It is equally common, and equally disfiguring. In fact it is to be found everywhere, from the head of the Persian Gulf to Aleppo, Mardin, and Diarbekr.

I was so done up on my arrival at Bagdad that I intended to take a considerable rest before I started to Babylon and Kerbela, which, although only some seven days' ride, I felt would be a pretty severe tax in the state of health I was in. The arrival at the Residency of Mr. C—— a lieutenant in an English regiment stationed in India, who wished to make the same excursion, decided me to set out as soon as possible, and we arranged to hire horses, and make the excursion in company. I had sent word immediately after my arrival to an interpreter, of whom I had heard at Aleppo, one Yusuf Antika, a Chaldæan Christian, who was indeed, so far as I could learn, the only professional dragoman in Bagdad, and who had been employed frequently before by English travellers. Yusuf promptly turned up, and having shown me a series of excellent testimonials, I engaged him for the journey, and also for a few extra days for shopping in the bazaar and making preparations. He was a short, square-set man, with a snub-nosed, good-natured, but very shrewd countenance, on which was always lurking a comical grin that set everyone laughing who talked to him. Although no beauty, he turned out a man of very great experience, and an excellent manager. He was, in fact, the most capable Oriental servant I have ever seen. He had travelled in Persia, India, Palestine, and of course knew the Mesopotamian routes well. English he had in some extraordinary way acquired to a very fair degree in Bagdad, and why, with his varied acquirements, he did not move to Beirut or Damascus, where he could have commanded high salaries as a travelling interpreter, I cannot understand. In Bagdad he wore a light-coloured cloak with gold embroidery, and a tarbush, a costume that suited him well; but on the journey he assumed a most extraordinary European kit, consisting of various articles of apparel which had been bequeathed to him by various travellers, and which, joined to an Arab kaffieh, caused him to present such an extremely comic appearance that he was to us a source of great amusement during the whole trip. Unlike most Orientals, his action and speech were rapid and vivacious, and he had a fair memory. In addition to these good points he was an excellent cook. With Yusuf, C—— and I perambulated the bazaars, laying in for our trip the usual commodities neces-

sary for travel in the East.   C—— who had a journey
through Persia in front of him, had his own saddle,
a convenience with which I was unprovided.   I was
strongly advised not to trust to a native saddle,
which is generally a cumbersome affair, and galling
in the extreme to one unused to them.   Fortunately
I was able, in the bazaar, to pick up a fairly good
English saddle for two pounds, which, when I had
done with it, Yusuf accommodatingly took off my
hands for half that sum.   Yusuf also undertook to
see about animals for the journey, and the day before
we started they were brought to be inspected.   We
had in all five horses, three for ourselves and Yusuf,
and two for the light baggage and tent that it was
necessary to carry along with us.   To look after
these were two attendants, the katterji, as mean
and irritating an old villain as ever existed, and a
younger man.   The horses were but poor specimens,
but might have been worse; and we accordingly
arranged that all were to be in attendance at six
o'clock the next morning, the sixth of April, in
order to make a start.

CHAPTER XI.

HISTORICAL SKETCH OF BAGDAD.

Foundation—The Early Caliphs—The Buyides—Degradation of the
Caliphate—First Appearance of Turks—Removal of Bagdad to
the East Bank of the Tigris—Ghenghis Khan—Al Mostanser—
Hulagu—End of the Abbasides—Persecution of the Christians—
Tamerlane—Shah Ismael—Capture of the City by Amurath.

BAGDAD was founded A.D. 763 by Abu Jafar al
Mansur, the second of the Abbaside Caliphs, who
traced their descent from Abbas, the uncle of
Mohammad. There was, however, a village on the
site at a considerably earlier date, founded no doubt
by the Persians, as the name denotes.* For the first
hundred and fifty years from this time the history of
the Caliphate is one of uninterrupted magnificence,
although, owing to the unceasing disputes arising
from religious and other causes, and from the
Turkish military ascendancy which so early set in,
it is never one of prosperity. In the time of Harun
al Rashid (786-809) the empire included Irak,
Syria, Arabia, Mesopotamia, Egypt, North Africa,

* D'Herbelot: "*Tarikh Mirkond*" (Teixeira).

Persia, Kerman, Khorassan, Armenia, Natolia, Geor-
gia, and Circassia, which on his death were divided
among three of his sons.   It was in his reign that
the powerful Barmekis, or Barmecide Wezirs, were
disgraced and deposed.   Amin, who succeeded Harun
at Bagdad, quarrelled with his brother Mamun, whose
general Tahir thereupon marched upon the city and
besieged it (812 A.D.).   The siege lasted a year, with
terrible sufferings to the inhabitants, and ended in
the total ruin of the city.   Amin was slain, and
Mamun took his place, but other intestine troubles
followed, during part of which time the city was at
the mercy of the soldiery; and his reign, which
was otherwise glorious, was broken by rebellions
brought about by his Aliite proclivities.   In the time
of Mostasim (833-842) commenced the degradation of
the Caliphate by the importation of Turkish mercen-
aries, which was so rapidly to gain ground; though
a long time was to elapse before the external bril-
liancy of the Caliphs' court was to be dimmed.   During
the days of Mustain, Mutazz, and Mohtady (862-870)
the city was the constant scene of siege, riot, or other
disorder, and in each case the Caliph was either
deposed or murdered by the turbulent Turks.   Yet
in the Caliphate of Moktader (908-932) the court is

described as of surpassing splendour. Seventy thousand eunuchs, we are told, lived in the palace. In the Audience Hall was a golden tree, upon which birds of precious metals fluttered their glittering wings and sang.* In 917 the Buyide dynasty, originated by three Persian brothers, usurped the country between the Caspian Sea and the Persian Gulf, and by the time that Al Radhi ascended the throne (934) the Caliphate was almost reduced to the province of Bagdad. The emirs and sovereigns of the provinces which formerly acknowledged the suzerainty of the Bagdad Caliph, now claimed independence, allowing only to the Caliph a spiritual authority. In 940 a pestilence and famine left the capital weak and partly depopulated, and six years later the Caliph, seeing the city surrounded by its enemies and with supplies cut off, invoked the protection of the Buyide chief. This was the beginning of the end. A short time saw the Caliph dethroned and blinded (as his two predecessors, who still survived, had been), and another raised in his place. Before the time of Radhi, each Caliph had remained at least the true " Commander of the

---

* Statistics and descriptions from Oriental sources must always be taken *cum grano.*

Faithful," and was in some sort a priest-king, but he instituted a head wezir, called the *Amir el Omra,* or Emir of Emirs, in whose hands these duties were placed. This post the Buyide seized, killing the Emir in office, and taking his place under the title Sultan Muiz ed Daulah. From this moment the fall of the Caliphate was complete, and instead of being, as once, the heads of the greatest Oriental despotism, the Caliphs sank to the position of abject slaves to their wezirs, if so the Buyides can be termed. Not long after one of these, Adod ed Daulah, assumed the title of Shah in Shah (King of Kings). This Adod, a brother of the first Buyide, had succeeded to the supremacy by defeating and killing Baktear, his predecessor's son, and in A.D. 980 he rebuilt the city, and founded and endowed a magnificent hospital.

These Buyides appointed their own wezirs, while the Caliphs themselves had only secretaries. At the beginning of the eleventh century, Mahmud, Sultan of Ghizni or Khorassan, besieged Bagdad, and mulcted the Caliph Kader in an enormous fine. A few years later (1027) the Turks appeared on the scene, and plundered the city; and in the following years the Turkish soldiers who remained in the city

U

kept it in a continual state of disorder by their
turbulent behaviour.   In or about 1037 they
revolted against the Buyide Emir, and burnt Bagdad.
In 1040, according to the *Tarikh Mirkond*, there fell
in Bagdad such a snow that it lay on the ground
three spans in depth; and the Tigris was frozen
over for twelve days — a most amazing state of
things, if it is to be believed.   In 1055, Togrul Beg,
whose aid had been sought by the Caliph Kaim
against Sultan Masud, entered the city and
plundered and destroyed it.*   The Buyide supremacy
was overthrown, and Togrul, having married the
Caliph's daughter, was proclaimed Sultan of Iran,
although not Caliph.   The Abbaside dynasty were
indeed destined to exist in this debased condition
for two centuries to come.   Yet, although the
Caliphate was moribund, the city was by no means
so.   It was, indeed, able to take under this new
dynasty a fresh lease of life, for in the time of
Caliph Mostader (1094-1118), and the Sultan Barkiarok, " the city of Bagdat, which was at first seated
in Mesopotamia on the banks of the Tigris, being
ruined by the overflowing of that river, he (Mostader)
removed it to the other side of the said river, which

* Authorities differ.   Some say he was well received.

was more commodious."*   The situation of the tomb
of Queen Zubeidah on the west side of the river
bears this out, but long before the city itself was
moved, a suburb called Rusafa existed on the left
bank.   Ainsworth states that a son of the founder
Mansur built a town called Mahadi on this side,
and that the two joined became Bagdad : but I am
ignorant of his authority.

About this time we get Benjamin of Tudela's
glowing description of the condition of Bagdad,
as he saw it in the twelfth century.   " The palace of
the Caliph of Bagdad," he writes, " is three miles in
extent.   It contains a large park filled with all sorts
of trees, both useful and ornamental, and all kinds of
beasts, as well as a pond of water carried thither by the
river Tigris."

Again : " The Caliph never leaves his palace again
for a whole year.   He is a pious and benevolent man,
and has erected buildings on the other side of the
river, on the banks of an arm of the Euphrates, which
runs on one side of the city."†

This interesting passage shows that although the

* Teixeira's translation of the *Tarikh Mirkond*, edited by Captain
John Stevens, 1715.
† " Early Travels in Palestine," ed. Thos. Wright, M.A., F.S.A.,
Bohn's Antiquarian Library.

city and Caliph's palace were on the east side, the
west bank was not discarded, and building operations
were in progress there. The arm of the Euphrates
must be the Saklawieh or Seglawieh Canal, or a
branch which joined that river with the Tigris about
this place.

In the time of the Caliph Nasir, the new city of
" Bagdat throve much: " but in these troublous times
when Ghenghis Khan was ravaging Asia, although
at one time he entered into alliance with the Tartar
against Mohammed, Sultan of Kharazm, he found
time to build or rebuild the walls of the capital,
which bore till their destruction the date of 1221, the
earliest dated structure in Bagdad.*

But the last blow was about to be struck. In 1227,
during the Caliphate of Mostanser, Ghenghis Khan,
recking nothing of his covenant with Nasir, having
ravaged Persia, made a descent on Bagdad. Mostanser, scholar as he was, was also a worthy representative of the early Caliphs. An army was collected,
and the tyrant was compelled to retire. In the short
reprieve that followed, the famous Medrassah el
Mostanser was founded. Of this building, of which
there still remains a small portion, dated 1232, many

* Buckingham : " Travels in Mesopotamia."

accounts remain. Four hundred pupils were regularly taught, clothed, and fed. There were four professors, a physician, and apothecary. But the end now came. Into the seat of the scholar Montanser stepped the effeminate coward Mostasem. This degenerate prince, heedless of the cautions of his friends, refused to take any measures of defence against the Tartars. Hulagu and his horde, surfeited with blood, did not wait long. At last a feeble army was raised, only to be destroyed, betrayed, some say by the perfidy of the Wezir himself. An attempt at defence was made, but the town was easily captured; the wave of blood-thirsty Mongols swept through the " abode of peace," and the last of the Caliphs was slain on the 13th of February, 1258. According to some accounts he was, by order of Hulagu, dragged through the streets in a sack until he died. The new dynasty was baptised in human blood, for at the massacre which followed a million and a half human beings are said to have been butchered in the city and surrounding district. So ended the Abbaside Caliphate, which had lasted for five and a half centuries, during which time thirty-seven Caliphs had occupied the throne.

About this time Marco Polo visited the city, and has left an account of the richness of the city, which does not tally well with the stories of the bloodshed and spoliation of the Tartar conquerors. "In Baldach or Bagdat are many manufactures of gold and silk. There are wrought damasks and velvets with figures of various creatures. All the pearls in Christendom come from thence. In that city is a university, where is studied the law of Mohammed, physic, astronomy, and geomancy. It is the chief city in these parts."*

According to Marco Polo, the capture of Bagdad was effected by stratagem, for " Ulan having a great army of one hundred thousand horse, besides foot, used policy, and having hid a great part of his men, brought, by pretending fight, the Khaliff into his ambuscade, and took him and the city, in which he found infinite store of treasure, insomuch that he was amazed. He sent for the Khaliff, and reproved him that in that war he had not provided himself with soldiers for defence, and commanded that he should be enclosed in that tower where his treasure was without other sustenance."

The writer then proceeds to tell a story about the Caliph, which, proving as it does that the Bagdad Christians were at that date subject to oppression, I here reproduce: " This seemed a just judgment

* " Pinkerton's Travels."

from our Lord Jesus Christ on him, for in the year 1225, seeking to convert the Christians to the Mohammedan religion, and taking advantage of that place of the gospel ' That he which hath faith as the grain of mustard seed, shall be able to remove mountains,' he summoned all the Christians, Nestorians, and Jacobites, and propounded to them in ten days to remove a certain mountain, or turn Mohammedans, or be slain as not having one man among them which had the least faith. They therefore continued eight days in prayer, after which a certain shoemaker, in consequence of a revelation made to a certain bishop, was fixed upon to perform it. This shoemaker, once tempted to lust by the sight of a young woman in putting on her shoe, zealously had fulfilled that of the Gospel, and literally had put out his right eye. He now on the day appointed, with other Christians, followed the cross, and lifting his hands to heaven, prayed to God to have mercy on his people, and then with a loud voice commanded the mountain, in the name of the Holy Trinity, to remove, which presently, with great terror to the Khaliff and all his people, was effected, and that day is since kept holy by fasting, also on the evening before it."

As Marco Polo commenced his travels in 1250, he was probably at Bagdad shortly after its capture by Hulagu, or Ulan, as he calls him. His description, therefore, of the condition of things at this epoch is of value, and tends to prove that the accounts of the destruction of the city are highly coloured. The critical reader may question the accuracy of the mountain anecdote, on the score that the country round is for miles one level plain; but the evident answer to this is that the very absence of the hill only proves the truth of the story. According to the *Tarikh Mirkond* (Teixeira), Bagdad was after Hulagu's death rebuilt by one of his wezirs, in accordance with instructions left by his master.

For a hundred and forty years it remained in the dynasty of Hulagu, and then the conquering Timur Beg, our Tamerlane, Sultan of Samercand, appeared on the scene. Twice did Bagdad fall into his hands; first in 1392, in a campaign in which he reduced both sea and land from Ormuz to far up the Tigris. Leaving it for new fields of conquest, the ambitious Tartar ravaged Turkestan, Kipzak, Southern Russia, and part of India, and in 1400, having sacked Aleppo and Damascus, he returned to Bagdad, where, finding that the former governor had regained possession, he marched on it, reduced it, sacked it, and raised on its ruins a pyramid of ninety thousand heads of slaughtered citizens.

From this time it seems to have become for a lengthened period the subject of strife among contending races, and dynasties of Turcomans and Persians. This is the period of the warlike Turcoman hordes of Black and White Sheep, under the power of each of which Bagdad fell at different times. In 1508 Shah Ismail Sophi or Safi captured it. Torn and rent thus by the continuous tide of discord, it must have slowly but surely gone to decay. Still it remained a great city with a great trade, and travellers' descriptions remain which show its opulence in these times. Master Ralph Fitch, in 1583, describes it fairly accurately, but by the name of Babilon.

" Babilon is a town not very great, but very populous, and of great traffic with strangers; for that is the way to Persia, Turkey, and Arabia; and from thence do go carovans for these and other places. Here are great store of victuals, which come from Armenia down the river of Tygris. . . . Babilon in times past did belong to the kingdom of Persia, but is now subject to the Turks. Over against Babilon there is a very fair village, from whence you pass to Babilon upon a bridge made of boats, and tied to a great chain of iron, which is made fast on either side of the river. When the boats are to pass up or down the river, they take away certain of the boats until they be past."

That by this is meant Bagdad and not Hillah or Babylon, is proved by the ensuing passage : "The tower of Babel is built on this side the Tygris, towards Arabia from the town about seven or eight miles, which tower is ruinated on all sides, and with the fall thereof hath made, as it were, a little mountain, so that it hath no shape at all. It was made of bricks dried in the sun, and certain canes, and leaves of the palm tree laid betwixt the bricks. It doth stand upon a great plain between the rivers Euphrates and Tygris."

The last sentence conclusively points to the ruin of Akar Kuf, which is between the Euphrates and Tygris, and towards Arabia, whereas Birs Nimrud, the tower of Babel of most early travellers, is west of the Euphrates.

In 1624 and 1630 it was unsuccessfully besieged by the Turks, but in 1638 it fell before Amurath IV., after a siege of nearly two months, since which time

BAGDAD AND THE BRIDGE OF BOATS, FROM THE WEST BANK.

it has been Turkish territory, and the capital (it may be said) of Turkish Arabia. Captain Alexander Hamilton, early in the eighteenth century, describes it as a " prodigious large city, and the seat of a Beglerbeg, who governs a very great province."

CHAPTER XII.

BAGDAD TO BABYLON AND HILLAH.

Leave Bagdad—Khan Ez Zad—Khan Mahmudieh—Pilgrim Caravan
—The Kajaweh—Khan Birunus—Reach Khan Haswa—Archi-
tecture of Persian Khans—Sleep in a Coffee-house and are
Worried by Fleas—Leave Khan Haswa—Sight the Ruins of
Babylon—Meet two Americans—Reach the ruins — Babel—
The Mujelibe and Kasr—Amran ibn Ali—Leave for Hillah—
Knock Down an Old Woman.

SOON after six o'clock, as I was getting ready, Yusuf
appeared in my room with the news that the horses
were in the courtyard, and everything was ready for
a start.   Yusuf's " get up " was certainly sufficiently
business-like, for he was habited in a leather riding-
coat, a pair of breeches that must have at least
been built for a six-foot man, and stockings and
boots.   If it had not been for his red kaffieh and
akal he might have passed for an ugly little city man
going out grouse shooting.   Our traps were carried
down into the court, and then began the usual fuss
of an Eastern start.   The katterji immediately gave
out that our baggage was too much for the two
horses we had hired, and refused to start unless we

ordered another. This was a lie, the katterji's real
reason being that he wished to have one animal
lightly loaded so that he could ride himself. However, the old sinner held out, and as we considered
that we should be able to travel more rapidly with
the third animal, we gave in. As a matter of fact,
we had no alternative, as we should never have got
away without. At last, at about twenty minutes
past seven, bags, tent, bedding, and provisions were
loaded up; and leaving the Residency, we proceeded
slowly through the silent bazaars and across the
bridge of boats.

After passing through the streets of the western
suburb of Bagdad, which already contained a good
many people, we reached in an hour and twenty
minutes another bridge, crossing what I was then
told was a backwater of the river, but which, as far
as I can ascertain, was in reality the outlet of the
great Saklawieh Canal, connecting the Tigris and
Euphrates. Across this our little party stumped,
and on the far side were brought to a halt to pay a
toll, and to receive from the keeper of a khan called
Khan Khirr a not unwelcome cup of coffee.

The country we now entered upon was an immense
level plain, endless to the eye, hard under foot, which

fills for miles the space between the two great rivers, and which at one time, under the management of an active though barbaric civilisation, yielded up its riches, but which now, under an effete Oriental government, is as barren and as unproductive as the North Pole. Yet, strange to say, as we rode along we were at once in touch of the most modern invention of the Western world and the most cherished superstitions of el-Islam. On one side of us was the telegraph wire running from Bagdad to Kerbela, Hillah, Nejef, and Busrah, and along the track close to it wound strange groups of pilgrims from Persia, India, and the Gulf, all bound for, or returning from the shrines of Meshed Ali and Meshed Husein, the pilgrimage which to the Sheite Mohammedans ranks only second to the Mecca Hajj. Of animal life little was to be seen. Occasionally great flights of sandgrouse crossed over head, and often we saw on the telegraph wires beautiful green birds of the kingfisher tribe, which live on the frogs of the Babylonian marshes.

After four hours' ride we came to the first khan upon the road, Khan Ez Zad, an enormous mosquelike structure built of brick. To my surprise, there was not a soul to be seen, and riding through the

entrance I perceived that the place was unused and
in a state of considerable dilapidation. It would
seem that these caravanseras, which are mostly due
to the charity of wealthy and pious Sheites, are now
more numerous upon the road than is necessary. A
new khan is founded and built upon the plain, and
the tide of pilgrims turns to it, and the adjacent
one is abandoned and falls to ruin. Khan Ez Zad,
which Buckingham found " so crowded with animals
and their riders that we could scarcely press our
way through," and " capable of accommodating at
least five hundred persons," and which Layard calls
"habitable," is now abandoned for Khan Mahmudieh,
one and a half hours further on, which, as it is not
mentioned by either of these travellers, is perhaps a
modern structure. Khan Ez Zad is an enormous
building of brick, of quadrangular plan. From the
centre of one side rises a square block containing the
entrance and four recesses, two of which, with the
entrance, are decorated with stalactite work. The
external wall facing the road has a series of deep
obtusely pointed arched recesses, in which, when
the interior was full, travellers could shelter and
sleep. The few Arab huts around were also abandoned.

After riding for another hour and a half we came to Khan Mahmudieh, similar to the last, and opposite to which was a coffee-house, where we reined in and stretched our legs while Yusuf unpacked the lunch and our animals munched their well-earned fodder. While we sat over our lunch of cold chicken, Arab bread, and excellent Kerkuk wine, a continued stream of arriving or departing "kafilahs," or pilgrim caravans, passed before our eyes.

Wild-looking Persians, with black elf-locks (like those on the coins of the early Edwards), escaping from under their black or white skull caps, came trudging up to the khan leading or dragging weary mules, on whose backs the heavy "kajaweh" or double pannier with its living burdens rested. The kajaweh consists of two boxes, with an arched and curtained framework above, which, being secured together, rest on the sides of an enormous pack saddle. I have seen a man and a child reposing in one and a woman and child in the other, a cruel load for one mule. The usual load is two adults, but a man travelling alone will stuff into the opposite side an equivalent weight of baggage to trim the kajaweh.

Women in blue gowns and trousers and white veils, perched high up on an enormous saddle like

x

clumsy bundles, and looking as if they might at
any moment topple off, formed no inconsiderable
portion of these pilgrim parties. Mules jangling
with bells, donkeys absolutely covered with pans
and domestic utensils; wild travel-stained figures
and forms, both human and animal, dragged together by the great magnet of superstition from
many a distant quarter of the East, to join into one
unsavoury, but picturesque medley at the gates of
Meshed Husein and Meshed Ali.*

After a halt of some three-quarters of an hour,
during which we were the objects of a good deal
of curiosity on the part of the natives, we remounted
and set out again. A ride of an hour and three-
quarters brought us to another large unused khan,
called Birunus, or, as some say, Bir Yunus, or the
well at which the Prophet Jonas halted to rest
As to the correctness of this derivation I hazard no
guess, but the name is pronounced as one word—
Birunus.

When we had passed this, we were in sight of
another distant khan, which Yusuf informed us was

---

* All this country has been intersected by ancient canals joining
the Euphrates and Tigris. The remains of one close to Mahmudieh
is supposed to be the Nahr Malka of the Babylonians, and the chief
canal even in the times of the Caliphs.

to be our resting place for the night. We therefore put spurs to our animals, and galloped on at a better pace, with Yusuf thundering at our heels on his sorry nag, which he encouraged to increase its speed by a mixture of English and Arabic curses. A funny enough spectacle he presented in his absurd costume, with a small saddle-bag or khurjin, which contained one or two immediate necessities for the road, walloping up and down and battering the bony flanks of his steed. The old katterji and the baggage animals we left far behind, to follow at their leisure, and as the sun's heat was now subsiding, and the hard mud plain was pleasant enough going, the gallop was a pleasant change had it not been that seven hours in the saddle in a blazing sun had galled us somewhat in the seat. The khan was, however, much farther off than it appeared, and it was half-past four before we galloped up to the khan door, where the entire population of the invariable Arab village was turned out to receive us. We dismounted, and, tired and stiff with the exercise, we threw ourselves on a bench outside a coffee-house to await the arrival of the baggage. It remained, however, to secure accommodation for the night, and after looking

x 2

into the khan courtyard, thronged with sheep, cattle, and horses, we made an arrangement with the kafedji of the coffee-house to occupy it for the night for the consideration of a small sum, which ensured us a sort of privacy. It was, of course, as dirty as the khan, or nearly so, consisting of a long dark room, reeking with the smoke of the kafedji's fire, and full of fleas. Round the walls were a series of arched recesses, with platforms crossing them about two or three feet from the ground. When the katterji arrived, we spread our beds in two of these, and while Yusuf prepared our dinner we had a look round the place, and reposed our stiff limbs on benches in front of the coffee-house, before the gaze of an admiring crowd.

Between Birunus and Khan Haswa, where we were now, the road divides, the track going to the right or west leading to Musseyib, Kerbela, and Nejef, and being, in fact, the pilgrim road. The one to the left is the road to Hillah, and on both of these roads there is, shortly after the bifurcation, a khan or caravansera. These, although some distance apart, are within easy view of each other, and from the Khan Haswa we could plainly discern the fortress-like structure of the Khan Iscanderieh.

Tradition relates, with its usual wildness, that Scanderieh or Iscanderieh is the site of the tomb of the Macedonian, and though such a theory may be properly rejected, it is possible that the name may chronicle some episode in the hero's campaign. With regard to the sister khan—Haswa, Ainsworth has boldly hinted at an indentification with Cunaxa or Kuhnaswah of Zenophon and Plutarch, a theory which requires infinitely more erudition than I possess to discuss, although I must confess that the carving out of the Arab "khan" from the first syllable of an ancient name is a process which does not appear to recommend itself to me as a likely one. I would also suggest that Scanderieh may preserve the name of some pious founder of the Khan, for although Buckingham relates that this caravansera was erected in the last century at the expense of Mohammed Husein Khan, Emir ed Dowla to the King of Persia, this may easily have been a refoundation.

Into Khan Haswa I accordingly strolled, and examined with some interest the arrangements for accommodation within. The khans which I had seen in Northern Syria and on the Euphrates, bore indeed not the remotest similarity to the edifice I

TTA-K*

now stood in. The former, which I have already described, consisted of a small stone or wooden building, in which were a few rooms, to which was attached a miserable court for the reception of animals.

Khan Haswa, in which I now found myself, was similar to all the great khans on the Babylonian plains. The type is, indeed, Persian, and is the regular caravansera or place of public entertainment throughout that country. Passing through the invariable tower-like entrance, one enters an immense square or quadrangle, well built of brick, and round which on the inner side of the wall are deep arched recesses, in which the weary traveller can spread his bed, and thus avoid being trampled on by the throngs of caravan animals which are picketed around. In the centre of this courtyard, with a passage between, are two oblong raised platforms, built of brick. These are for the same purpose as the niches, to sleep on by night, or to picnic on, clear of the dung and litter of the animals. Of course in summer, when travelling is done chiefly by night, the arched recesses, affording some shelter from the broiling sun, would be preferred for the daily rest, but in the cool season, when the journey is made by day, it matters little whether sleep is taken under an arch or quite in the open, and these platforms form additional accommodation. In some khans there are on these, bars and niches for tethering horses, and some have a sort of cloister or covered stable running round behind the niches, which are approached from the four corners. Caravanseras of this description will contain from five hundred to a thousand guests.

What between the scream of the mule and the bray of the ass, the squabbling of dogs, the lusty snore of the pilgrim, and the incessant attacks of vermin, the English traveller could not expect to put in a very good night's sleep in one of these caravanseras, unless he was perfectly accustomed to the sights, sounds, and sensations common to them; and as I left the building, I congratulated myself that our snug coffee-house was engaged. Yusuf had been busy; the place had been swept and the fire extinguished, but the stifling smell that remained was not over pleasant. The dinner proved excellent, and after a pipe we coiled ourselves up in two of the niches and courted slumber.

In spite of our having had it carefully swept out, the " snug little coffee-house " did not prove the

most restful of bed-chambers. The insects absolutely swarmed, and my experience was that per-
sonally conducted parties of them took up their
quarters at different stations on my person, from
which excursions or tours were made under com-
petent guides to the most interesting points in the
localities. After one of these they would return to
their respective rendezvous, and after a brief
pause for refreshment and repose, they would set
out again to inspect some new attraction. The
most favourite trips seemed to be my knees, fore-
arms, and collar-bone, at the last of which a large
picnic was regularly organised.

Another source of annoyance was the old katterji,
who, I suddenly became aware, had taken up his
position on the floor of the coffee-room. As we
had specially engaged the coffee-house for privacy I
raised myself in my niche, like an offended deity,
and sternly bade him begone. The old man was
very impertinent, and did not retire until I tumbled
out of bed, riding breeches and all, in order to "chuck"
him. Yusuf also professed great fear of thieves,
and lay in the doorway on his stomach, as he said it
would not be safe for him to sleep. Once or twice
in the small hours of the night, when I was com-

pelled to sit up to disperse a specially large "Cook's tour," I found him puffing wildly at a big cigarette, in the same attitude. He said that this was for a bad cough he had caught, and he certainly was "barking" a good deal; but how a cigarette was to cure him I could not see.

Although I saw nothing of thieves, Yusuf assured me next morning that the police had caught one attempting to enter the coffee-house by stealth for the purpose of pilfering. This was one of the evanescent banditti of whom one hears so much and sees so little when travelling in the East.

Between these disturbances and bats, and the usual dog-fights, we were not over lively when we mounted the next morning at a quarter to six. It was cool and pleasant at this hour of the morning, and we accordingly pushed on at a fair speed in order to have as much time as possible in the ruins of Babylon. At about half-past six we passed some tents, which Yusuf said belonged to a tribe of Arabs called the "Baaj," and about fifty minutes later reached another khan called Nasrieh, a name which may have some reference to the town of Nassar, which formerly existed near Kufa, on the Hindieh canal. After leaving this we came to a nasty clay

marsh, which gave us some trouble to cross, having
to pick our way among the harder ground as best
we could, and getting well bespattered with the mire
for our trouble. This brought us to the Khan
Mahawil, eleven and a half hours from Bagdad, and
about an hour and a half from the mounds of
Babylon, which, indeed, are first sighted just beyond.
To ease ourselves and our animals we sometimes
varied proceedings by dismounting and leading our
horses for a mile or so. The poor brutes had but
little go in them, and Yusuf, equal to the occasion,
produced an extra pair of spurs, with one of which
both C—— and myself adorned a leg. It is a
sad fact that the spur in these parts is an absolute
necessity to the traveller if he wishes to get even a
moderate speed out of his jaded "crock." Immediately after leaving Mahawil we crossed a canal,
and came in sight, at three or four miles distant, of
the first of the big Babylonian mounds—the Mujelibe of Rich and Buckingham, and the Babel of
Ainsworth. From this trailed away to the right a
long line of palms, fringing, as we found later, the
muddy Euphrates. Closer at hand, on either side of
the track, were to be seen small and more unimportant
mounds, which, it seems probable, lay within, if,

indeed, they did not form part of, the northern boundary of the great city. Just as we reached these we met, to our astonishment, two Americans making their way back to Bagdad from Babylon. Of course we pulled up to have a chat, and they told us the best way to proceed. After leaving them we cantered on, passing on our way the numerous remains of ancient canals, all of which were dry. In these some travellers have seen rather the lines of ancient streets than irrigation water-courses : a theory which would seem to have little foundation, as the remains seem to differ in no way from those I noticed between Feluja and Bagdad, which could not have been anything but canals. At about ten minutes to ten we were opposite the mound, but as a canal containing water lay on the east of it and intervened, we had to proceed a short distance beyond, and then to cross it by a bridge. To this canal Yusuf gave the name of Nahr en Nil, the name which appears from Arabian geographers to have been applied to the great canal, or arm of the river that left the Euphrates and passed between the mound called Babel and the more extensive ruins to the south.

It would seem, as Ainsworth has pointed out, that

this Babylonian Nile was the river alluded to by
Herodotus, which intersected Babylon and divided
the Temple of Belus and the royal palace. I have
no wish or qualification to enter into the vexed
question of the identification of the different sites,
so I will content myself with describing briefly the
various mounds which the traveller sees coming
from the north to Hillah.

After crossing the canal we turned back, and
clambered over the hollow and banks of another
canal. We were now on level ground, and could
approach the great mound from the south.

To the untutored eye, this immense ruin seems
but a shapeless mass of ruined brickwork and earth.
It is, however, more regular than it appears, being
a rough oblong, of which the north and south
sides measure approximately two hundred yards,
the eastern one hundred and eighty yards, and the
western one hundred and forty yards. It varies
considerably in elevation, the highest part being
one hundred and forty feet above the plain.
Scrambling about on the rough surface of this
heap, I found in one or two places chambers
which had been partially excavated. In one of
these I noticed the peculiar style of building also

found at Akar Kuf, in which the layers of bricks are alternated with layers of reed matting. A gaunt jackal skulked off from his lair in a hollow, and not far off I kicked up a plump little hare. Jackals, by-the-bye, seem born antiquaries, and are generally to be found prowling about ancient sites.* Bricks with cuneiform inscriptions, and small fragments of bronze were found by searching.

This huge mass, which lies clear of all the other mounds, as a sort of outlier to the north, is the Mujelibe, Mukallibe, or Makloube, of Rich and Buckingham. Ainsworth, however, ascertained that the Arabs called it Babel, which name has been pretty generally adopted, and the term Mujelibe has been transferred to another part. It seems curious, but is apparently the case, that the Arabs transpose and transfer the names from one mound to another in the most haphazard fashion. A very recent traveller found this northern mound called Anana, a name that hitherto has only been applied to some ruins on the west bank of the Euphrates. To prevent confusion, therefore, I shall here adopt Ainsworth's nomenclature.

* "Wild beasts of the desert shall lie there, and their houses shall be full of doleful creatures." Isaiah, chap. xiii., v. 21.

Pietro delle Valle, Rich, and others have been inclined to identify this mound with the tower temple of Belus, and others have seen in it the ruins of the palace, or the hanging gardens. The Arabs themselves would appear to regard it as the ruins of the veritable Tower of Babel. Be it which it may, it is a wonderful ruin, and must have been one of the chief places in ancient Babylon. The excavations of Layard and others would appear to prove that all the chambers and tombs which exist or have been discovered on the top of the mound, belong not to the ancient structure, but to a comparatively modern period. The "piers and walls of brick masonry" found at the very base of the structure on all sides, prove that at one time, one or more imposing and massive edifices reared themselves straight from the plain level, and in the huge ruin we have, we see but the crumbling remains of these stupendous works of antiquity.

Looking south from the summit of Babel, we saw the rough outline of all the other mounds of Babylon lying one behind the other in a confused mass. To the newcomer's eye, no sort of regularity or order can be discerned in this rugged and unbeautiful group. But alongside of them to the

west, meandering through groves of waving palms,
lies the Euphrates, here but two hundred feet in
width, deprived of half its might by the various
water-courses and canals, ancient and modern, which
leave it to water the plains, both east and west,
between Feluja and this point.   Dreary and desolate enough the remains of ancient splendour
certainly looked, but alongside nature asserted herself in her most captivating form.

Leaving the mound of Babel we remounted, and
made our way by the river side for over a mile,
until we were opposite the more central mounds.
Here, under the shade of a noble tree, we sat down
to lunch, while Arabs from a neighbouring village
squatted round us with relics from the ruins for
sale.   Of these people I purchased several tablets
inscribed with cuneiform inscriptions, but I have
not yet had an opportunity of ascertaining whether
they are genuine or not.   It is well known that
these objects are fabricated to pass off on the
unwary, and it is not improbable that they are
supplied to the country people for this purpose.
But the ridiculous price at which they were willing
to part with them seemed almost to preclude the
possibility of their being objects of this class.   The

two or three which I purchased, I certainly did not
pay more than a rupee each for, and others were to
be had at the same sort of price. A few cylinders, of
the genuineness of which there was no question,
were also brought. C——, fagged out by the riding
and sun, snored placidly on the ground, while I sat
smoking, and meditating as one can only meditate in
such places as these, where a host of strange thoughts
rush unbidden to the brain, calling up before them
pictures from the most celebrated epochs of the
great world in which we live. Down the river,
borne on the tide of the most historical stream in
the world and wafted by the gentle spring breeze,
floated lazily an Arab boat, with its great lateen sail.
The crew were singing as we passed, and the little
vessel, fair and graceful as she was, only served to
heighten the loveliness of the scene. What a contrast it would be if one could have but for a
moment pictured correctly the appearance of the
same place when Babylon was at its glory. The
flotillas of river craft, the lines of quays and embankments crowded with busy throngs, the stately
bridges,* and the towering masses of temples and

* Pliny mentions a fine stone bridge spanning the river at
Babylon.

palaces, must have combined to form a striking and magnificent picture of wealth and power.   But truly the words of the prophet have been fulfilled. After lunch, I walked in company with one or two Arabs on to the mound opposite to which we had

ON THE WATERS OF BABYLON.

been resting.   This is the Kasr of Rich and Ains-worth, and the Mujaliba or Mujelibe of Layard.   It is a rough, uneven mass of brickwork, similar to the Babel, about seven hundred yards square, and rather

Y

over a mile south of the northern mound. Glazed
and inscribed bricks are lying about on the surface,
but the two principal objects of interest are the
great stone lion, described by Rich, Layard, and
others, and which still lies half buried in the rubbish,
a sorry memento of the ancient city.   A more
interesting relic is to be found in the remains of a
brick building, to which the name of " El kasr "
seems more correctly applied, and which is the only
piece of building which remains in anything like
preservation throughout the ruins. This remarkable
little ruin has been repeatedly described, but Layard's
concise and accurate account I here reproduce:
" Nearly in the centre, a solid mass of masonry, still
entire, and even retaining remains of architectural
ornament, protrudes from the confused heap of
rubbish.   Piers, buttresses, and pilasters may be
traced ; but the work of destruction has been too
complete to allow us to determine whether they
belong to the interior or exterior of a palace.   I
sought in vain for some clue to the general plan of
the edifice.   The bricks are of a pale yellow colour,
and are not exceeded in quality by any found in the
ruins of Babylonia.   They are firmly bound together
by a fine lime cement, like those at the Birs Nimroud.

Upon nearly every brick is clearly and deeply stamped the name and titles of Nebuchadnezzar, and the inscribed face is always placed downwards. This wonderful piece of masonry is so perfect, and so fresh in colour, that it seems but the work of yesterday, although it is undoubtedly part of a building which stood in the midst of old Babylon."*

It seems not improbable that this mound may, indeed, have been, as the name of " Kasr " signifies, the Palace of Nebuchadnezzar. It has been noticed that the bricks found throughout are of the finest quality, and for this reason it has been subjected to even worse treatment than the others, great portions of Hillah, and, indeed, even parts of Bagdad, having been constructed from the results of this unfortunate industry. Whether the term Mujeliba "The Home of the Captives," or Mukallib," The Overturned," be correct, it matters little, as nothing can be deduced from the name, applied as it seems to have been, to various parts of the whole series of mounds.

Returning to the river's edge, we remounted and

* "Nineveh and Babylon," 1882, p. 287. It may be remarked that the engraving which accompanies this account is thrown quite out of scale by a ridiculous little camel which is placed in the foreground, and which makes the ruin look several times the size it really is.

prepared to resume our journey. The road leads along a sort of hollow, closed in on the right by a long mound or embankment which borders the river, and on the left by another mound which leaves the south-west corner of the Kasr mound, and joins at about a quarter of a mile the great southerly mound, commonly called Amran ibn Ali, from a sheikh's tomb built upon it. This broad trackway, in some places a quarter of a mile wide, is continued round the south side of the Amran mounds, from the south-east corner of which another embankment can be traced round to close to the northern Babel, and is, perhaps, the remains of one of the three walls which are said to have encircled the palace and hanging gardens. There are interior lines of embankment, which may represent the others.

The mound of Amran, sometimes called Jumjuma, from an Arab village situated to the south of it, is irregular in shape, and, according to Buckingham, 1,100 yards long, 800 wide, and between 60 and 70 feet high at its highest point. From its position and dimensions, it has been conjectured, with a fair amount of probability, that here stood the celebrated hanging gardens. Layard's excavations to some extent appear to confirm this, as he found no sort of masonry in its ruins. It had, however, been used for burial and other purposes long after its destruction, and among the objects found were relics of the occupation of the Seleucidæ, and Greeks. Besides these great main mounds, there are others of considerable extent, but probably of less importance. To one of these, a rambling mound of considerably less elevation, situated between Babel and the Kasr, Ainsworth has applied the hardworn term of Mujaliba, or Mukallib, the fate of which seems to be tacked on to, and afterwards discarded by, every mound in the ruins.

The total dimensions, as given by Rich, of the enclosed space is two miles, six hundred yards in breadth, and two miles and a thousand yards from north to south. It is, therefore, plain on the face of it, that this enclosure is but a small, if important, quarter of the great city, which Herodotus describes as sixty miles in circuit, and the walls of which, he tells us, were three hundred and fifty feet high, eighty-seven thick, and that six chariots could go abreast upon them.

Allowing for error and Oriental exaggeration, there is no doubt Babylon covered an enormous space of country, and that the walls were of immense size.

The traveller Buckingham went in search of these, a
long and arduous ride in the heat of July, and after
riding from ten to twelve miles eastward, he found a
curious mound three to four hundred feet in circumference, and about seventy feet high.   On the top he
found a mass of solid wall, broken and ruined, but
still of great size, which had the appearance of being
indeed the remains of a great wall, and not of any
chambered building.   From the great central group
to this point the country was covered with the remains of ancient works, but from the summit, looking
east as far as could be seen, no vestige of canal or
mounds could be discerned.   From this he drew the
theory that this mound, Al Heimar, or " the red," as
it is called, was indeed a portion of the great city
wall.   It is remarkable, however, if, as appears to be
the case, there are no continuations to be traced
north or south, or in other words, that if this is
indeed a portion of the wall, the line cannot be
traced from it in either direction.   But those who
would argue against this identification must allow
that it is even more extraordinary if no trace of the
wall at all is to be found.   The question is one of very
great interest, but, until some further evidence is
forthcoming, it must remain in abeyance.

As we rode out of the ruins a stream of poor Arab women and children followed us with strings of beads and small relics which they had found in the ruins. It was now very hot, as it had indeed been when we were among the mounds. Putting spur to our horses, we set off for a gallop towards the welcome palm groves of Hillah. I was pounding along in the rear, attempting to keep up with C——, whose animal had a much better stride than mine, when a woman walking with a party of poor Arabs on the road suddenly stepped, as I was about to pass, right in front of my horse, and next minute was of course head over heels in the dust. I immediately pulled up and haloo'd to Yusuf to return; the woman was only shaken, and picked herself up, weeping dismally, though seemingly more with fright than anything. I told Yusuf to tell the men that I was sorry for the accident and hoped the woman was not hurt, but that it was her own fault. Yusuf was inclined to pooh-pooh the whole matter, and I fancy his version of my speech was to ask what an old Arab peasant-woman meant by getting in an English Sahib's way. The men, however, were far more concerned at a Christian's pulling up and staring at a Muslim woman (albeit the stare was one of compassion), than at any damage she might have received. Accordingly they shoved her behind them and entreated me to depart, which I did, having presented them with a bakhshish to cover damages, which of course the lady was not allowed to receive in person.

CHAPTER XIII.

HILLAH AND BIRRIS NIMRUD.

Arrive at Hillah—Sayyid Hassan—Hillah—Start for Birris Nimrud—
Remarkable Appearance—We meet Russian Travellers—The
Birris—Description of the Ruin—View from the Top—Benjamin
of Tudela's Account—Theories about its Origin—Borsippa—
Nebbi Ibrahim and Arab Traditions—Disappearance of my
Umbrella—The Power of the British Name—Return to Hillah—
Visitors—Leave for Kerbela—Yusuf's horse makes some Pressed
Beef—Road to Musseyib—Owlad Muslim—Arrive at Musseyib.

AT the entrance to Hillah we were met by an Arab
gentleman, a friend of Sayyid Hassan, whose hospitality we were going to partake of. This individual
who was dressed in his best clothes for the occasion,
proved to be one Ahmed Ebn Saad Hubba, a merchant
of the town. In company with him we made our
way through the palm groves and eastern portion of
the town to a bridge of boats, which is even more
rotten than that at Bagdad. Crossing the river, we
passed through more bazaars, similar, but inferior to
those of Bagdad, and turning into a narrow by-
street, we alighted at the house where we were to
rest for the night. The Sayyid soon appeared, and

greeted us with a cordiality which was certainly not feigned, in spite of the artificialness and formality of Persian manners in general. Sayyid Hassan is a Persian gentleman of means, whose own home is at Kerbela. I am not quite certain whether the house at which he entertained us at Hillah belonged to him, or whether it was put at his disposal for this purpose by a friend or relation. At any rate he acted towards us here in the capacity of host and a kinder host we could not have found. The Sayyid is, as this title denotes, a descendant of the Prophet through Fatimah, his only daughter, and her husband Ali. The title is therefore equivalent to the "sharif" of the Sunni Muslims. His appearance and manner are noble and dignified to a degree. He has singularly refined and intelligent features, aquiline and aristocratic in cast, and a high forehead, upon which, well set back, he wears a large dark green turban. In spite of his descent he is absolutely without any feelings of fanaticism towards Christians, and the great courtesy and hospitality he has shown to more than one English traveller shows the feelings he entertains towards our nation. He showed us with pride several letters he had received from the Hon. G. Curzon, M.P., author of " Persia and the Persian

Question," Col. Tweedie, late resident at Bagdad, and other Englishmen. We were shown into a comfortable room, fitted, of course, with divans at each end, and were much amused at the Sayyid's servants bringing in chair after chair, which, from their varied and antiquated appearance, I cannot help fancying had been rummaged up from different parts of Hillah as a concession to our English tastes. Some of the notables of Hillah then appeared to call on us. They were a very varied assortment — a dark individual who Yusuf said was a sort of native judge, and one or two Turkish officials. I had also asked Yusuf to inquire of the Sayyid if there was anyone who had antiques from Babylon to sell, and accordingly there turned up a rich Jew with his pockets full of cylinders and Babylonian knick-knacks. He also produced a magnificently preserved aureus of one of the Roman Emperors—if I remember rightly, of Commodus—but we could not come to terms for the purchase of it. When these gentlemen departed we took the opportunity to have a bath, C—— fortunately carrying with him an india-rubber camp bath. While this was in progress Yusuf kept " cave " (as the old Harrow term has it) at the door, lest more notables should arrive suddenly, and break in upon this very un-Moham-

medan ablution. This over, the table was laid, (knives
and forks in deference to C——'s prejudice against
eating with his fingers,) and an enormous dinner was
placed before us. Our host, although kindness and
hospitality itself, excused himself from eating with us,
and even helped a little in the waiting, which we of
course, through Yusuf, entreated him not to do. I
cannot but suppose that his refusing to eat with us
was in consequence of the Sheite prejudice against
eating with Christians. Of course he pleaded as an
excuse that it was Ramazan, and that he could not
break his fast until after sunset, but only a short
time before he had accepted cigarettes, on the score
that he might smoke, as he was on a journey; making
his way, in fact, home from Bagdad to Kerbela. He
then left us, and we could not resist getting out the
bottle of good Kerkuk wine, which after the long
day's journey was most acceptable, and which we had
not liked to produce when we were partaking of his
excellent fare, not wishing to irritate his Muslim prejudices. Unfortunately he returned immediately after,
and with much ado we smuggled it under the table.
I felt exactly like a naughty schoolboy, caught in the
act of smoking. Whether the Sayyid saw it or not I
do not know, but he asked Yusuf why his guests

were not drinking wine. He of course could not offer it to them, but Englishmen he knew drank it, and carried it with them. He begged we would not refrain from doing just as we would at home. Englishmen did not abuse the custom like swinish Turks. This made us feel more hypocritical than ever, but we acquiesced in the sanctified sobriety of the British nation, and Yusuf was made to perform a conjuring trick by producing a bottle of wine two feet high out of a saddlebag which did not contain it. This having been dexterously performed, we "had at" the pilaf, kabobs, and leben again, and all went as merry as a marriage bell. After dinner the Sayyid again made his appearance for a talk, which was chiefly carried on through the medium of Yusuf. Persian was, of course, his own language, which neither of us knew. He also knew Arabic, but my knowledge of it was insufficient to carry us very far. It afterwards turned out that he had some acquaintance with Hindustani, and after that C——was enabled to converse with him. We found out from him that Turkish rule was anything but popular among the residents of Hillah. This is even more the case at Kerbela. There is no love lost between the Arab population of these towns and the Turks, and putting aside the inborn dislike between

Persians and Turks, the fact that the latter are in
possession of the sacred Sheite shrines of Meshed
Ali and Meshed Husein, is a cruel thorn in the sides
of the Persians. I had wanted to take a stroll in
Hillah after my arrival, but the Sayyid would hardly
hear of it. " Hillah," said he, " is a wretched place :
there is nothing to see : the people are rude, and you
cannot go without an escort : wait till you get to
Kerbela. There, there is much to see." Hillah, it
would seem, has never borne a very good character,
and Buckingham has indeed made the statement,
"that they" (the Hillahites) "murder their governors,
and assassinate each other with impunity."

Hillah, which may be called the present representative of ancient Babylon, situated, as it almost certainly
is, within the ancient boundaries, and built of bricks
gathered from the ruins, is a place of considerable
importance situated on both banks of the Euphrates,
which is here less than two hundred yards wide, and
of a gentle current. The town is prettily set in palm
groves, and is surrounded by a mean brick or mud
wall. There are bazaars on both sides of the river,
but those on the right bank appear more extensive,
and that part of the town is indeed the principal.
The population seems to be increasing, as Layard

put it down at " about eight or nine thousand," and
Gratton Geary, in 1878, states that it was then estimated at twenty thousand.   I cannot but think,
however, that the last is a high estimate.   The population is chiefly Arab, but there is a considerable
fraternity of Jews.   It is indeed an interesting fact
that ever since the Babylonian captivity this remarkable race has dwelt in considerable numbers in the
vicinity of ancient Babylon.   Rabbi Benjamin of
Tudela, whose travels are greatly composed of statistics of Jewish population at the various places he
visited, says " Twenty thousand Jews live within
twenty miles from this place " (*i.e.*, Babylon), " and
perform their worship in the synagogue of Daniel,
who rests in peace."   A still more astonishing statement is " Hillah . . . contains about ten thousand
Jews and four synagogues," a number probably equal
to two-thirds of the entire present population.   He
also says that Bagdad contains one thousand Jews, and
Buckingham notices that this was the exact reverse
of the state of affairs in his time, the Jews of Bagdad
being estimated at ten thousand, and those of Hillah
at one thousand ; so that, as he remarks, " there seems
to have been only a change of place, without an aug-
mentation or diminution of actual numbers in both."

The next morning we were up betimes, and on our way to Birris Nimrud. I write it Birris, as that was the only pronunciation of the name I heard either at Hillah or at the place itself. No traveller or writer that I am acquainted with spells it otherwise than Birs, so that the curious question arises whether the local pronunciation has changed recently. The word Nimrud, which is, however, only occasionally applied, carries with it no more evidence than it does when applied to the singular ruin in the vicinity of Bagdad, called Nimrud, or Akar Kuf. Immediately after we got clear of the wall of Hillah, on the road or track which leads south-west, we saw, standing up on the desert plain, the remarkable pile to which we were bound. Its distance is between five and six miles from Hillah, and at this distance it presented the appearance of a ruined pyramid, or possibly of the débris of a tower of such dimensions, that it is easy to understand how so many travellers have mistaken it for the veritable Tower of Babel. As we cantered forward over the arid plain it seemed to slowly increase and expand before our eyes, forming a truly extraordinary feature in the landscape. We were not, however, destined to have good going far, as the ground became spongy and boggy, and presently we had to make a great detour to avoid a big lake, caused by the overflowing of the Euphrates, or, speaking more correctly, of the branch of that river called the Hindieh canal, or river of Borsippa. These vast swampy lagoons, which in winter and spring are formed between Hillah and Birris, were presumably to some extent checked in olden times by the excellent system of canals, which carried superfluous water away and utilised it for the production of cereals, and agriculture: nowadays the Euphrates is unharnessed, and her waters invade the country and render traffic over the plain difficult and unpleasant.

Working round this lake we at last turned due west, and made for our destination, from which we were now but a short distance. Here we were again baulked by several very awkward canals, which intersected our path, and which were deep enough to come up to our horses' bellies when we were fording. Here we met one or two poor Arabs who told us that Europeans, some said French, others English, were encamped in the ruin. Although we could not imagine who they were, this was pleasant news, and we pricked forward to make their acquaintance.

Riding round the base of the great mound which

z

lies east of, and unconnected with, the Birris proper, we emerged into the wide open space that lies be- tween the two.   Here we caught sight of a tent and a crowd of people, which was evidently the party of European travellers we had just heard of.   Riding up to these, we found that, although it was then half past eight o'clock, the party was just preparing to make a start.   Twenty mules stood about with their packs on, or being loaded up, and a perfect crowd of muleteers, servants, and interpreters were fussing and gesticulating in the manner that always accom- panies an Eastern start.   In the midst of this throng, dressed in the daintiest of sun hats, the neatest of riding breeches, and most polished of smart boots, with odoriferous cigarettes between their lips, stood two Russians, looking exactly as if they had just stepped out of some tropical Rotten Row, instead of being in the ruins of an ancient Mesopotamian city, seventy miles from anywhere.   Oh, how dirty and untidy I felt in my stained riding dress and un- polished boots, bestriding my sorry nag, in the presence of these beautiful Moscovs. We alighted to have a talk and found them both able to talk English, the elder, indeed, Baron something or the other, speaking it very fluently and accurately.   My

friend C—— had met them but recently in India, so
that an old acquaintance was renewed. They told us
they had been there two days, and were now leaving
for Bagdad, whence they were going to travel to
Mosul, and *viâ* Sinjar to Deir and Damascus. It
struck me rather forcibly that if they intended to
take all these mule-loads of pretty clothes and cham-
pagne across the Mesopotamian and Syrian deserts,
there would be some nice picking for the Shammar
and Anazeh Arabs. Also that if they intended to
make nine o'clock starts on these same routes, during
the time of year they would be there, they would get
nicely toasted for their pains. We found them,
however, pleasant and agreeable men, in spite of
their peculiar ideas about Oriental travel. I afterwards heard that when they were hiring their animals
at Bagdad for the journey, the muleteers of that city
made a ring against them, their wealth being of
course well known, and they had to pay a perfectly
fabulous price for their caravan.

When we had left them we saw them mount their
valuable steeds, and the whole party disappeared in a
cloud of dust, leaving us in undisturbed possession of
the Birris. A big white object lying near we found
to be the body of an immense pelican that they had

z 2

shot, a wantonly cruel form of sport, as their bodies are perfectly useless for diet or anything else.

We now approached the Birris from the south and proceeded to climb to the top. The appearance of the mound from this, and indeed from all other sides, is that of an irregular ruined mass of building material, in which it is not easy to see any definite plan or arrangement. Here and there among the hummocky heaps of débris of brick, pottery, and slag, may be seen faces of brick walling jutting out, showing that there is within at least portions of the structure left. The south, west, and north sides are all climbable, but somewhat steep; on the east the hill trails off into a lower ruin which lies below but is attached to the main mass. On the summit of this cone, which is said to be about one hundred and sixty feet above the plain level, rises a ruined mass of brickwork, which I estimated at forty feet high, twenty feet thick, and about thirty feet broad,* which is rent in twain by an enormous fissure or crack. The facing of the bricks shows that it is a portion of a western wall, but it is only a fragment, being broken away both on summit

---

* Layard gives thirty-seven feet high and twenty-eight feet broad. Buckingham, fifty feet high, thirty feet broad, and fifteen feet thick.

and sides. Immediately west of, or behind this, lie several enormous masses of slag-like fused material, which have all the appearance of being portions of masonry vitrified or bound into a solid mass by the action of intense heat. In these the courses of brick-work can still be discerned. The extended portion of the mound lying at the eastern base is occupied by a series of brick walled chambers, which are now excavated. The Birris appears to have been built of kiln-burnt bricks, every one of which is inscribed with the name of Nebuchadnezzar.

Standing beside the brick ruin on the summit, a wide and curious panorama unfolds itself before the traveller's eyes. Away to the north extends the wide green lake, formed by the spring floods coming down from Armenia. On the left or west runs, at no great distance, the Hindieh canal, which, full of water now, does not appear to the eye much less than the parent river itself. To the east lies the other enormous mound of rubbish, of much less elevation indeed than that on which we stood, but still of immense size. Due south, about seven miles away, there rises from the plain a group of palms, which shade the tomb of Ezekiel, called Kiffl, a contraction, it would appear, of Kiff el

Yahudeh, "The Tomb of the Jew."*   Far as the eye can reach on every side lies the plain, unbroken except by the gigantic efforts of ancient civilisation, and the puny works of modern cultivation.   One or two scarecrows of Arabs were climbing about the ruins watching our movements, and a couple of fine jackals skulked away when I looked over the northern side, and except for this all was ruin and desolation.† From the remarkable character of this ruin, it was naturally enough supposed by early writers to be the Tower of Babel itself. The remarkable passage of Benjamin of Tudela, which has been quoted by nearly all who have written on the subject, is too interesting to omit.   "Four miles from hence" (Hillah) "is the tower built by the dispersed generation. It is constructed of bricks called al Ajurr. The base measures two miles, the breadth two hundred and forty yards, and the height about one hundred canna. A spiral passage built into the tower (in stages of ten yards each), leads up to the summit, from which we have a prospect of twenty miles, the country being one

---

* Buckingham gives among other bearings from the summit, Mujellibe (Babel) N.E. by N., ten miles; Mesjid esh Shems, Hillah N.E. by E., five miles; Kiff al Yahooda S., seven miles, etc.

† Birds and animals seem common about the Birris. I noticed pelicans, wild gcose, hares, and jackals, during a few hours.

wide plain, and quite level. The heavenly fire, which struck the tower, split it to its very foundation."

Rich and Buckingham formulated the theory, a theory which obtained largely, that in the Birris we have the remains of the Babylonian temple or tower of Belus. The tower of Belus had eight stages or turrets, one apparently behind the other like a gigantic staircase. Buckingham counted four at the Birris, and concluded the remainder had disappeared. Oppert and Rawlinson fell in with this theory, and Layard gives an imaginary restoration* of the Birris on the same lines, but without attempting to identify it. Lastly, Ainsworth suggested that it was not in Babylon at all, but the remains of the adjacent town of Borsippa, a theory which Sir Henry Rawlinson more or less corroborated by finding clay cylinders in the ruins, describing works at Borsippa. Of the name spelt variously Bursif, Borsiph, Barsita, and Byrsia, we may then probably trace the present representative in Birris. It is probable enough that the curious ruin we see is indeed the remains of a temple, possibly dedicated to Belus, and built on the same lines as that of Babylon. When Buckingham

---

*" Nineveh and Babylon : A narrative of a Second Expedition to Assyria," by Sir Henry Layard.   London, 1882.

visited the place, he enquired of the Arabs about a
ruin called Brousa or Boursa, which he, believing the
Birris to represent the Babylonian temple of Belus,
expected to find a separate ruin. The Arabs examined,
however, with one exception, maintained that Birris
and Brousa were identical, " different ways of pro-
nouncing the same word." One Arab however, not
improbably in the hope of reward, maintained that
another ruin existed about four hours away to the
south-east. I cannot, however, learn anything of
this site, so that the account was probably incorrect.

It will be remembered that Byrsia or Borsippa was
the town to which Alexander turned aside when
warned by the Chaldæan magi not to enter Babylon
from the east; he accordingly went across the
Euphrates for the purpose of entering from the west,
but was compelled to desist, as he found it an impass-
able morass. This all corroborates the Borsippa
theory, as north of Birris lie immense tracts of
marshes formed by the Hindieh canal, and which
extend to north-west of Hillah, along what may
be presumed to be the western boundary of ancient
Babylon.

The remarkable condition of the fused masonry at
the summit was, of course, sufficient to cause early

travellers to write down this ruin Babel. This certainly has the appearance, taken into consideration with the rent wall, of divine fire or lightning; various theories have been lavished upon the subject, and it would be desirable that an accurate scientific examination were made of this extraordinary mass.

Having prowled about on the Birris, and admonished the two Arab scarecrows, who followed us about like shadows, for attempting to wrench bricks out of the ruin to bakhshish us with, we descended to the base of the mound, and instructing Yusuf to convoy the lunch to some snug place near or on the other mound, we set off to examine that ruin. While Yusuf was performing this duty we made our way across the bare space which divides the two mounds, and which may be (I speak from memory) a quarter of a mile wide. In shape the second heap resembles perhaps more the Babel, the northern ruin of Babylon, than anything else, being apparently a fairly symmetrical oblong.* The surface is uneven, rough, and stony, or rather bricky, in places, and covered with soft débris in others, that made travelling on it difficult. I rode all over it, but failed to see any sign of brick masonry in sight, although the ground was everywhere

---

* Buckingham says a quarter of a mile long, and one furlong wide.

covered with broken potsherds and bricks. On the summit of it are two small Arab sanctuaries, the larger of which, a pretty little domed shrine, was crowded with Arabs when I arrived. I learnt on enquiry that this place, called by the Arabs Nebbi Ibrahim, is regarded with sanctity by the Arabs in these parts, who resort to it as a sort of place of pilgrimage all the year round. They have, indeed, traditions with regard to it, of which the following are examples. One, which Sayyid Hassan told me on our return to Hillah, was to the effect that Nimrud who was the enemy of Ibrahim, or Abraham, attempted here to destroy him by fire. With this in view, an enormous pile was constructed, and Abraham was about to be immolated, when God interfered, and by a miracle transformed the all-devouring flames into budding flowers.* Less poetical than this was the other which Yusuf got from the Arabs in my presence on the spot. According to this, the king of the place (presumably the eternal Nimrud of local Arab tradition), actuated by an infernal lust for blood, gave orders that all women with child should be ripped open.

---

* The story of Abraham being cast into the fire is found in Chapter XXI. of the Koran "The Prophets." This course was taken against him for breaking the Idols. The commentators say the fire was turned into a pleasant meadow. *See* Sale's "Koran."

The mother of Abraham, in fear of this barbarous edict, fled to and concealed herself at the spot where this sanctuary now stands, and here the patriarch was born. Crude to a degree as these stories are, they are worth noting, and other legends bearing on the same subject should be compared.

The Arabs about here are of a tribe called Khafaja. At the tomb and within it were many of these people, both men and women, who seemed poor, and, indeed, of a degraded intellectual type generally. Within the little building were many praying and repeating from the Koran, and I noticed that the walls of the edifice itself were decorated with barbarous drawings and prints. Yusuf had spread our lunch beneath the west wall, but the driving dust, thrown up by a high wind which had now arisen, rendered our chicken, dates, and bread anything but a pleasant feast. Attracted by the spectacle, the poor Arabs, who did not in the least degree seem to mind our " devouring our food " under the shelter of their chapel wall, gathered round us in a fantastic and squalid group, an attention which my travelling companion did not appreciate, although I pointed out to him that if a couple of Zulus sat down to breakfast on the steps

of St. Paul's, he would, and perfectly justifiably,
stop to have a stare if he was passing that way.
Although I chivalrously championed these poor
folks, I have my doubts if they were deserving of it,
for when we rose to make our departure, my trusty
umbrella, which to me, as I possessed no sun-helmet,
was of the greatest value, was nowhere to be found.
In vain I sat on my horse and scowled, and vented
my wrath upon all knaves and traitors. In vain
Yusuf and the cawass scoured about and poked under
Arab cloaks and into ancient crannies. In vain was
the sheikh of the tomb brought trembling before me
to be questioned and threatened with instant annihi-
lation. At last my friend, with inspiration in his
eye and command in his tone, rode to the front and
in a voice of thunder told the recreant sheikh that
unless the "gingham" was produced, the Pasha of
Bagdad would, through the British Resident, be
moved, and an armed force of Turkish soldiers would
descend on the devoted Birris and its inhabitants
and raze it, or rather Nebbi Ibrahim, to the ground
and all that therein dwelt, so that no stone should
stand upon another, and the place should be cursed
from one generation to another. In an instant all
was activity; trembling forms hurried hither and

thither, and the very abode of El-Islam itself was
ransacked.   Suddenly a scarecrow uttered a cry of
triumph, and from beneath a heap of dirty straw
was dragged my poor old Oxford Street umbrella,
which had only been hidden there five minutes before, and if it had not been for my friend's presence
of mind and the might of the British name, might
have remained to whiten its skeleton in the
Babylonian desert like a worn-out caravan mule.
But the prestige of Great Britain was upheld, and
with triumph in our hearts and scorn at the in-
fidelity of the Saracens on our brows, we departed
for Hillah.

The evening, which was partly wet, we spent
at the Sayyid's house. Our dinner, which consisted of about twelve courses, including soup,
keubbeh, pilaf, joint and vegetables, the Sayyid
apologised for, saying he was sorry he could only
give us so poor a dinner; when at Kerbela (his
home), he would provide a more worthy entertainment. After dinner we had a long chat with him,
and I could not but admire the facility with which,
though sitting on an ordinary chair, he could place
both his feet on the seat with no appearance of
inconvenience or awkwardness. Our conversation,

chiefly carried on through Yusuf, was about the Turkish Government and the state of the country. We asked him why he did not travel and visit England, easy as it was at the present day, and C—— mentioning at the same time that in London there was an institution where distressed or outcast Orientals were always received, he unfortunately connected the question and remark, and gravely replied, "Thanks to God, he was rich enough, if he did visit that great country, to do it with a retinue of servants and retainers, and would be in no need of such help." We then astonished him by describing to him funicular railways, and C——told him about ballooning, of which he had had some experience. Our host was considerably astonished at these things, and though I believe he did not credit much we said, he was much too well-bred to say so. Yusuf was much less well-bred, and we found it difficult to keep our countenances when, after translating some long Persian tradition or anecdote of our host's, he would finish up with a gloss of his own, " Dam nonsense," or " All lies, I think."

Afterwards came "two gentlemen of Medina," clad in gorgeous costumes, and whose visit, which we first thought ceremonial, proved to be because

they wanted our advice as to the value of a certain
shoddy-looking German watch that they meditated
purchasing. I told them that the value of a watch
depended upon its time-keeping qualities. A European watch which would not go was as worthless as
an Oriental one in the same condition.

The most trying part about intercourse with a
Persian of the better class is the formality, especially
the high-flown compliments that it is necessary to
receive and return with due gravity. Even with the
Sayyid, whose kindness and hospitality left nothing
to be desired, and which was, I have no hesitation in
saying, completely genuine and unselfish, we found
conversation for any lengthened space of time somewhat trying. The last item of the evening was a
call from Ahmed and the judge, and the five of us
kept up a sort of five-sided duel of exaggerated compliments for about an hour. C——— and I cudgelled our
brains for fine speeches, but no matter how fine and
polite they were, they were immediately " capped "
by our Oriental friends, who were indeed much more
skilled in this peculiar sort of fence than we poor
dull Saxons were. Gradually, as the visit wore on,
we collapsed, and feeling all the politeness thus
sucked out of our natures in this fierce struggle of

manners, we would have given worlds to have been allowed to go out into the street, and to have grossly insulted by word and deed the first people we met.

The true cause and meaning of this visit, however, we did not arrive at till about half-past nine, when it transpired that Ahmed and the judge were a sort of deputation to inform us that the Governor of Hillah was somewhat exercised as to the meaning of our presence. He could not understand, it seemed, why so many Europeans had visited Hillah of late years. It would seem, indeed, that his shallow brain suspected that under the guise of archæology there lay a more sinister and hidden signification in the visits of Englishmen to the ruins of Babylon. The judge suggested we should call, but as it was so late, and an early start was necessary the following morning, we excused ourselves, and sent our cawass to him to present our respects, and explain who we were, and what was our reason for visiting Hillah.

At six o'clock next morning we bade adieu to the Sayyid, who was going by a short cut across the canal and lake of Hindieh to Kerbela, and rode out of Hillah in the direction of the mounds of Babylon. At half-past nine, having passed in sight of these, we arrived at Khan Mahawil, where we were com-

pelled by heavy thunder rain to shelter for half an
hour. The rain came down so heavily that I found
my old volunteer great-coat of the greatest service.
As soon as we got into the khan gate, and alighted
for a smoke, Yusuf's horse, carrying the small saddle-
bags containing our lunch, deliberately retired into a
dark corner and proceeded to roll on that valuable
institution, an act of malice which was perfectly un-
called for. The people in charge of the khan
collected round us, and gave us an account of the
road we were now to enter upon that was anything
but encouraging. It was, they said, a mire and
morass the whole way ; unless we took a guide to
show us the way through the snares and pitfalls that
beset it, assuredly we should be bebogged, and eaten
by the birds of the air and the fowls of the sea, or
else we should, like Pharaoh and his host, be overcome and drowned by the might of the waters. In
addition to this, the road was full of thieves, Arabs,
veritable Arabs without conscience or mercy, with
spears five yards long, and imbued with a bloody lust
for rapine, which would stick at nothing. We ought
to take a guard, they said, but as there was no
guard to take, we overlooked the irony of the suggestion, and set out as soon as the rain stopped, with

AA

a tall, lanky young Arab, who was to perform the double duty of piloting us through the maze of marshes, and of destroying the marauders who might venture to meddle with us.

After leaving Mahawil, we struck off to the left, abandoning the Bagdad road, and making straight for Musseyib on the Euphrates, where we were to pass the night. A little before eleven o'clock we arrived at cultivated ground, muddy and even marshy in places, but over which the going was not on the whole bad. All about the track we were following, and indeed everywhere, were numbers of bodies of yellow locusts, killed, our guide told us, by crows and other birds. As the insects did not appear in most instances to be eaten, I am inclined to doubt if this explanation was the correct one. After lunching in a delightful green field, a most refreshing change after the dusty khans at which we had lunched on the Hillah road, we set out again, and reached, about one o'clock, an encampment of Arabs, who, Yusuf said, were Shammar fellahin, who till the ground between Mahawil and the river. The huts which these people occupied were built of brushwood, and roofed with matting, which is made near Busrah. I saw also for the first time the humped cattle, similar, if not identical, with the Indian species.   Close by this village was a sheikh's tomb called Mohammed ibn Hassan, and a little further on we passed over an ancient site consisting of low mounds, which the guide only knew by the name of " Kasr."   Soon after we struck the river, and I galloped off to a matting encampment of Arabs in the hope of getting some milk.   The Arabs turned out to be of the Nusirieh tribe, a nomadic people, and they willingly brought us excellent new milk, for which they refused any payment.   Were these the terrible Arabs of which we had heard?   They had a handsome chestnut mare, of the Seglawieh strain.   The owner of this said he would sell it to me, whereupon Yusuf facetiously offered the sum of half-a-crown, an evil jape after the man's friendly gift of milk.

Immediately after, we came in sight of a long line of palm trees, in which lay Musseyib.   On the extreme right of this line we noticed two blue domes side by side, without minaret of any sort near them.   On inquiry I learned that these are called " Owlad muslim " or the " Mohammedan boys," I presume from their appearance, and not from any legend or story. We were now close to Musseyib, and the country we had been riding across during the day was a clay plain intersected at intervals by large canals. There were mud marshes, but in spite of the account we had got at Mahawil, we had had no difficulty, which was due most probably to our having a guide with us.

Entering Musseyib, we contrived to lose our way, and got among some brickfields, where we saw large flat bricks, similar to those of ancient Babylon, being made. The town is built of these, and it is said to be a considerable industry here, so that it is perhaps incorrect to say that all the towns and villages between Euphrates and Tigris are made up of materials stolen from ancient sites. After retracing our steps a little, we passed through the eastern part of the town, for, like Hillah, it is built on both sides of the river; crossed the usual bridge of boats, and pitched our little tent opposite a small coffee-house, the owner of which undertook to carry on his business outside for a consideration, and to give up the building to us.

PERSIAN PILGRIMS AT MUSSEYIB.

CHAPTER XIV.

THE PILGRIM ROAD.

Musseyib—The Pilgrim Traffic—A Storm in the Night—Arrive at
Kerbela—Meshed Husein—Kerbela Stones—Fanaticism—The
Martyrdom of Husein—Corpse Caravans—Kerbela—We Visit
a Nawab—Martyrdom from Mosquitos—An Awkward Incident
—We part with our Host—Leave Kerbela—Musseyib again—A
Hot Ride—Khan Iscanderieh—Reach Bagdad—Rumours of an
Arab Revolt on the Tigris—The Barber of Bagdad—The Hunch-
back of El Busrah—Go on Board a Tigris Steamer.

MUSSEYIB seemed to me to be about the funniest
place I had ever seen. It is certainly, owing to its
peculiar situation, a very interesting one. It is the
last stage on the road to Kerbela, and the Arab inhabitants drive a roaring trade in fleecing the poor
travel-stained Persian and Indian pilgrims, whose
caravans are continually arriving or departing either
on their way to or from Kerbela. The town itself,
although built on either side of the river, is no great
size, and its stationary population must be small ; but
besides this, there is the fluctuating mass of pilgrims
who are always present in greater or less numbers,
and who, I should be inclined to think, sometimes

number between two and three thousand. This is
only guesswork, but on the night I was there an
immense khan was full, and a great open space before
it was entirely occupied by caravans and encampments of pilgrims. This pilgrim population has also
the peculiarity of being only a nightly one. If you
ride through Musseyib in mid-day, as we did on our
return, the khan and town seem nearly empty. The
caravans arrive in the afternoon or evening, "out-
span" for the night, and depart at sunrise on their
next stage. The busiest time seems from three to
five in the afternoon, when the town is all alive with
the music of the bells of incoming caravans. I have
mentioned the great khan, near which we encamped
on the Arabian side. After the tent was pitched I
peeped into this, and found it absolutely thronged
with people and animals. At the doors were stalls
with bread and dates for sale; at pretty high prices,
too, for everything at Musseyib is as dear as it can be.
I looked into one or two of the side streets and
walked a little way along the bank of the river. The
sanitary state of the town can be imagined when I
state that both streets and river bank have abundant
evidence of being used as places of public convenience
by the pilgrims. As the evening advanced, fresh

caravans were continually arriving, and as the khan was full, they encamped for the night around the open space in front. The unceasing noise of the neighing and braying of the animals, the jangling of the bells, as droves of mules were taken to the river-bank to water, and the hum of a hundred tongues in half-a-dozen different languages, all combined into an odd enough medley of sound.

We brought out a bench and sat down to gaze at this extraordinary kaleidoscopic scene before us. Among the people we saw, Persians predominated. There was many a wild-looking fellow with black elf-locks, clad in his blue tunic reaching to the knees, and sometimes wearing big shoes and stockings. Here came a group wearing the Persian astrakhan cap, probably holders of some official position under the Persian Government. Not uncommon were men with their beards dyed a bright red, to conceal the fact that they were grey or white. A couple of kajawehs, each containing a couple of blue bundles, which, when they alight, prove to be white-veiled and trousered Persian dames. A party of Indians, some in white, or wearing black frock coats, and carrying umbrellas, a sort of European veneer which struck the eye oddly in this hotbed of Sheite Mahommedanism. Three

Persian beggars with long staffs, and hands out-stretched for alms. Another wild and nearly naked form, with an orange in his hand, apparently his only luggage—a durwish who had begged his way from khan to caravansera, from far-distant Meshed near the Caspian to the Masheds in the Arabian desert; and a throng of houris from India, a glow of bright red drapery.

Behind the coffee-house was a small mosque; and a mullah living in the adjacent house invited me on to the roof where he was sitting, to get a general view of the place. Little more was to be seen thence than from below, and as Yusuf was cooking the dinner, I was not capable of holding a very lengthened conversation, and soon descended. After dinner Yusuf insisted on re-packing everything before we turned in, as he said there were so many pro-fessional thieves in the place, something was sure to be lost. Remembering the last night we had spent in a coffee-house, we anticipated a better night in our tent, a hope which, however, was not very well realised as far as I went, for the noise of the party who had been turned out of the coffee-house for our benefit, and had ranged themselves on five or six

long forms just in front of our tent door, combined
with the shindy caused by a crowd of children who
were holding a sort of Ramazan carol procession,
kept me awake a long while. When these sounds
subsided, which I think they did about midnight, I
went to sleep, but about two hours later I was
awakened by a storm of wind and rain, which
threatened to flood us out, if indeed the tent escaped
being blown down. I sprang to my feet, and hung
on to a tent pole in case the tent pegs gave, and
halloo'd to C—— to do the same by the other. That
gentleman, who, I believe, would not wake if a
Queen's birthday *feu de joie* were fired off in his
room, calmly opened his eyes and told me not to
fuss, and then reclosed his eyes, and slumbered
once more. Much to my disgust, for I would then
have given worlds for the soaking tent to have come
flop on his recumbent form, the storm stopped as
suddenly as it began, and I had no alternative but
to retire to bed growling. Yusuf, as confirmed a fib-
ber as C—— was a snorer, stuck his ugly face in at
the tent, and solaced me by repeating the everlasting
story that he dare not sleep as there were thieves all
round the coffee-house. So telling him to keep his

weather eye open, I once more fell asleep, only to be
awakened at sunrise by the bustle of the departing
caravans.

At six o'clock we rode out of the town, and after
crossing a very steep canal bridge, so steep and
rough that we dismounted to effect the crossing,
we found ourselves among more marshes, on which
could be seen various sorts of waterfowl. The road
traversed these on a causeway, on which we met a
large party of Anazeh Arabs, with many camels
and horses. As I had not seen any Anazeh for a
long time, and imagined that by this time the whole
tribe ought to be in the desert near Aleppo, I
inquired what they were doing. The reply was
that they were taking the animals to Bagdad for
sale, and that they, the Anazeh, were to form part
of the escort for the Bagdad caravan on the pilgrimage to Mecca.

The sky cleared soon after we had started, and by
half-past seven it was getting very warm. Just
before ten we arrived at a sheikh's tomb, designated
Nebbi On Ebn Jaffa, which by the quantity of pilgrims who were collected at the spot, seemed to be
considered a place of some sanctity.

Proceeding on, and passing continually innumerable caravans, we reached the palm groves around Kerbela about eleven, and halted to lunch in a very beautiful place. Here we found a mounted servant of our host's, who had ridden out to meet us, and to escort us to the town.

It was nearly one o'clock when we rode up to the Sayyid's house, which is situated in the more modern part of the town, and without the walled precinct which contains the sacred mosques and the bazaars. The house, built in the Persian style, is handsome and large, similar but not so ornate as the Residency at Bagdad, and surrounds a spacious courtyard. Our host greeted us kindly, and we were shown into a pretty room, furnished with divans, chairs, and a table, which groaned beneath an enormous load of different sorts of oranges. We were introduced to the Sayyid's little son, Sayyid Mahdi, a nice little boy with a pale but interesting face, who wore a big green turban wound over a bright-coloured kaffieh. This youngster amused us a good deal by his funny old-fashioned ways. He coiled himself up in a chair, and gazed at us and our proceedings with a sort of serious curiosity. Forgetting it was Ramazan, and wishing to make friends with him, we offered him an orange, which he refused by somewhat haughtily

waving it away, and making the peculiar little sound
with the point of his tongue which English people
generally do when slightly shocked.   After a rest we
were shown on to the roof of the house in order to
get a view of the mosques and town.   From here
we saw the gilded dome and two minarets of Meshed
Husein.   It is similar, but hardly as fine as Kazemein, which has four great minarets, and, like that
mosque, it has a hideous modern clock-tower.   The
domes of other mosques could also be seen, but only
that of Imam Abbas, which is covered with fine tile
work, is worthy of attention.   We then photographed
the Sayyid and little Mahdi with our hand cameras,
a proceeding that seemed to please our host much.
I had been somewhat doubtful as to how he would
take the suggestion, knowing the objection which
good Mussulmans are commonly supposed to have
to representations of life.   But the fact of the matter
is that this ordinance of the Prophet is almost a dead
letter. The wise men of El-Islam, who by nature are
as fond of pictures as anybody else, have, indeed,
decided that photographs and paintings are not
representations of people in the meaning of the
Koranic law, as they show but one side of a person.
How can that which represents but the face of a

man and totally omits the back of his turban be
called a true representation ? A statue is different,
and an abomination of abominations. But a photograph is a trivial, incomplete affair, which the Prophet evidently did not intend to include. We then,

MY HOST AND HIS SON.

accompanied by the Sayyid's brother and Yusuf,
went to get such a peep as might be possible of the
gates of the shrine. We passed through crowded
streets and bazaars, and stopped at a money-changer's

TTA-M

shop opposite the main gate, with the ostensible purpose of getting money and enquiring about coins or
antiquities, but really in order to get a glance at
the structure. While Yusuf was haggling, I turned
round and took a good look. What I saw was a
large tiled gateway, decorated with Persian or Arabic
inscriptions. Within there was a blaze of blue and
red tiles, and a row of people sitting at booths, with
things for sale. That was all. The people did not
appear to resent my looking, but our guide hurried
us away through more bazaars, pointing out several
other gates as we went, which, however, were chiefly
down crowded streets, and being built up with other
buildings, were not imposing. After we seemed to
have made a circuit of the building we came opposite
a large gate, the sixth, our guide said. Within this I
saw a gold-plated "mihrab," or niche for prayer
towards Mecca. We then passed through more
bazaars, where I stopped at a shop and bought,
for about fivepence, four pretty little baskets and
three trays, all made out of palm fibre. At this
shop were also exposed for sale, to the faithful only,
the curious stamped earthenware tablets commonly
called Kerbela stones, which the pilgrims to Kerbela buy and carry home with them as souvenirs

of the shrine. As these are supposed to be made of earth taken from within the shrine itself, they are regarded with a superstitious veneration that is absurd. Sheites are said, in praying, to place the forehead in the position of prostration upon these stones, and no one, of course, but a true believer is allowed to touch them. Those we saw in the shops we were told by the Sayyid's brother on no account to touch; and he even advised us not to look at them too curiously. Our host, however, who, as I have said, was singularly free from bigotry, undertook to obtain us examples, and I now possess two. One is an octagon under four inches in diameter, the other a circle half as wide, both made of a light-coloured unbaked clay, and impressed with neatly stamped patterns. Other shapes are made, and a blank space is left at the centre, in which something is often written—I fancy the name of the pilgrim, and the date on which his visit to the shrine was made.

During this walk, and, indeed, throughout the time I was in Kerbela, I saw little or no trace of the anti-Christian intolerance which the inhabitants are usually credited with. To this town, where, until quite lately, it was quite unadvisable for a

Christian traveller to enter, several Europeans probably come every year now. In consequence, the townspeople are getting more or less accustomed to the sight. The old prejudices are wearing off, and the presence of well-behaved travellers is not actively resented. An attempt on the part of a visitor to enter or sketch, or, perhaps, even to examine curiously, the mosque, would, however, probably lead to very uncomfortable results even yet.

Kerbela is the fourth most sacred shrine of Sheite Muslims, and many thousand pilgrims annually visit the site.*

The origin of the pilgrimage may be briefly recounted as follows:—In the year of the Hijra 60, Ali the Caliph, son-in-law of the Prophet, having been murdered in the mosque at Kufa, the inhabitants of that place sent to Husein, his son, at Medina, an invitation to come and assume the reins of government. But in the meanwhile, Muavia, an enemy of Ali during his lifetime, had usurped the caliphate, and, dying, had been succeeded by

---

* Mr. Curzon gives the following as the order of sanctity, from information he received from a Sayyid of Kerbela, who I believe to have been my friend Sayyid Hassan himself:—1. Mecca. 2. Medina. 3. Nejef. 4. Kerbela. 5. Kazemein. 6. Meshed (in Persia). 7. Samara. 8. Kum.

his son Yezid, who was now in power. Husein set out on the 8th day of the month of Zu-el-Hejeh, with his family, and accompanied by a body of armed retainers. When he arrived at the place where Kerbela now stands, he was met by an army of the treacherous Kufans, sent out in the absence of Yezid, who was at Damascus, by the governor Obeidallah, and commanded by his general, Amer ibn Said. After some parley, the hostile troops posted themselves between Husein's party and the river, and thus cut off from water a force already weakened and exhausted by a long and arduous march through the Arabian desert. Husein, in this fearful predicament, is said to have offered to return, or to have gone under escort to Yezid at Damascus; but in answer to this the general only demanded an unconditional surrender.

Tradition then relates that in the night Husein had visions and dreams which apprised him of his fate, and during the following day or days his little army, worn out with privations, and dying from thirst, dwindled away, chiefly by desertions, until it consisted of but seventy-two. Amongst these were several members of his family, including Ali Akbar, his eldest son, two younger sons, Abdallah, and Ali, afterwards known as Zain-al-Abudin. There were also his brother, Abbas Ali, his sister Zeinab, his daughter, his nephew Kazem, and his aunt. A series of skirmishes took place, but the prince's little party, though they fought well, had no chance, and were at last surrounded and massacred. Ali Akbar, the first to die, was wounded with a lance, and then cut to pieces; and a still more horrible tragedy followed, when Husein's infant son, Abdallah, was pierced by an arrow in his father's protecting arms. Zain al Abudin escaped, as he was lying ill. Wounded and bleeding, the unfortunate prince rushed on his enemies, and soon after fell, pierced, it is said, with over thirty wounds. His head was cut off, his body trampled into the dirt, and the tents in which his family were, were pillaged, and the women insulted. His head and the prisoners were sent to Damascus, but his body was interred at Kerbela; and on the site was afterwards erected the shrine which has for ages attracted concourses of the faithful Sheites.* In the ninth century, the anti-

---

* A detailed account will be found in Ockley's "History of the Saracens," and Muir's "The Caliphate." But authorities differ as to details of the massacre. For the disputed point as to the ultimate place of burial of the martyr's head, see a note in Burton's "Mecca and Medina," Memorial edition, vol. II., p. 40.

Sheite Caliph, Motawakel, tried to stop the pilgrimage by letting the Euphrates into the country
between Bagdad and Kerbela. It is also said that
he attempted to destroy the mosque, but the Sheites
were much too enthusiastic to allow such tyranny
to have any lasting effect. Unlike the Mecca Hajj,
the pilgrims arrive at all times of the year, but
the months of Zu-el-Hejeh and Moharrem, in which
the martyr's expedition and death took place, are
most affected. Many pilgrims, however, coming as
they do from the colder climate of Persia, time
themselves to arrive on the Babylonian plains in
the winter season in order to avoid the heat, and
Yusuf also told me that Ramazan was a particularly busy month, which certainly seemed to be the
case, although there seems no reason why this
month should be a favourite. The pilgrims, who
come mainly from Persia and India, are said to
number some two hundred thousand annually; and
as to be buried in the sacred earth of Kerbela is
considered to ensure admittance to Paradise, many
hundreds of bodies are brought by caravan or
steamer every year to be interred at the spot.
During my journey to and from Kerbela, I saw
many of these ghastly processions. A rickety

wicker coffin fastened across a mule's back was the usual sight, and, as many of them have been brought hundreds of miles from Persia or India, it is commonly supposed that a very unsanitary state of things exists in these corpse caravans. In many cases, however, the bodies have been long buried at the place they died, and the relations have been saving up until they could afford the pilgrimage and burial fees, which at Kerbela are very high. It is also not improbable that in other cases where death has been more recent, the heat and drought of the climate dries up the corpse, without making it offensive in the way it would become in a different climate. Some time ago, the Turkish authorities raised such difficulties in the way of the passage of corpses through Bagdad, that friction ensued, and the Shah stopped the Kerbela pilgrimage in a great measure. In consequence of this, Meshed, in Persia, was resorted to in place of Kerbela, and a great source of revenue to the Turks was for some time lost. The road has, however, again been opened, and as many pilgrims as formerly now come.

The devotion with which all Kerbelais or pilgrims, and indeed all Sheites, regard the name of their martyr, Husein, is truly remarkable. In the month of Moharrem, both in Persia and India, the painful tragedy of Shahid Husein is regularly enacted before crowds of people, and never fails to work up the observers to an agony of passionate grief.* I have myself witnessed on a Tigris steamer a recital of the tragedy by a Kerbelai to a group of fellow-pilgrims, which wrought them up to such an extent that they all were sobbing with unfeigned distress.

The town of Kerbela, originated in such a strange way, is a thriving place. Formerly a waterless desert, it has been converted by the aid of a canal, called the Nahr Huseinieh, brought from the Euphrates, into an oasis, inhabited, according to some authorities, by some fifty or sixty thousand people. On this canal can be seen many boats, and a certain amount of trade is carried on by its means, but the pilgrim traffic keeps of course to the caravan track. The town experienced a serious reverse when in 1801 it

* See Gratton Geary, "Through Asiatic Turkey," Appendix C, for an account by Sir Lewis Pelly of one of these plays at Bombay; and "A tour from Bengal to Persia, 1786-7," by William Francklin; (Pinkerton's "Collection of Travels," 1811, vol. IX., p. 274.)

was sacked, plundered, and many of the inhabitants massacred by Saud ibn Saud, the Wahabite general. The ancient part of the town, in which the shrine is situated, is comparatively small, and is contained within a brick wall with round towers at intervals. Outside this have grown up large suburbs, in which can be seen one or two fine and wide streets, almost worthy of some of the second-rate parts of Alexandria. In one of these is the Sayyid's house. As at Musseyib, yellow bricks are made at Kerbela. After we had been round the town, we visited an Indian Nawab, an agent of the British Residency at Bagdad. He received us politely, but struck us as being a very conceited and affected old thing, and although, no doubt, a person of importance, seemed a good deal of a bore. His idea of furnishing a house seemed to be to crowd every available space in each room with innumerable paraffin lamps, a scheme of decoration which does not recommend itself to all tastes. Our entertainment consisted of cigars, sherbet, and tea, all of which politeness demanded I should accept, although I was again suffering severely from a return of my illness.

In the night a fearful storm of rain, accompanied by incessant thunder and lightning, broke over the

town. Hour after hour the deluge descended, and
so continuous and vivid was the lightning, that
through the windows of our room everything in the
courtyard could be discerned as clearly as by day. In
addition to this, which alone was enough to have
scared away sleep, our room was absolutely filled with
immense and very venomous mosquitoes, which
attracted by our European blood, were intent on
making a night of it. I do not think it an exaggeration to say that at no time of the night was I without
several upon my face. In vain I rubbed my face
with lemons, until I was a living lemon squash; in
vain I buried my head beneath some article of
apparel, and wooed asphyxiating slumbers. Sleep
would not come, and I lay for most of the night
slapping my face and cursing C——, who, with his
head enveloped in one of somebody or other's patent
mosquito nets, slept and snored in an irritatingly
peaceful manner, for which I felt there was no
excuse. Hour after hour the vile clock-tower of
Meshed Husein tolled out the hours, making one
think, if it had not been for the incessant " ping " of
the innumerable and implacable mosquitoes, that one
was rather in an English country town than in sacred
Kerbela.

An awkward incident happened as we were about to leave next morning. Yusuf, to whom we had given some money to tip the Sayyid's servants, came to us saying that it had been stolen from his pocket when he was asleep, and he accused a servant, who was certainly a hang-dog looking personage, of the theft. This man had, Yusuf said, repeatedly pestered him the previous day for bakhshish, and argued that he was an avaricious brute who would stick at nothing. We told Yusuf he had not the slightest proof of the man's guilt, and that as he had lost the money he must bear the loss himself, and ordered him to hand the man the present we had intended for him, in our presence. The servant, however, who no doubt had been blackguarded by Yusuf, refused to accept it until I handed it him in person. It was impossible to tell from such evidence as we had whether Yusuf was lying or the man was guilty. Much to our regret, and owing to Yusuf's continual grumbling, the matter came to the ears of the Sayyid, who had made his appearance to see us off, and he wanted to refund the money and tips. All we could do was to assure him that we did not for a moment believe in the theft, and that it was either due to a mistake or dishonesty on the part of Yusuf himself, but as almost everything we said had to be translated by Yusuf, it is hard to say what the Sayyid understood. Yusuf, driven to desperation by our wrath, protested that he told our host that he himself was a " damn liar," and the money was really safe in his pocket. But we could see from the expression of the Sayyid's face that he was, and naturally, put out. However, there was nothing more to be done, and we all rode out of Kerbela in mud six inches deep. Turning a corner, C——'s horse slipped and came a sprawling cropper, covering him with mud, but fortunately not hurting him. The Sayyid was off his horse in a minute, helping him up and brushing away the dirt. When we parted a short time after, I wanted to make a present to him of my sheath knife, the only object I had with me worth giving, but he would not hear of taking, as he said, anything from travellers who might want such things on the road. Anything I might like to send him from England he said he would gladly receive. I really felt truly sorry to leave this delightful man, whose kindness and courtesy to us had been absolutely unlimited. We exchanged addresses, shook hands warmly, and soon were out of sight.

We were now fairly set out on our return journey.

Indeed, from this point I felt I was turning homewards.
The desert country we had ridden over, dry and
parched the previous day, was now covered with mud
and large pools of water.   The day, however, was
fine, and, indeed, as the sun rose, became oppressively
hot.   We passed several caravans with corpses, and a
small encampment of poor Arabs, and at about eleven
we stopped to lunch close to a large tribe of Massaud
Arabs, a tribe who cultivate the land a little and keep
large flocks of sheep.   Shortly after noon we reached
Musseyib, at that time of day comparatively empty,
and here we had a row with the old katterji, who
wanted to stop for the night, and so make a three
days' journey of the return to Bagdad.   We insisted,
however, on going on, and after about an hour's rest
we ordered Yusuf to saddle the horses and rode out of
the town.   The heat had by now become very trying,
and although we saw Khan Iscanderieh, where we
were to sleep, apparently about half an hour distant,
yet it took two and a quarter to reach it.   So deceptive
is the atmosphere on these vast level plains that the
traveller is continually being taken in in matters of
this kind.   The broiling rays of the sun poured down
on us, and seemed to penetrate us like a knife, and
our party moved slowly and wearily along the track.

sitting or hanging on to our saddles too fatigued by the heat to speak, and more indeed like logs than human beings. The country between Musseyib and and Iscanderieh is chiefly the usual mud plain, but near the latter place it becomes gravelly. At about four we rode into the little village, and pitched our tent opposite a small coffee-house some little distance from the khan itself.

We resumed our journey next morning at half-past five. After about half an hour's journey, we saw far away to the right a speck on the horizon, which Yusuf said was Ctesiphon. This was probably correct, but from that point the ruin must have been distant some seventeen or eighteen miles.* A party of Turkomans soon after appeared on the road, wearing strange-looking astrakhan caps. They said they were from near Tabriz. Next a volume of smoke far away to the left attracted our attention, which looked like a steamer on the Euphrates, but was probably made by lime burners.

When we got near Bagdad we heard that the waters

---

* Layard (" Nineveh and Babylon," 1882, p. 328) describes on riding between Iscanderieh and Bagdad, seeing Ctesiphon under the effect of mirage, and plainly discerning arcades, columns, and masses of masonry. Either he must have ridden a long way off the caravan track to the east, or else the mirage had magnified the ruin strangely, for from the road the distant ruin is hardly perceptible, as above stated.

of the river had risen so much during the last few
days that the Tigris bridge was cut. Indeed, we were
warned that unless we hastened the bridge at Khan
Khirr would be also missed, as it would probably
have to be cut very soon. We galloped forward,
finding the watercourses of irrigation which we passed
all bursting their banks and swamping the roads. At
one place we met a woman wailing over a little dead
girl who had been swept into a flooded canal and
drowned. The agonised sobs and groans of the poor
creature were most painful to hear, but we could give
no help, and hastening forward crossed the bridge
and arrived in Bagdad at two o'clock.

My journey was now in a way over. I had seen
Aleppo, Bagdad, and Babylon,—the three tasks I had
set myself, and all that now remained was to make
my way home as comfortably as possible. The long
and fatiguing hours in the blazing sun had by no
means improved my complaint, and on my return to
Bagdad I felt incapable of facing another overland
march to the Mediterranean. Besides this, I was
anxious to see the lower Tigris and the Persian Gulf,
and as both of these could be done on steamers, and
amidst European comforts, I resolved to make my way
home by Bombay.

Our arrival in Bagdad was on the 12th of May, and the same afternoon we summoned the old katterji to pay him off for the animals. He had throughout behaved so badly that we resolved to mark our disapprobation by giving him no present, although, of course, the young muleteer who accompanied him would receive his accustomed bakhshish. When this was communicated to him the old rascal became extremely violent and abusive, and refusing to take the hire money for the animals, departed in a passion, making a great disturbance in the courtyard of the Residency as he went. We put the money aside, and next morning the young man came and the business was settled.

Immediately on my return, I began making enquiries about the next steamer to Busrah, where I hoped to get a steamer for England. One of these ought to have sailed about the 14th, but in consequence of its being Ramazan, little was being done at the custom house and dock, and I was informed that she would not leave until some day in the following week, as she had to be unloaded, a slow process, like everything else in the fasting month. Under these circumstances, I should have liked to have filled up the time by an excursion to the ruin of

Ctesiphon, and the mounds of Seleucia, but I felt too enfeebled by continued bad health to attempt it. Besides this, I was told that the river steamers passed close to the ruins, and very often time was allowed for passengers to visit the great arch of Ctesiphon, so that I hoped to be able to see it in that manner. The heat also had now become so great, that active exercise in the sun between ten and four was extremely fatiguing; so that I resolved to spend the two or three days before the steamer left in peace and quiet.

The river had now reached such a height that it threatened to flood the Residency garden. The long lane leading out of Bagdad to the south was occupied by great pools of stagnant water, which, under the heat, soon began to emit an effluvium which was anything but pleasant, and which, with the soaking gardens around would be very likely to breed fever and ague from its miasma. Evident signs were present that the increased heat was telling upon the faithful fasters of Bagdad, and the ong lines of closed shops in the bazaars, and increased activity in the evenings, showed that Bagdad found business an arduous task under these circumstances.

One day, walking in the bazaar, I met one of my
Aleppo friends, the Greek doctor, who followed
close on my heels down the Euphrates to Bagdad.
He informed me that an Arab tribe on the river
between Bagdad and Busrah were in revolt, and were
firing on steamers. Some of those of the Turkish
company, he said, had been actually turned back,
and steam traffic was now at a standstill. Although
I did not believe much of this, I found on enquiring
that it was in some degree true, although the English
steamers had not so far been molested. My steamer,
I finally learnt, would start on the 19th, so I settled
my things, gave away to Yusuf my pots and pans,
and an old pair of riding breeches, which were not
more than six inches too long for him; and finally
summoned a barber of Bagdad to cut my hair. This
worthy, who appeared with the regulation basin
and a bushel of scissors and razors, was, I presume,
the descendant of the original of the "Thousand
and one Nights"; though I was greatly relieved to
find that he did not dose me with idiotic anecdotes,
and astrological problems. On the contrary, he cut
my hair well and neatly, received his pay, and
departed with a praiseworthy demureness, which
shows that the breed of barber has improved

in Bagdad. The same day I saw, on the edge of Tigris, the Hunchback of El Busrah, whose aspect we are told in that delightful old yarn book, " was such as to excite laughter in the angry and to dispel anxiety and grief." I cannot say that the poor little chap, who had apparently come up from his home on a day's outing, excited quite that sort of feeling in me. He was a strange little creature with his head in his chest, and short curved legs about a foot long, springing out of his body; and from his dress was apparently a man of some position.

On the night of the 19th we went on board, having previously sent on our heavy baggage with plenty of bakhshish to push it unmolested through the Customs.

CHAPTER XV.

BAGDAD TO BUSRAH[1]

Steam Traffic on the Tigris—A River Steamer—Chaldæan Sailors—
Itinerary—Leave Bagdad—Ctesiphon—Arab Tribes—Paucity
of Traffic—Flooded-out Arabs—Amara—Sabæans—Deck Scenes
—The Revolt of Sheikh Saud ibn Munshid—Ezra's Tomb—
A Scare—Kornah—The Shat el Arab—The Port of Busrah—
Visit the Town—Escape of Prisoners—Historical Notes—
Health of Busrah.

THE history of the steam traffic on the Tigris and
Shat-el-Arab does not go, of course, far back. There
are at the present day two lines of steamers navigating the river between Busrah and Bagdad : they are
respectively Turkish and English. The Turkish
line has about seven steamers, and was started by
Midhat Pasha. They are, of course, avoided by
Europeans, as they are small, accommodation is bad,
and you have to bring your own food. The English
line was started thirty years ago, by the enterprising
firm of Lynch & Co., and is a very fair river
service. Their steamers are three in number, the
Mejidieh, the *Calipha*, and the *Blosse Lynch*, and are

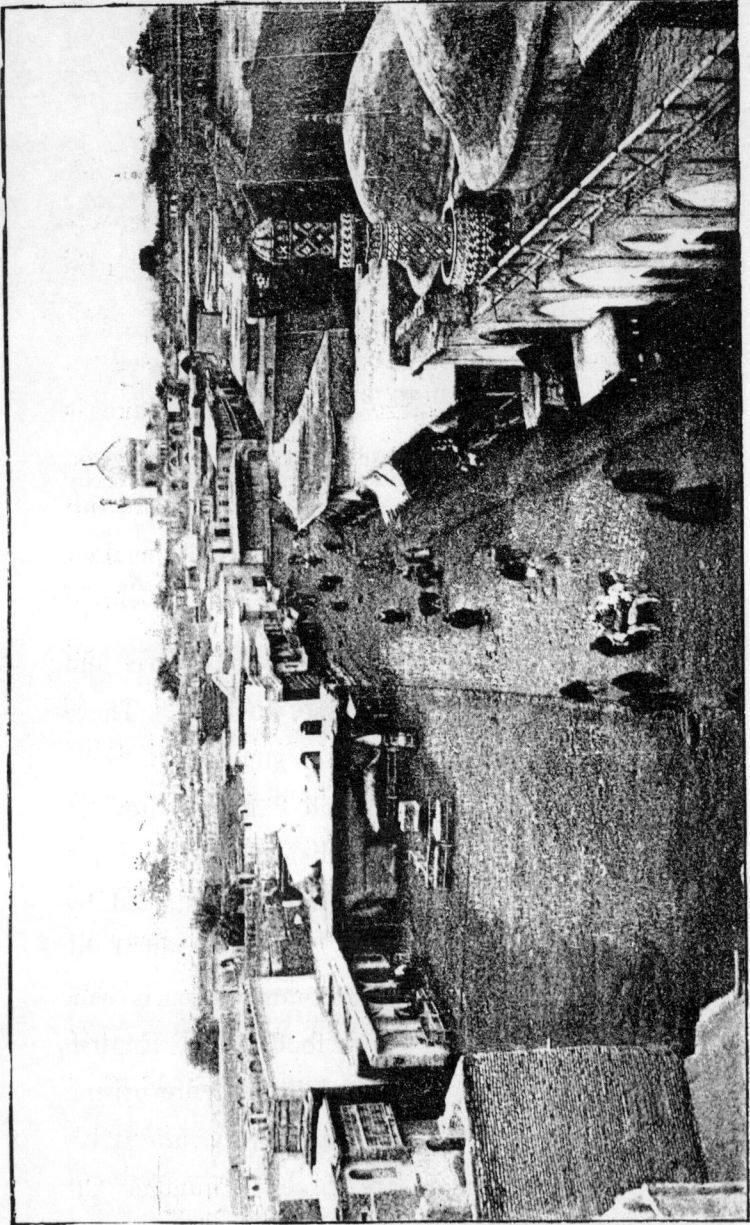

A STREET IN BAGDAD.

much larger, more powerful, and in every way superior to the Turkish steamers.

These vessels are of a somewhat curious build, drawing, of course, but little water, but immensely wide. From the main deck, which is but little above the water level, rises a long series of deck houses, two-thirds of the length of the vessel, on the top of which is a large upper deck, which is generally occupied by the numerous deck passengers. The cabin accommodation is forward, and in the *Mejidieh* consists of several comfortable single-berthed cabins, and a snug little dining saloon. The *Mejidieh* could take over six hundred deck passengers, and the *Blosse Lynch* I believe, a greater number.

These steamers are manned by Chaldæan Christians from villages near Mosul—tall, handsome men, who from their faces might be Europeans rather than Orientals. It was a pleasure to see these fellows at work. They worked like men, and had none of the sneaking and deceitful air that is usual among Oriental Christians. In spite of their fine, honest faces and manly forms, I was told by an officer of the steamer that they are soft, and are quite unaware of their strength. Left to themselves these indolent giants would probably be no good in a scrimmage.

and would, perhaps, act on the adage, "He that fights and runs away." Their costume of blue tunics and white turbans hardly distinguishes them from Mussulmans, and their language is Arabic. The navigation of the river is anything but easy, and when the river is low the steamers sometimes stick on the mud banks. Some of the corners to be turned are also very sharp, and in going down stream at the flood-time very smart steering is necessary. Of course a native pilot is always carried. There is, naturally, a great difference in the time occupied in the up-stream and down-stream journeys. From Busrah to Bagdad occupies a minimum of about three and a half days, though it generally takes a good deal more, and sometimes, when the stream is strong, a full week. The minimum of the seaward journey is two days, though generally even in flood-time six to ten hours more are required. In the saloon of the *Mejidieh*, the following notice is posted :—

Names of places on river.	Time of steaming interval. Average. Up river. Down river. hrs. mins. hrs. mins.		Explanation and particulars of the places on the River Tigris.
Basreh		4 30	Lat. 30° 30' 9 " N
Kurneh	5 30	3 0	The junction of Rivers Euphrates and Tigris, and supposed Garden of Eden

Ezra's Tomb	4	15	4	40	Ezra the Scribe, and a Jewish holy place of pilgrimage. A green dome on bank of river, west bank.

Location					Description
Ezra's Tomb	4	15	4	40	Ezra the Scribe, and a Jewish holy place of pilgrimage. A green dome on bank of river, west bank.
Abu Sedra	9	30	1	10	A small grove of poplar close to the bank, with a tomb inside a reed hut, of an Arab saint, west bank.
Amara	2	0	4	15	A village founded in 1861. There is a coaling depot for the Company's steamers on east bank.
Ali Sherghi	6	15	4	0	High poplar grove on east bank, and tomb of Arab saint inside of it.
Ali Gherbi	5	45	3	10	A small village on west bank, called after the name of a tomb of an Arab saint below village.
Sheikh Saad	5	0	4	30	A small village on west bank, called so after the name of a former Arab sheikh.
Kut el Amara	6	0	4	30	A village on east bank. There is a coaling depot for the Company's steamers.
Bughela	7	0	5	0	Village on west bank, the property of the Sultan; built in 1885.
Azizieh	9	0	1	45	A small village, with mud houses on east bank.
Baghdadieh	3	45	4	0	An old mud fort on a mound on west bank. It was built by a sheikh of the Zobeid tribe to levy blackmail on native boats.
Bostani Kesra	6	30	2	30	Ancient mounds, the ruins of a Parthian town of Ctesiphon.
Diala River	5	0	1	50	Emptying into the Tigris, it runs down from the Persian Hills of Lohristan.
Baghdad	3	15			In Lat. 35° 20′ 0″ N.

Steaming hours up river, 78 45; Steaming hours down river, 47 10.

As a comparison with this it may be mentioned

that sailing craft take from seven to fifteen days on the downward journey, and upwards, frequently above a month.

Before leaving Bagdad the next morning we cast off from the quay on the east bank and crossed to the opposite side of the river. Here the bank presented a somewhat lively appearance. One or two hulking buggalows* lay fast to the shore, and kofa boats and long snake-like canoes were paddling about. These buggalows are the largest native sailing craft in the Persian Gulf and Arabian Sea. They are excellent seaworthy vessels, varying greatly in size, but all built on the same pattern. Both fore and aft they are very high out of the water, while amidships they are quite low. There is a cabin astern, generally painted in bright colours, and the one great mast rakes forward in a very odd way. These vessels sometimes come from Zanzibar to Bagdad. I believe they are not much good at tacking, and navigation is principally effected by coasting along in sight of land.

We left at noon, and were soon clear of the palm groves and mud-brick coffee-houses of Bagdad. As I sat ensconsed in a comfortable chair on the lower

---

* *Buggalow*—the Anglicized form of *baghlah*, *i.e.*, a female mule.

deck under a thick awning, I could not help thinking of the immense difference between this style of travelling and that which I had been experiencing during the last month. How different was the luxury and speed of the comfortable English river steamer to the weary hours of jogging through the desert in the fierce sun on a sorry horse, or in the confined space of my takht-i-rawan. Past scrub, palm plantation, and reed-built village, past miraged plain and squalid Badawi encampments, we seemed to fly with the speed of lightning. Now close to the bank, against which our wash furiously rushed ; now dashing along in midstream ; now charging wildly round a bend in the river, churning up the turbid waters of the Tigris with our paddles into a brown froth. Soon after one o'clock we passed an open bridge, Jisr Gerarah, a place at which passengers Bagdadward bound sometimes alight and walk to the town, for, as there is a great bend between here and Bagdad and the steamer is steaming against a rapid current, the journey can thus be shortened. With the current, at this time of year, downward steamers make eleven knots to the hour. A few miles further we passed the mouth of the Diala river, spanned by a bridge of boats.

An hour later we were opposite Ctesiphon, and, greatly to my disappointment, the officer in command of the steamer refused to allow us to land to walk across the bend, and thus get a close view of this wonderful ruin. As Ctesiphon is situated in a loop of the river, which after passing close to its west side makes an enormous bend and then passes about two miles from it on the east, this is continually done ; as it takes the steamer an hour to get round on the downward journey, and a great deal more when travelling up stream. Unfortunately the captain of the vessel was ill in Bagdad, and the first officer, " clothed in a little brief authority," did not see his way to allowing us that gratification. Consequently we had to content ourselves with seeing all we could from the steamer's deck.

The Taki Kesra, or more correctly Takht-i-Khusrau, the throne of Khusrau, appears even from the river, and in its present dilapidated state, a wonderful ruin. The first view we had of it, from the west, appeared like a huge Norman keep, jammed up against a mammoth arch. Round this colossal palace of the Parthian empire we could see the pigmy encampments of the Arabs. Just before reaching this place we passed on the west bank a

large mound or rampart of earth, sliced away by the
action of the river. This is all that remains of
Seleucia, the Macedonian city, which rose upon the
ruins of Babylon, and which afterwards, with
Ctesiphon, became known as " Al Modein," the two
cities. An hour later we were opposite the eastern
front of the Takht, and though much more distant,
we could plainly discern the tiers of niches and
pilasters which adorn the façade on this side. The
other façade, which balanced the building on the
opposite side of the great arch, has fallen in the last
few years, and it is said that the rest of the ruin
may go at any time. One enlightened Bagdad
Pasha, indeed, was only compelled to desist from its
destruction by the representations of European
consuls to the Ottoman Government; and as the
general pilfering of bricks from the lower portions
of the walls is continually progressing, some antiquarian traveller anxiously gazing from the
steamer's deck may any day see, instead of the noble
and majestic arch, nothing but a mound of débris
like those on the opposite bank.

The desolation of the country on either side of
the Tigris, between Bagdad and Busrah, is almost as
complete as upon the Euphrates above Deir. There

are occasionally villages or matting encampments of Arabs, but throughout the whole distance there is one place only (Amara) that could be called a town, and two or three other villages big enough for the steamer to stop at. There is patchy cultivation here and there; but it is evident that the inhabitants of the district take no interest in it. Below Ctesiphon none of the thick scrub of the Euphrates is to be seen, and its absence is accounted for by its use as fuel for the steamers. Before these were put on, there were lions to be shot in the jungle, but now they seem to have entirely disappeared, though they are still to be found on some of the reaches of the Karun river. Wild pig and pelicans are numerous, and the former are sometimes shot from the steamer's deck.

The Arabs inhabiting the banks of the Tigris belong either to the Zobeide and great Montefik* tribes on the right bank, or to the Beni Lam and Albu Mohammed tribes on the left. They are all properly nomads, living a pastoral life, and the villages seen, with their patches of tilled land, belong to small sections of these tribes, who have been

---

* The Montefiks, however, properly belong to the Euphrates Valley.

induced to try an agricultural life. On the whole
these experiments seem to have borne but little
fruit, and it is probable that many of these Arabs
relapse into their former state of existence. At the
villages seen from the steamers, buffaloes, cattle,
goats and sheep seem numerous, but camels are
hardly ever seen. Some of the Albu Mohammed
tribe, about whom I shall have more to say, inhabit
the wilderness of marshes that extends for miles
above Kornah.

Another feature on this magnificent stream is the
extraordinary paucity of traffic upon it. Occasionally
we passed a clumsy lugger-rigged vessel, laden
with fire-wood, being "tracked" along the bank
by a crowd of singing naked Arabs; but for hour,
I almost said days, together we would see no sort of
craft. To be sure the river was at the time I passed
along it, in an exceptional, but by no means unique,
condition, owing to the revolt of Arabs lower down
and the consequent suspension of traffic; but in
ordinary circumstances the traffic is ridiculously
small. Mr. Geary, who narrates his experiences
going over the same route in 1878, noticed that he
met only two little steamers, and a score of buggalows of no great size. When one considers what

this great waterway, extending as it does from the Persian Gulf to the mountains of Armenia, might be made, the absolute incompetence of Turkish rule is brought more clearly home to one than in any other way.

The Zobeide or Zubeide tribe were formerly a powerful and numerous community, but now are in a broken up and weak condition. It was from this tribe that Harun-al-Rashid obtained his fair wife Zubeidah. In the evening of the first day we passed the modern mud village of Jezirah of these people and soon after an earthern fort called Bagdadieh, built by one of their former sheikhs for the purpose of intercepting and levying blackmail on the river craft.

The marshes are entered on the first afternoon after leaving Bagdad, and from the ceaseless noise of the frogs when we went to bed at ten o'clock, we seemed to be still in them. In these marshes mosquitoes are very troublesome, and I noticed that the ordinary fly inflicted a sharp and painful bite, although no swelling followed.

In the night we stopped at Kut el Amara, and when we rose in the morning we were tearing along against a brisk head breeze, with a wide plain,

grassy and green, on either side of us. Far away
to the left we could now discern Jebel Hamrin, the
mountain range dividing Persian Luristan from
Turkish territory, and beyond which lay the town
of Dizful.

At about half-past ten we passed Ali Gherbi or
"Ali of the West," a wretched mud village on the
west bank. Both sides of the river swarm hereabouts with Arabs, those on the east being Beni
Lam, whose village encampments are a mixture of
matting, reed, and mud.* These people are said
to be much intermarried with Kurds, and speak
both languages. The children seen on the banks
are often dressed in red, instead of the eternal Arab
blue. At one place we came upon a large crowd
of these people standing absolutely naked on a spit
of land surrounded by water. They carried a green
flag, and gesticulated and screamed to the steamer. I
gathered from one of the crew that the poor creatures
were in great distress on account of the river flood
having broken a dam, flooded their village, and
destroyed their crops. At another very large encampment further on, it was quite easy to see that

* Some of the matting encampments of the lower Tigris Valley
are built with great regularity, almost like a military camp.

the river was higher than the plain on which it flowed, so that the wretched embankment had only to give way for the inhabitants to be served in like manner.

In the evening we found ourselves sailing between banks lined with orchards, and young palm groves contained between mud walls. Strange-looking canoes, extremely long and absurdly narrow, could be seen punting about and tacking up stream. These are called " ballums," and are the pleasure boats of the lower Tigris and the Shat-el-Arab. Soon after, we were at Amara, opposite which we swung round in midstream, so as to make fast to the quay, with the vessel's nose up stream. Although I could persuade none of my fellow passengers to accompany me, I immediately went ashore to stretch my legs and have a look at the place. Amara is a considerable town of about five thousand inhabitants, amongst whom there are a good many Jews, but very few Christians. It has a governor, and there are barracks in which one Turkish regiment is generally quartered. On the river front there are some very good and clean-looking houses. A bridge of boats, telegraph-office, and fairly roomy and well supplied bazaar complete its attractions.

At Amara a river flows into the Tigris from the
east, the identity of which appears to be somewhat
doubtful. Kiepert marks it as the river Tib which
takes its rise in Jebel Hamrin, and other maps are
similar. Mr. Yusuf, however, the clerk of the
Mejidieh, informs me that this was incorrect, and that
it was the northern mouth of a canal or back-water
running out of the great series of marshes called
Samida and Samargha which extend almost to
Hawizeh over the Persian border. The stream is
called the Shat or Sid al Khud. Mr. Yusuf assured
me that from here Hawizeh could be reached by
boat from Amara, traversing *en route* these immense
lagoons. The real truth of the matter seems to
be that this is one of the mouths of the Persian
river Kerkah, which after passing Hawizeh spreads
over the country in a vast series of morasses, from
which the Khud empties itself at Amara, another
mouth further down at El Ozeir or the tomb of
Ezra, and one or more some sixty miles south close
to the junction of the Tigris and Euphrates. Into
the Khud the Tib would appear also to flow, not
close to the Tigris, but further east, in the vicinity
of the marshes.

The ballums I have spoken of, which are seen here

and even more at Busrah, are built of teak from the Malabar coast; the wood is riveted with iron nails, and the whole is covered with bitumen. A moderate sized one can be worked by one man sitting in the stern with a big-bladed paddle.

In Amara, as indeed in many of the towns of the lower Tigris, there are considerable numbers of the people called Sabæans, who claim descent from the ancient Chaldæans, and regard St. John the Baptist with peculiar reverence.* Their physical characteristics, at any rate in those I saw, differ from those of the Arabs and Persians, although there is nothing peculiar in their costume; such as I saw had dark beards and fine eyes. Just as the *Mejidieh* was casting off, a Sabæan, apparently a person of importance, was standing on the lower deck; on the quay a crowd of his friends had gathered to see him off, and each in turn hurled on board a cloak or abbah, in which a farewell gift of walnuts or dates was tied up; as fast as they tumbled on board the tall Sabæan emptied the contents on the deck and threw back the cloak to the struggling crowd. At last the steamer was too far from the shore to throw any more, and

---

* For an account of the Sabæans, their tenets and peculiarities, see Ainsworth, "Personal Narrative of the Euphrates Valley Expedition," 1888, vol. II., p. 243.

the excited friends waved their companion a wild adieu.

A more curious scene than the upper deck of a Tigris steamer cannot well be depicted : hundreds of sitting and recumbent forms of various nationalities and in multi-coloured raiment throng the space, and so thickly, that it is difficult to make one's way from one end to the other. Of these a large proportion are Persian pilgrims returning home from Kerbela and Nejef ; in the groups of skull-capped men and veiled women I saw but a repetition of the groups on the pilgrim road, saving only that here I saw them at their ease, lolling on their untidy and travel-stained beds, sipping their tea and puffing the eternal kalian ; also it was possible, by making a sudden sally into a quiet corner of the upper deck, to catch some of the houris of the Orient unveiled. I cannot say that I was much impressed by such as I saw, and as the ladies hastily donned the necessary apparel, it became necessary for me to become vastly interested in the mechanism of the paddle boxes. Besides these there were Arabs of Busrah, Mussulmans from Bombay, and one or two adventuresses from Bagdad on their way to Bombay, where they hoped to reap a fortune from their charms. All this odd mixture lived, smoked, cooked, fed, and slept on the deck, without discord. The place where a deck passenger deposited his bundle when he embarked at Bagdad, that must he occupy until he landed at Busrah ; very seldom did any individual rise from his or her place, except to reach the tea-pot or pipe, and as for a walk, why, there simply was no room had anyone wished it.

In one place the Tragedy of Husein was being enacted. Around a lamp (for it was dark) sat a ring of a dozen Persian pilgrims, among whom the teapot rapidly circulated ; at one end of the ring, sitting on a box so as to command the attention of his audience, was a noble old Sheite, narrating in a sort of nasal chant the story of their revered martyr. He began in a monotonous and prolonged monotone, and then suddenly his tone changed, and with rapid and sympathetic utterance he worked himself up into a graphic and theatrical exposition of his narrative. When he got to a certain point, I presume the murder of Husein, his voice faltered and sank into accents of unutterable grief, and at the same moment his audience, one and all, burst into the deepest sobs and groans. The narrator then paused, and with his right hand wiped from his eyes what seemed to be the tears of unfeigned grief. At certain parts of the narrative the Persians would raise their hands, palm upwards, and piteously repeat the names Husein and Allah.

We anchored for the night in mid-stream, and slept heartily to the croaking of the frogs.

It now became evident that there was at least some possibility of trouble from the Arab tribe in revolt, whose country we were about to pass through. The officer in command of the steamer gave orders for the bridge of the vessel, on which the pilot, steersman, and officer on duty were stationed, to be defended with bales of wool, in view of possible hostilities. The history of the disturbance was this : Two sons of Sheikh Saud Ibn Munshid, the sheikh of the Madan Arabs, were seized and thrown into prison at Amara by the Turkish authorities for non-payment of taxes. The Madan Arabs are a sub-section of the great Albu Mohammed tribe, which occupy a great part of the country on both sides of the Tigris, between Amara and the Karun river. The Madan Arabs are a buffalo-breeding tribe, and are said to number about forty thousand. The sheikh, with whom all who have any knowledge of the Turkish policy towards the Arab tribes must feel more sympathy than anything else, had gathered together a large body of armed men,

including some four hundred with Martini rifles, and
was venting his wrath in intercepting, plundering, and
often burning, the grain boats and other traffic upon
the river. The infuriated chieftain, after the manner
of his ancestors, did not stick at lopping off the
heads of his prisoners, and even fired upon and
turned back one of the Turkish steamers on her way
to Busrah. As he had not yet interfered with the
English boats, and had no reason for hostility towards
our nation, it was probable we might pass unmolested.
But in a similar affair some years back one of the
commanders of a Lynch steamer was shot in the chest
and severely wounded, so that precautions were very
necessary. The Turkish authorities, of course, were
attempting to repress these disturbances, and expeditions were sent against the turbulent ones: but the wily
sheikh, who knew the ins and outs of the vast series of
morasses and reedy fens which border the river, had
only to retire with his forces like water rats to their
fastnesses, and no troops in the world could follow
them. In sore straits, therefore, were the Turks what
to do, and although there was a price on Saud's head
that would no doubt, sooner or later, bring him to
account, there was at present no apparent likelihood

of capturing the rebel, and thus restoring tranquility.*

Early the next morning we stopped at the village of Kalah Salah, on the left bank. Here a detachment of twenty Turkish soldiers came on board as an escort—a somewhat questionable sort of protection, as Saud would be more likely to fire on us with Turkish troops on board than if we were without. They brought with them accounts, which if they were at all true, looked as if the rebellion was assuming serious proportions. A party of Turkish soldiers (according to this account) had proceeded the previous day, in company with a friendly Arab sheikh, one Yesser, and some of his people, across the river, and had attacked Saud's party somewhere on the right bank. Fifty rebels were killed and fifteen Turks. How far this was true it is hard to say, and I have never learned what had really happened. Probably a skirmish, and a few lives lost. At any rate, it was evident we must not be napping till we were past

* Mr. Geary, who passed up the river in April, 1878, found the same tribe engaged in a similar, but less malignant revolt. According to his account, the sheikh was a piratical ruffian, for whom there was no excuse. I am unaware if this man was Saud, or of the details of Saud's case, but as a general rule in disputes between the Turkish government and Arab tribes, the latter merit the sympathy, the former the opprobrium of right-minded people.

" Castle Dangerous." As we left Kalah Salah, I noticed no less than thirty-five buggalows made fast to the bank in a line. Some of these had been the previous day at Amara, but on arrival here they were forbidden to proceed by the authorities. Below this place the banks were swarming with Madan Arabs, whose appearance was certainly not calculated to inspire terror into our hearts. Most of them were literally as naked as the day they were born, and others had simply a rag over the head or a cloth girt, not round the loins, but round the chest. Of the males, fully grown men only were fully dressed. The lads and hobble-de-hoys raced furiously along the shore for about a mile, the race continually augmented by newcomers, for few of course could keep up with the steamer for any time. At intervals, the passengers would throw towards them a cake of bread, and then the wildest scene would take place, half a dozen brown slippery forms would fly plump into the water together, like a school of porpoises, and have a rough-and-tumble together in the river for the spoil. I thought from their behaviour they must be in great want, but was told that the babies always behave like this when the steamer passes. Soon after, we came to the sanctuary called Abdallah ibn Ali, a small tomb, close to which were what appeared to be ancient mounds. Round the tomb were to be seen a crowd of Arabs with flags. This place is held to be very sacred by the Arabs, who make pilgrimages to it, and bury here as at Kerbela, though what its history is I could not learn.

Just past this we came to the sharpest turn in the river, where, as the stream is very narrow, very quick steering is necessary. The steamer seemed almost to swing on a pivot as we whirled twice in succession round corners, our stern so close to the bank that one might have jumped ashore.

At a quarter past nine we were at Ezra's tomb, called El Ozeir by the Arabs, prettily situated on the right bank, among palm trees. A considerable time before reaching this place, we could see it away to the right, apparently in the open country, and far away from the river, which makes a huge bend, and passes close to it. This place, at which, according to Jewish tradition, Ezra the scribe died on his way from Jerusalem to Susa, is, and has for a very long time been, a great place of pilgrimage for the Jews. Benjamin of Tudela writes: " The sepulchre of Ezra the priest and scribe is in this place, where he died on his journey from Jerusalem to King Artaxerxes

In front of the sepulchre a large synagogue and
a Mohammedan mosque have been erected, the latter
as a mark of the veneration in which Ezra is held by
the Mohammedans, who are very friendly towards the
Jews, and resort hither to pray." A pretty blue
dome now exists, and there are two big modern
houses facing the river for the reception of pilgrims,
but there are no ancient remains now standing, and
Layard has conjectured that the real site has been
washed away by the river.*

Jewish pilgrims visit this place in considerable
numbers—four to five thousand annually; but this
year, in consequence of the disturbances amongst the
Arabs, there were hardly any. As the steamer only
stopped for about two minutes, I had no opportunity
of landing, as I should have liked. A crowd of
Turkish soldiers were standing in front of the
building, and a small Turkish gun-boat lay in the
river, having been sent up from Busrah to render
any assistance possible.

By breakfast time we were told we had passed the
only place where any danger was to be apprehended.
Immediately after, however, an absurd scare happened. I was looking over some books in the cabin,

* " Early Adventures in Persia," &c. vol. ii., p. 215.

when I suddenly heard shots. Bang, bang, bang went rifle after rifle, and I rushed hurriedly on deck, fully believing that we were being fired upon, and that I was about to see a little active warfare. Much to my surprise, perhaps satisfaction, I found the Turkish soldiers engaged in the peaceful occupation of firing at a big wild pig, that was scrambling through the reeds on the western bank. Fortunately they were not very good shots, and piggy saved his bacon.

The marshes through which we had been passing were filled with reeds, few of which seemed more than three feet high. Through my glass, however, I could see, further back from the river, a taller growth, something like bulrushes. Birds of many sorts abound, including hooded crows, snipe, kingfishers, and pelicans. Herons were plenteous, and there was a species of white bird I was unacquainted with.

At mid-day we were at Kornah, where the Tigris and Euphrates, after their long course from the neighbourhood of Lake Van, at last join and flow together in one grand stream to the sea. The village of Kornah, for it is nothing else, is situated on a narrow point of land, amidst luxuriant palm groves. An interest attaches to the site from the local tradition that here was the Garden of Eden. It is certainly a charming place, and calculated to attract to itself a halo of romance. The water of the Euphrates where it joins the Tigris is not turbid, as I had always hitherto seen it, because a few miles above this place it is lost in marshes. Kornah is nearly fifty miles above Busrah as the crow flies, and twice that distance from the sea. A Turkish gun-boat was stationed there when we passed.

The Shat-el-arab, between Kornah and Busrah, is a magnificent stream varying from two hundred and a fifty to three hundred yards in width, and with a depth of ten to fifteen fathoms. Throughout the distance are palm groves, some tall and stately, others but recently planted. The dates of this district are of most excellent quality, and the cultivation of the date palm is one of the standard industries. There are a great variety of species cultivated, the Arabs asserting that there are forty or even seventy distinct sorts; great quantities are annually exported to Europe and America. Fish-traps, composed of semi-circular enclosures of upright reeds, are to be seen on the river's edge. Into these the fish rush at high-tide, and at the ebb are unable to escape. The tide, by-the-bye, is felt as high as Ezra's tomb. An occasional raft of reeds, built into the shape of a boat of immense size, can be seen floating down to Busrah. The reeds are chiefly used in the manufacture of the matting which I have already noticed as in use in Arab encampments.

We arrived at Busrah on the evening of the 22nd of April, and at this point my Turkish journey came to an end. I had some idea of accompanying C—— up the newly-opened Karun river as far as Shuster, but this proved not feasible, as Messrs. Lynch's steamer was temporarily taken off, and a wretched launch was running in its stead. As this vessel did not start till the middle of the following week, and had no sort of passenger accommodation, I decided to go at once on board the British India steamer *Simla*, which was lying in the river, and which would sail early on the morning of the 24th. The port of Busrah, a modern growth (for the town itself is some distance away from the river, up a creek), is an odd mixture of East and West. The British Consulate, and one or two business premises of English companies ; the steamer *Simla*, and an opposition Persian liner : a hulking Turkish steamer all canted over to one side ; the smart English gunboat *Brisk*, and a dirty Turkish one ; and several river steamers represent the civilisation of the latter; while the gesticulating crowd of Arabs, Persians, and negroes, the snake-like ballums, and the crowd of buggalows represent the old East. The ballums, which I have already noticed at Amara, are flitting about all over the river like gondolas, each manned by two boatmen, who use poles or paddles, as necessity dictates. There are so many near the shore that you cannot proceed in one a hundred yards without half-a-dozen collisions; these neither boatmen nor passengers take any notice of, and the unwary newcomer must look to himself, or he will get harpooned in the eye by a long bamboo pole.

With C—— I called on the British Resident, Major Jennings, at whose house I also met the agent of the British India Steamship Company. The latter said that the Arab rising was the most obstinate that had occurred for the last five years. Saud had a price on his head, and sooner or later would be killed. All traffic on the river was temporarily at an end, which meant great loss to the Company. He pointed out to me several wrecked and dismantled native boats, which had floated down from the scene of the disturbance.

The following morning we rose early, and took a ballum to visit the town of Busrah itself, which lies some two miles from the river, at the head of a narrow creek or canal. At that early hour the air was fresh and delightful, and nothing more pleasant than this early morning trip could be imagined. We turned into the creek between houses, and having passed under a rickety wooden bridge, we entered a charming vista of palms. It was a sort of eastern Venice. To and fro on every side flitted the gay ballums, covered with gaudy awnings, and directed by dusky gondoliers. That one collided every other minute didn't matter one jot; it rather added interest to the voyage. Throughout the whole distance the canal is shadowed by palms, and the banks are in places strengthened with palm logs or bricks, which swarm with minute crabs. In half an hour we reached the creek head, around which a few houses are situated; and in company with one of our boatmen we walked through the town. A long, covered rope-walk, a second-rate bazaar stocked with English goods, and a telegraph-office, from which I attempted to telegraph, but couldn't, as everyone was asleep, and all was seen. I had imagined that in Bagdad I had seen almost the lowest pitch of degradation to which a great city might come, but evidently I was mistaken. Where is the rich and magnificent Balsora of the Caliphate ? Warfare, disease, and the alteration of trade routes have brought it to what it is, and yet

A BALLUM OF BUSRAH.

some writers assert that it is becoming prosperous.

Among the dogs in the town I noticed some, quite different to the ordinary bazaar dogs, and resembling close-haired English sheep dogs. I fancy they are really Persian. What I noticed

most at Busrah was that, for the first time since
I had landed at Scanderun, English was a language
of which nearly everyone knew a smattering. The
ballum men touted at the steamer's side in pidgin
English; the telegraph clerk and the shopkeeper
all knew a word or two. How was this? Busra
is not, like Alexandria or Beirut, invaded during
certain seasons of the year by hordes of English-
speaking tourists. The fact of the matter is that
English is at Busrah and the Gulf ports what
French is in northern Syria, and this is of course
due, not to English, but to Anglo-Indian influence.
Messrs. Lynch's river steamers, and the weekly
British India boat from Bombay, as well as the
Anglo-Indian mail service that is kept up between
Bagdad and Bombay, all tend to keep English
before the notice of the natives. Although on
Turkish territory, Indian or Persian money is much
preferred in the bazaar to Turkish, and a quantity
of small piastres I had brought from Aleppo, and
which were so much prized at Bagdad that I
could have got rid of them with profit, I was
told here were useless; and would have been
obliged to keep them, had not the British India
agent obligingly taken them off my hands.

A serious incident, showing almost as clearly as the Arab revolt, the Turkish mismanagement in these parts, had taken place a day or two before my arrival at Busrah. Some occupants of the prison, numbering over twenty, and all either convicted of murder or murderous theft, had managed to break down their prison wall, and having tied their sentry and warder back to back, they forded or swam the creek in their heavy irons, and escaped into the open country. Three were shot by the police or soldiers, and the remainder were supposed to be at large, in the vicinity of Busrah when I was there.

The present city was founded by the second Caliph, Omar, in the seventh century, and therefore takes precedence of Bagdad as a Saracenic city. An earlier town, however, existed on the site of the present Zobeir,* or old Busrah, a few miles west, on a canal which is supposed to be the old mouth of the Euphrates, called the Pallacopas. From time immemorial, indeed, must there of necessity have been a port here, where all trade of the East would make its way to Babylon and Seleucia in the earlier days, and to Ctesiphon, Kufa,

---

* Zobeir must be identical with Obolla.

and Bagdad in later times. It was this trade which raised the mediæval Balsora to such importance, and as Layard has remarked, it was the discovery of the Cape of Good Hope route which ruined its trade. In the time of Rauwolf (1574) a pigeon post was maintained between Bagdad and Busrah for commercial purposes. The East India Company established their factory here in 1738. Like the cities of the Babylonian plain, it has always had its quota of Jews, of whom Rabbi Benjamin reported two thousand when he travelled. Though Busrah of old is moribund, it is not impossible that a new Busrah is springing into existence. The traveller Buckingham wrote : " It (*i.e.*, trade) is said to have increased within the last ten years from two annual vessels to six under the British flag, besides those sailing under Arab colours." Layard describes how, fifty years ago, an English merchant-man with Manchester goods would occasionally anchor in the river, but had difficulty in finding a return cargo. About twenty years later there was a six-weekly steamer from Bombay, to which port there is at the present day a weekly service, and regular but less frequent sailings to Europe. There is also a Persian line between Busrah and India.

EE

The romantic journeys of " Es Sindibad of the Sea "
are things of the past, and the merchant can now
set forth from Busrah for Hind or Sarandib in a
spacious and well-fitted British India steamer, in
which he need have but little fear of the gigantic
and revengeful " Rukh," or of the other perils that
Es Sindibad faced and surpassed in such a wonderful
manner.*

Busrah has had its share of struggles and difficulties. Arab, Turk, Zanzibari, Persian, and Omani
have in their turn captured and lost the place. In
1777 it held out eight months against the Persians,
and though taken, the Turks repossessed it the
following year. In 1787 it was actually seized
and held from April to October by an Arab sheikh
of the Montefik tribe, whose brief reign was suddenly put a stop to by the Porte. A similar state
of things existed at Busrah shortly before the
Euphrates expedition, when the Sheikh of Zobeir
managed temporarily to seize the reins of government.

Westward of the Shat-el-Arab, from a point
above Kornah on the Euphrates to south of Busrah,
lie, at no great distance from the river, an elongated

* See Appendix No. VIII.—*Romance of the Persian Gulf.*

series of marshes which separate the river valley from the Arabian plain. These seem to be formed by the superfluous waters of the Euphrates, which, in spring-time, bursting its banks above Kornah, tries to make its way to the sea by another channel, the Nahr Salah (perhaps the Pallacopas), which flows past the town of Zobeir, or old Busrah. It is these marshes that give to Busrah the feverish and unhealthy reputation it not unjustly bears. At the same time, I was confidently assured that it is much more healthy than formerly, owing perhaps to the reclamation of some of the sur-rounding land. It is probable that formerly the Euphrates, tapped by innumerable canals, and also finding a second outlet to the sea by the Nahr Salah, (which probably does its work inefficiently at the present day),* did not inundate the country as now, and in consequence the country was much more salubrious. Besides the curse of marsh fever, the date mark is here as rife as at Bagdad. The natives also suffer grievously from stone, which may be due to drinking brackish water.

* Ainsworth, who visited Zobeir, gives the width of the Nahr Saada, or Salah, as forty feet

CHAPTER XVI.

THE PERSIAN GULF.

Mohammerah—Native Craft—Fisheries—Shusteris—History—Fow—
Crossing the Bar—The Persian Gulf—Piracy—Climate—Winds
—Health—Bushire—A Persian Whiteley—Description of the
Town—Killi—Reach Bahrein—Submarine Fresh Water—The
Pearl Fishery.

Soon after five o'clock on the 24th of April we were
steaming down stream towards the sea. At about
half-past seven we came opposite the outlet of the
Karun river. On the north bank stands a large
modern house, the residence of Sheikh Mizal, the so-
called independent Sheikh of Mohammerah, who is
a somewhat interesting person. As we passed this
we fired a gun as a salute, which was somewhat
tardily answered. Some years since, a British India
steamer was attacked by Arabs, and this salute is
always accorded by vessels of this line, in return for
the Sheikh's timely interference. Opposite the mouth
of the river, or rather canal, for this opening is artificial, we stopped, and as the skipper said there was
time, I lowered myself into a ballum and was rowed

up to Mohammerah, which is situated under a mile from the Shat el Arab on the right bank of the Karun. Some of the canoes I saw at the entrance to the canal are real " dug-outs," which come from Persia, or occasionally, it is said, coasting from Bombay. The ballums are carved with interlacing band patterns, exactly like the Celtic designs seen on the early crosses of Cumberland. Very odd patterns of sailing vessels are also to be seen, some with high poops like old English ships. At Mohammerah some of these native craft are built. There is a considerable fishery; soles are common, and there is a fish known as " sabur,"—patience, a piece of Arabic irony, as the fish, though sweet, is extraordinarily full of bones. A large net is most usual, but the casting net is also in use. In summer, sharks are common at the entrance to the Karun, and accidents are frequent. These plagues, by-the-bye, are found up the Tigris, as far as Amara. Opposite the town I saw the skeleton of an old paddle steamer, which belonged to one of the late sheikhs. The appearance of this ruin, high, dry, and rusty, on the bank, was a strange contrast to the surroundings, and recalled to mind similar scenes on the mouth of the English Thames.

There are pretty gardens extending along the north
bank until Mohammerah is reached, but the town
itself is a miserable place. Built of mud and bricks,
squalid, half ruined and dirty, with narrow bazaars
which could almost be spanned with the arms, it
does not seem to have one solitary redeeming feature.
Although in Persian territory at present, the people
are chiefly Arab. A good many negroes are also
seen, and there are some Shusteris, uninteresting-
looking people with big noses. Very different
accounts are given of the character of these people.
Layard found them kind and hospitable, but on the
opening of the Karun river for traffic, the commanders of Lynch's steamers had considerable trouble
with them. They seem, anyhow, to have an exceedingly bad reputation on the Shat el Arab. The
tradition is, that when everything was created, God
found that more men were required. So he took the
blood of a dog, and the blood of a Jew, and from this
rich blend was formed the Shusteri.

The old and natural outlet of the Karun river is
the Bahmeshir channel, which runs parallel with the
Shat el Arab from Mohammerah, and empties itself
into the sea at a point east of Fow on the latter.
This outlet is still navigable, but the Haffar canal,

which connects the Karun with the Shat el Arab, carries away a good deal of the water. It is remarkable that the Karun water has often a red tinge.

The history of Mohammerah is unique. On or near the site where it now stands, have existed in succession an Alexandria, an Antiochia, a Charax, and an Astrabad.* The present town, which is on the border line of Turkey and Persia, was erected in 1812 by a sheikh of the Muhaisen Arabs, a subdivision of the great Kaab tribe. The place proved, as Ainsworth has termed it, a " bone of contention " between the two powers, until it was decided by a boundary commission to belong to the Persians. The Turks sacked it in 1837, and in 1857 the Anglo-Indian expedition bombarded it with mortars placed on floating rafts, and the Persian garrison was soon routed. Various Arab sheikhs, under Turkish protection, ruled the place, and the present governor, Sheikh Mizal Khan, of the Muhaisen tribe, and chief of the Kaab Arabs, is now in authority. This independent Arab chieftain, for independence he claims, has jurisdiction over a large region east of Mohammerah. He pays an annual tribute to the Government, and he himself levies taxes on his

* Curzon : " Persia and the Persian Question."

subjects.   Of the former he lives in bodily fear ; and
they have, it is said, made more than one attempt to
carry him off.   His position seems somewhat anoma-
lous, as, although holding the Governorship under the
Persians, he at the same time asserts the independence of his tribe, who inhabit Mohammerah.
And the Persians, who have appointed him governor,
are anxious to get him quietly out of their way,
although they are not in a position to supplant him
at present by a new governor.   He is probably the
last of the independent Sheikhs of Mohammerah.   A
portrait of him in Mr. Curzon's "Persia and the
Persian Question" shows a handsome and dignified
Arab with a face full of intelligence and character.
Mohammerah is notoriously unhealthy, though
probably not so much so as the Persian Gulf ports.
In the vicinity it is said to be swampy ; but the
palm groves do not extend any distance up the
Karun.   Good sport, lion, fallow deer, and other
game is to be got by a trip to Shuster.

In spite of the misery of the present town, its site
is of the greatest importance, commanding as it does
the waters of the Euphrates, Tigris, and the Persian
Karun, and it must have a great future before it.   So
much has recently been written about the Karun new

trade route, that it is unnecessary to go into the question here. It was opened to commerce in 1888, and Messrs. Lynch, and the Bombay and Persian Gulf S.S. Company soon placed steamers upon it. The latter soon gave up the matter as a bad job, and the former, although still maintaining some sort of service on the river, are doing so at what is probably a dead loss. One of their larger steamers was replaced by a stern-wheeler from the Nile, and when I was there, connection with Ahwaz was only maintained by a small steam launch. Persian pigheadedness will probably for some time stand in the way of the successful development of trade.

The river between Busrah and the sea is uninteresting and unpicturesque. The banks are level and almost continuously planted with palm groves. It is, however, deep and wide, and capable of floating ships of any size when they have once passed the bar at the mouth. In the afternoon we arrived off Fow, or Fao as it is generally spelt, consisting of a small barrack, a custom-house and quarantine, and the Indo-European, and Turkish telegraph stations. There is also a pole to carry a light, and a flag-staff. One of our passengers, an English doctor, who was leaving Turkey for India, went ashore, and returned with a trophy in the shape of a Turkish government flag, which he had deliberately hauled down under the very noses of the Turkish authorities, and pocketed as a memento of the country. An hour later we were out of sight of land and stuck on the great bar which closes the entrance to the river. Looking over the vessel's side, we seemed to be motionless, although the propeller was at full speed. We were, however, moving slowly, and in two hours we were clear, having forced our way through the soft mud. This has frequently to be done, as there is only some eighteen or twenty feet of water over the bar at high tide, and at low water only half that amount. The strong shemal (north west wind) was blowing, and perhaps helped us a little : but it made our initial experience of the Persian Gulf rather a surprise, for as soon as we were clear, it became so cool that we were not sorry for light overcoats.

The Persian Gulf, situated between Lat. 30°, and Lat. 24° N., is perhaps, considering its historical interest, and future commercial importance, less known to the average Englishman than any other sea of equal size and equal accessibility. This is due of course to very good reasons. It possesses a climate almost unbearable to Europeans except during

certain seasons, and, although it can hardly be said to
lead to nowhere, the places it does lead to are so
unprovided with the comforts of European travel,
that the ordinary tourist shuns them, and so wound
up in the net of Eastern bigotry and backwardness,
that as yet trade has not been able to make great ad-
vances in the centres of population.

In shape an irregular oblong, it stretches diagonally south-east from the Shat-el-Arab to the Strait of
Ormuz, where the Ras Mussendom of the Arabian
coast projects boldly northward, and forms the
southern point of the Gulf. South of this the Gulf
of Oman widens boldly to the Arabian Sea. The
length of the Persian Gulf itself is only about five
hundred and forty miles, but the total distance
navigated by the British India Steamers from Bombay
to Busrah is close on two thousand. The eastern
littoral of this is occupied by Arabistan, Farsistan,
and other Persian States as far as Gwetter, where
Baluchistan comes in and extends to Anglo-Indian
territory at Karachi. The eastern coast is entirely
that of Arabia, portions of which are nominally under
Turkish Government. As a matter of fact, such
prosperity as the Gulf possesses is due to British influence.

In the fourth century B.C. Nearchus, Alexander's Admiral, navigated the Macedonian fleet from the Indus to the Tigris, supporting his master, who marched through Baluchistan and Southern Persia, after his Indian campaign. In the sixteenth century the Portuguese established a commercial supremacy, which remained unshaken for a hundred years.

The piracy of the Persian Gulf is, thanks to British energy in the early part of this century, practically at an end.   Inhabiting, as the pirates did, the western coast of the Gulf, no settled trade was possible so long as their depredations were suffered to continue. From 1805 till 1825 the work of pacification was carried on, but it was not until the treaties of 1835 and 1853 that the Gulf became really safe.   The huge scale on which these buccaneers carried on their trade may be judged by the fact that in 1809 their fleet numbered sixty-three large, and eight hundred small vessels, the total of crew being nineteen thousand.

The native trade of the present day is carried on by buggalows, which ply between the Gulf, and the African coast, Red Sea, and India.   These vessels vary from one to three hundred tons, and are rigged as a rule with mainmast and lateen sail, and a small

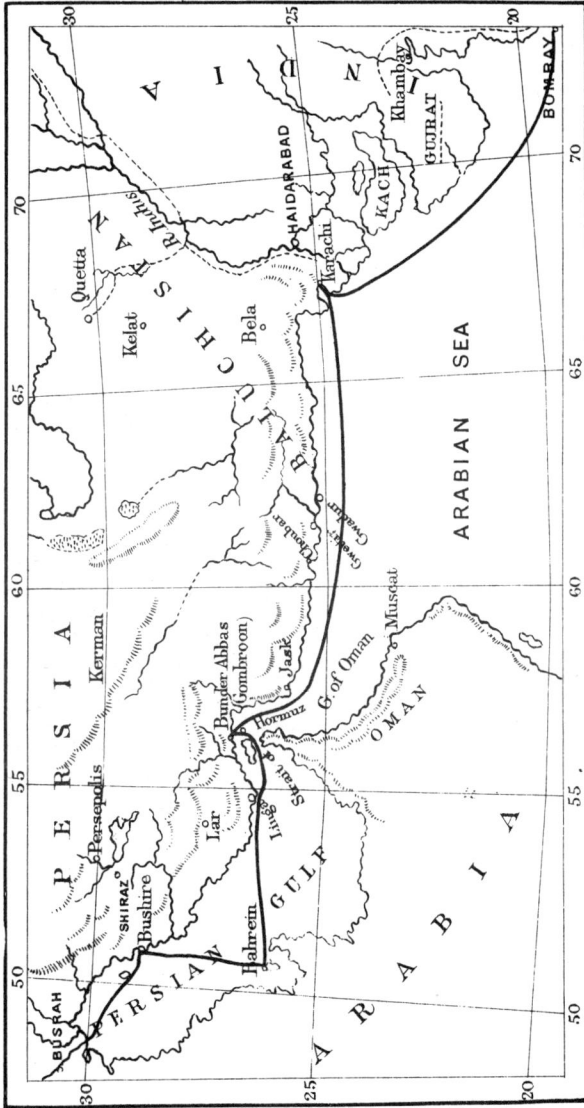

THE PERSIAN GULF AND THE ARABIAN SEA

Miles
100 80 60 40 20 0   100   200   300   400   500

To face P. 428.

TTA—O

lateen mizzen. For their size they require a large crew, and, though excellent sailers in moderate winds, they are unable to tack or sail close to the wind.

The following notes of the temperature and winds of the Gulf are abstracted from the "Persian Gulf Pilot," published by the direction of the Lords' Commissioners of Admiralty, 1870, which the captain of the *Simla* kindly lent me.

Table of Fahrenheit temperature taken on board ship, from observations extending over four years ; on shore the range would be more considerable.

Month.	Average Max. 4 p.m.	Average Min. 4 a.m.	Month.	Average Max. 4 p.m.	Average Min. 4 a.m.
Jan.	69	65	July	91½	89
Feb.	67	63	Aug.	94	89
Mar.	75	69½	Sept.	90	83½
Apl.	80½	75	Oct.	85½	81
May	85	81	Nov.	80½	76
June	89½	85	Dec.	74	70

Although this shows a pretty warm condition of things at sea, the heat on the shore and in the stifling towns must be much more oppressive. The amusing account of the fifteenth century writer, Abdin Rezak, quoted by Mr. Curzon in his " Persia and the Persian Question," is so highly comic that it will bear re-quotation. This refers to the climate of Muscat :

" The heat was so intense that it burned the marrow in the bones; the sword in its scabbard melted like wax, and the gems which adorned the handle of the dagger were reduced to coal. In the plains the chase became a matter of perfect ease, for the desert was filled with roasted gazelles."

The Gulf has its winter rains like Europe, and in winter is sometimes very cold. The rainfall at Bushire is eight or nine inches, at Muscat but three and a half.

The prevailing wind in the summer months is the north-west shemal, which follows the curves of the Gulf. Frequently this wind is loaded with minute particles of dust from Mesopotamia, and several times during the voyage we found cabin windows, deck, and rigging coated with a thick deposit of this.

The south-east wind in winter is called the " koss," and blows from December to April. It is a stormy and wet wind. The north-east wind in winter is also wet and is called " hashi." The south-west " saheili " often follows a " koss," and generally blows but a few hours It is accompanied with thunder and lightning.

A peculiarity in the Gulf is that the worst weather is sometimes unaccompanied with any change in the barometer. During summer there is, however, a permanent depression.

All the Gulf ports may be said to be very unhealthy; to Europeans, indeed, almost fatal; the ill supplies of water, absolute lack of sanitation, and great heat soon telling their tale on any who try residence. Gulf fever, a remittent and dangerous form of malaria, is prevalent, and restoration to health can only be obtained by seeking a new climate. The natives themselves suffer much from it. The fearful scourge of Guinea worm* is painfully common at Bunder Abbas and other of the ports, and is probably due to bad water. Elephantiasis is also often seen. Cholera is said to be never absent, but is worst at Bahrein.

The next morning found the *Simla* under a strong northerly shemal, and a highish sea, heading towards Bushire. Instead of the placid sea and broiling heat we expected, the general appearance was more like blowy summer weather in the Bay of Biscay. With a wind like this we might, of course, have made Bushire very much sooner, but the British India service in "the Gulf," is not, although carrying mails, noted for its speed, and a full fortnight is

* Filaria Medinensis, or Dracunculus.

consumed between Busrah and Bombay. About
eight o'clock we sighted the island of Kharak, behind which we could discern snow-covered peaks
of the Persian mainland. This Kharak, now inhabited by a few fishermen and Gulf pilots, was
occupied in the early part of last century by a
Dutch factory. The brief history of this settle-
ment, from Baron Kniphausen, the first director,
who was inducted by Sheikh Mir Naser, to Mr.
Van Houting, the third and last, who was summarily
kicked out by Mir Mahenna, the successor of Mir
Naser, for meddling in Perso-Arabic politics, is
told by Carsten Niebuhr in his "Travels in Arabia."

As we approached Bushire at noon, a magnificent
panorama of Persian mountains rose up behind the
town. The principal point is Kuh Hormuj, a noble
peak towering 6,500 feet above the sea level, and
succeeded to the left by another fine range. These
mountains are, they say, three days' journey from
Bushire, and beyond them lies the town of Shiraz.
The anchorage is two miles from the port, and is
somewhat difficult of approach, a big detour having to be made to reach it. As we steamed up,
I was struck by the extreme greenness of the
sea ; more intense than any I had seen elsewhere.

The town occupies the northern edge of a long sandstone ridge, some twelve miles in length, and raised, it would appear, above the sea in recent times. At high tides it is separated from the mainland by the sea, and at other times by a salt swamp. Bushire itself presents, from the sea, an appearance somewhat like what Alexandria must have had, before it put on its present rather European aspect. As the whole of the following day was spent here, I deferred my visit to the next morning. Having gone ashore in the mail boat, I took a donkey, which can be hired as in Cairo, and proceeded round the town : and first, as I was informed that Bushire possessed a shop where European goods of all kinds might be purchased, I proceeded in search of a sun helmet, and civilised pipe tobacco, a luxury I had not smoked since leaving the Mediterranean. To my surprise, I was put down at a shop, well-stocked with English boots, tinned provisions, and sun hats; in fact, a regular Persian Whiteley, where everything, it seemed, could be purchased, from a cigar case to a bottle of pain-killer. Mr. Goldsard, the proprietor, was politeness itself, and for a quarter of an hour I revelled in the luxury of European shopping. It certainly seemed strange, that here, in a wretched,

FF

squalid Persian port, an enterprising trader can run a shop containing more civilised luxuries than the bazaars of Aleppo and Bagdad combined. I afterwards rode along the shore past the British Residency, where a guard of Sepoys is maintained as at Bagdad, and then, crossing the spit of land to the other side, I returned through the bazaar. This was the narrowest and perhaps the dirtiest I had yet seen: and although crowded with Persians and Persian-speaking Arabs, there was not much of interest in it. The usual amount of Manchester goods, sugar, and shops full of very elaborate sweets were the principal commodities. I purchased some rather pretty sherbet spoons, carved out of wood, for a trifle. My donkey boy spoke some English, and the people stared less at the sight of an Englishman than at Aleppo. Altogether, in spite of the smelly squalor, I felt nearer home in the bazaar of Bushire than I had done for many a day. The houses are chiefly built of mud and stone, and all of the better class have double verandahs. There are no serdabs, as the climate here is too damp, but many of the houses are supplied with peculiar towers to catch the wind and conduct it into the rooms. These are called " bajirs ": from July to October the heat is so

great that the inhabitants sleep on the flat roofs.
The costume of the inhabitants being rather Arabic
than Persian, is not characteristic as that up country.
Along the shore, near the sea wall, I noticed a line of
well-built fishing vessels. The Bushire boats, by-
the-bye, have their own colours, a red flag with the
two-bladed sword of Ali depicted in white in the
middle. I was hospitably entertained to lunch at the
comfortable office of the company, where I was able
to inspect a chart of Bushire and its surroundings.
Reshire, about six miles down the peninsula, contains the telegraph-station, and the summer residence of the British Resident lies beyond at a
place called Subzabad. This part had recently no
houses, and was reputed dangerous, but residences
of the few Europeans and others have recently
sprung up at this place. There are here, also, some
ancient remains in the shape of mounds containing
a quadrangle of three hundred yards in diameter.
The mound, about thirty feet above ground level, is
said to be strongly ditched towards the landward side.
Other mounds are found in the vicinity, and cuneiform inscribed bricks and urns have been turned up.
It is variously conjectured that these remains are of
the Babylonian age, or the remains of a Portuguese

fort. In 1856 the site was occupied by the British forces.* The curse of Bushire is its water supply. The ordinary quality, which is so ordinary (or " ornery," as a Yankee would have it), that the Europeans will not touch it, is two miles distant, and the best over five miles away towards Reshire.

Standing on the verandah of the comfortable office, I saw in a neighbouring courtyard a lot of boys playing a game which seems to be one of the chief amusements of the " street arabs " of this place. It is called " Killi." A circle is marked on the ground, and one player, armed either with three sticks or a stick and a sack stands in front of it; another boy, from about twenty paces distant, throws up a short stick, or a piece of bone, which it is his intention to get into the circle, while the stick and sack man has to keep it out; the latter stops it as best he can with stick, sack, or his body, and then he takes it up and strikes it as far as he can away with one of his sticks. This he generally does so that it strikes the ground and rebounds off it with considerable force. From wherever it then falls the thrower has again to try to shy it into the circle, whether it is close to or far

* See, " The Persian Gulf Pilot."

from it. When he succeeds in this, the stick and sack man is out.

Horse sales in Bushire are conducted in a funny way. An English traveller had just ridden in from Persepolis, and his animal was to be disposed of. The auctioneer was sent for, and he proceeded to walk through the town leading the animal and continually shouting out his merits, in order to get bids. He at last arrived under the windows of the B. I. office, where he had a bid or two, and after walking his animal up and down the street, yelling the price offered, it was at last disposed of.

Although there was an earlier Mohammedan town upon the peninsula, the port of Bushire is modern, having been founded by Shah Nadir in the last century. Mr. Curzon has pointed out that the common derivation of the name—Abu Shahir, "The Father of Cities," is incorrect, one of these words being Arabic and the other Persian. Soon after 1761 the East India Co. established their factory here. It soon rose to be the first port on this part of the Persian Gulf, and during this century has about doubled its population, which may now be 13,000. In the Persian war it was captured by the British troops on the 10th December, 1856, and was held till the

termination of hostilities with Persia in the ensuing
year. Like Mohammerah, it was held during the
late part of last century and beginning of this, by
Arab sheikhs, but the Persians have for some time
appointed a regular governor, who at one time, and
probably still, holds the special title of Darga Beg, or
" Lord of the Sea." There is a small Armenian
community, in whose church there are the graves of
some English officers who lost their lives in the
Persian campaign. The town was formerly strengthened by a good wall and towers on the south or
landward side, but very little now remains.

We did not leave Bushire till five in the evening,
as we were somewhat delayed by the mails. The
north wind still held, and was very cool and refreshing, the thermometer on deck at nine p.m. showing
the pleasant temperature of 75°. We made a rapid
passage across the Gulf and arrived at Bahrein just
before noon the following day. The captain wished
to leave soon, and, in consequence, I was not enabled
to land, so all I saw was a long sandy waste, dotted in
some places with palm groves, and the two towns of
Maharak and Bahrein, which at high water are separated by the sea. The former is one of the chief
head-quarters of the pearl fishery, but it goes on all

along the Arab coast. The boats used in this industry could be seen piled up high and dry on the island,
as no fishing is done before the end of May. The
sea-water at the anchorage, which was a long way
from the shore, is beautifully green, and when calm
exceedingly clear. The remarkable phenomenon of
fresh water springs at the bottom of the sea exists in
many places near the islands, and the inhabitants
dive for their water as they do for their pearls, and
having filled leather bottles which they carry for the
purpose, they are hauled to the surface. This remarkable water supply would probably never have
been found if the pearl fishery had not enticed the
Arabs to be always prowling about the bottom of the
sea. Besides the harmless pearl oyster, the sea is
also occupied by sharks and sawfishes, for which the
poor diver has to be on the look-out. I noticed also
very large jelly-fishes, and many water crows, a sort
of cormorant.

The pearl fishery is carried on from May to
September, and at Bahrein there are several thousand boats from four to ten tons burden at work
in the season. Two to three hundred thousand
pounds' worth of pearls are said to be raised
annually at Bahrein alone. The diver, with his

ears filled with wax, an instrument like a clothes peg on his nose, and his feet weighted, descends in water not deeper than thirteen fathoms. When he has collected his oysters, he is hauled up by a rope. The extreme time they can remain below water is one and a-half minutes. Most of the pearls make their way to Bombay. The horrible system by which the poor divers—who ruin their health and strength in this unnatural existence—are kept in poverty and dependence by scoundrel Indian and Arab merchants, is well known. Unfortunately, the "Truck Act" is unknown in the Persian Gulf; and the wretched Arabs, compelled to sell their pearls to their master at his own price, and to hire their boat and provisions from him at a hideously extortionate figure, are sometimes actually starving, while their labour is making others millionaires. A more vile form of slavery does not exist.

Bahrein was, like other Gulf ports, occupied in the sixteenth century by the Portuguese, who were, however, expelled in 1622 by the Persians. After that time, it was a continual source of dispute between the Persians and various Arab sheikhs (including the Sultan of Oman), who in turn possessed it. At the present day it is practically under British protection.

CHAPTER XVII.

THE PERSIAN GULF.

Mountains round Lingah—Lingah—Water Supply—The Straits of Hormuz—Situation of Bunder Abbas—The Town—Tremendous Heat—The Island of Hormuz—Its History—Old Accounts— Beautiful Scenery—Flying-fish and Sea-snakes—Turtles and Black-fish—Bombay—Leave for England—Wild Weather in the Red Sea.

FROM Bahrein we steered almost due east across the Gulf for the Laristan port of Lingah. Captain Robertson told us the wind would drop, and heat would follow, and so it turned out. And the next day we lunched and dined with the flat-topped skylight of the *Simla* for a table (a delightful arrangement in tropical seas), and felt none too cool, although we had the punkah going in the open air. After lunch we had beautiful views of the desert coast of Laristan. First appeared a long range of red mountain far away to our left, behind which another and much higher range towered. At half-past two a small island, somewhat mountainous and apparently uninhabited,

was on our right. This is called Farur. Later on
another noble chain, apparently volcanic, rose to
the left, at the base of which, by means of my
glass, I could discern a small town, with a wretched
little date grove at one end. This range is Jebel
Bustaneh, 1,750 feet in height, but the table-topped
mountain seen shortly before, is Jebel Turanjeh,
5,150 feet. Over all the mountains lay a heavy
haze, for the climate of this part of the Gulf, in
spite of the desert-like appearance of the shores,
is exceedingly damp, and soaking dews fall every
night. Fogs are very common.

Lingah, which we reached in about twelve hours
from Bahrein, looks fair enough from the sea : it is
situated on a plateau of the coast, behind which the
mighty mountains rise as a background ; in the haze
which hung over it as we steamed up to the anchorage,
the white line of houses, the solitary minaret, and the
fishing boats looked very pretty. At the anchorage
lay two English full-rigged ships, some sixty years old,
now the property of an enterprising Arab merchant.
It occured to me that it would be interesting to
examine the present condition of the once trim
cabins of these old clippers. The anchorage is

about a quarter of a mile from the land. I went
ashore with the mail officer, and we landed near a
small walled dock where a lot of buggalows were lying
up, high and dry, for repairs: others, some of considerable size, were being built here, as there is a
very active coasting trade carried on at Lingah.
Sanitary considerations seem to have less attention
here than even at other Gulf ports, and the moment
we landed our noses were assailed by a stench arising
from the shore which was, in fact, covered with filth
of all sorts. It was perfectly pestilential. I walked
through the town and bazaars. The latter are narrow
and irregular in the extreme; fish, grain, and sweetmeats seem to be the chief commodities. At one
stall I saw a row of little Chinese pots, used for kohl;
these are probably brought overland with tea by the
caravan routes. The people are mongrel Persian
and Arab of the pirate Jowasmi tribe, and some
wear a turban of native cloth which is large and
pretty. Negro sailors and negro beggars loaf about
the little harbour, adding not a little to the picturesqueness of the place. Women, in a totally
different costume to anything I had seen, marched
about, wearing a veil something like a mask, with

apertures for the eyes. The total population may be about ten thousand. The sights of Lingah are few and far between; there is one small modern mosque built in the Bagdad style, with a little tile ornamentation. Outside the town on one side, I was pointed out a lot of curious domed structures, scattered over the plain, which are tanks formed for the purpose of collecting the rain-water, the only supply Lingah boasts, for there are no springs; the domes, some forty feet in height, are roughly constructed, and are intended to prevent evaporation. The rainfall at Lingah is rather heavy, and these " birkehs," as they are called, will contain an ample store for the purposes of the town. After this we went to the British post-office, quite a smart structure, like all in the Gulf, under the management of a native of India. The deliberation of this individual in making up the mail bags made it late before we got on board.

Lingah is even now said to be a lawless and not altogether safe place to walk about in; formerly it was a stronghold of the Persian Gulf pirates—many an East Indian Co. man-of-war was lost in following these phantoms among the perilous shoals and islands of the Gulf. The town was, till recently, governed by an independent Arab sheikh. It is said that a foot messenger can go from here to Bushire in ten to fourteen days, according to the season of the year.*

Early on the following morning we rose to find ourselves within sight of Bunder Abbas, without doubt the most interesting part of the Persian Gulf. We had now got into real heat, and most of the passengers had elected to sleep on deck; as I was yet far from well, and the dews in this part of the Gulf are so great as to render everything on deck wet through in a very short time, I preferred to remain in my cabin, although the heat there rendered sleep difficult enough. In a climate like this, however, one can hardly avoid, at sea, taking prolonged naps in one's deck chair in the heat of the day, so that sleep at night is not of the same importance that it is in Europe, where each day is a day of activity.

Bunder Abbas, or Gombroon, as its old name is, lies in an immense bay cut out of the Persian coast. Opposite it from the Arabian side projects a peninsula, the extreme point of which is called Ras Mussendom, and the channel dividing the two coasts, the Strait of Hormuz. I do not know if I am correct, but a glance at a map or chart suggests to me that this channel, half crossed by the Arabian

* The " Persian Gulf Pilot."

peninsula, and dotted as it is by islands and islets, is but a comparatively modern geographical development. At one time, surely, before some subsidence let in the water, these coasts were joined, and the islands now projecting off the Persian coast mark but eminences in the level of this Perso-Arabian land. If this is so, the gulf was then, like the Caspian, a land-locked sea; and as at that epoch, probably, there were neither Assyrians, Persians, nor Arabs to seek an outlet to the south for trade, no caravan route nor canal would cross this spit of land, which parted the inland sea from the great ocean which stretched away to the southern polar regions, and whose tides washed the shores of countries which were to become the richest, perhaps, in the world.

The approach to Bunder Abbas is, in its strange way, absolutely lovely. The steamer, after passing the island of Kishm, which is perhaps seventy miles in length, turns north to make the harbour, which is placed at the most northerly point of the great bay. As she approaches vast desert mountains rise in rugged and sterile confusion on all sides. Right behind the town itself is Jebel Jinao (7,690 feet), peeping over whose shoulder to the right can be descried the majestic Jebel Bakhur, which dominates the Gulf from a height of 10,660 feet. Further to the right lies Jebel Shimal (8,500 feet), while to the left of Jinao lies Khamir. Behind us are the cliffs of Kishm, once held by the Portuguese, and still sustaining a population of ten or twelve thousand. In 1820 a British force was placed here to check the Jowasmi pirates, and as late as 1879 a force of Sepoys was still maintained.* At the present day a coal depôt only represents British influence. Out to sea and closing the harbour are the islands of Hormuz and Larak, the former, which played so important a part in the history of the East, showing from here a low crinkly outline and at its south end a spit of land terminated by the old Portuguese fort. On the left before entering the harbour are a few small and unimportant islands.

---

* I have a curious memento of this English occupation in a fine old Koran in its original binding, on the fly-leaf of which is written :
"This book was found on board a pirate vessel destroyed in the Persian Gulph, near the Island of Kishmé, by H.M.'s ship *Eden*, on the 10th of January, 1819. The thermometer was not lower than 64° though in the dead of winter."
As the expedition did not leave Bombay till the end of 1819, the date is evidently a clerical error for 1820, a common enough mistake even in England in the new year, with newspapers and almanacs on all sides. Interesting details of the expedition are to be found in Mr Curzon's work on Persia. The date of the Koran is A.H. 1061.

At the anchorage, which is about a mile and three-quarters from the town, we found the steamer of the Persian line lying. The town is situated on a sandy plain, with a frontage of nearly a mile to the sea. At the east end of it lie mangrove swamps. In spite of its being a place of great trade (being the port of Kerman and Meshed, from which the trade routes pass to Teheran, and even Cabul and Herat) there is little to be seen in the town. There is a respectable little quay and sea-wall, on the former of which I found two old brass guns marked " Honi soit, &c., G.R." Of these relics I got different accounts. An Englishman, who had been resident in Bunder Abbas and who came on board the *Simla*, believed they had been brought from Bushire, and an Arab boy on the jetty said they had come from Muscat. Mr. Curzon notices that the Sultan of Muscat, towards the end of the last century, held the town by a firman from the Persian government, during which time he, by a treaty, gave the English leave to establish a factory and mount guns. He suggests that these old pieces are records either of an affirmative response, or that they were a present to the Sultan.

The bazaars were mostly closed, as it was a

festival or "id," but many of the inhabitants I saw were wild-looking creatures, with long locks trailing on their shoulders. Baluchis are also to be seen. Some of the houses fronting the sea have double verandahs, and many of the better class have bajirs on the roofs. Those in the town are wretched mud structures, and there are also reed huts built about in the open spaces. Altogether it is difficult to believe that Bunder Abbas was the greatest, and is still an important, commercial place on the Persian coast. I took a walk round the town with one of my Arab boatmen. The heat was terrific, and the perspiration poured off my face in torrents. The sand I walked on seemed to scorch my boots, and every few yards I was fain to sit down to rest. The place seemed a veritable oven, and it is easy to believe that this is the hottest place in the Gulf. It is also extremely damp, and sea fogs are very common. Fever is very bad here, and Europeans cannot live long in the place. Guinea-worm and elephantiasis are also common. There are the remains of an old wall and towers, and my boatman, who spoke Arabic, showed me a gateway on the landward side of the town called " Bab el Balao."*

* Query—Bab el Baluch—the Baluchistan gate.

GG

Although some Arabic is spoken, Persian and Hindustani are more common.

The chief exports from Bunder Abbas are fruit and grain to Muscat, carpets and asafœtida in large quantities to Bombay, and salt which is quarried and blasted in Hormuz. There is the usual import trade of piece-goods. The population has, it would seem, a very fluctuating figure, as many of the inhabitants retire to the country behind in the great heats, and as it also depends on the arrival and departure of caravans. The maximum in winter may be 10,000, and the minimum 5,000. Hamilton, in his account of the East Indies, says that in August the heat affects the sea so much, that "there comes a stink from it" that is "as detestable as the smell of dead animals on the land, and vast quantities of small shell-fish are thrown on the shore by the surges of the sea; . . . It tarnishes gold and silver as bad as the bilge water of a tight ship."

The wonderful island of Hormuz there was no chance of visiting, and I had to content myself with looking on its jagged outline and three white peaks from the steamer. From all accounts, although there is now but a fishing village of a hundred houses upon it, it is a most curious place. There is no sort of vegetation, and no fresh water, but salt, sulphur, and iron ore abound. Two of the white peaks seen from a distance are composed of sulphur, and the other of salt. It contains also many volcanic cones. The captain of the *Simla*, who had visited the place, said that in one part is the most extraordinary spectacle ; a broad stream of water can be seen flowing to the sea covered with a dazzling crust of salt, and in the centre, but not mixing with it, runs a blood-red streamlet tinged with iron ore. A Portuguese fort. and lighthouse still exist, the former said to be a wonderful construction of dressed stone.

Hormuz, or Ormuz, was originally founded in the third century by one of the Sassanian dynasty. This was succeeded by an Arab city founded by an Arab prince, Mohammed Dramku by name. These, however, were both upon the mainland, and it was not until the beginning of the fourteenth century that the island city was established, in consequence of the inroads of Turks on the mainland.* The Ormus of

---

* I would refer the reader to the " History of Persia .... written in Arabic by Mirkond....that of Ormuz, by Torunxa, king of that island, both of them translated into Spanish by Antony Teixeira,.... and now rendered into English by Captain John Stevens, MDCCXV." Hormuz was, according to Torunxa, or Turon Shah, founded by Ayza Sefin, 1302. Turon Shah wrote in the 14th century, but in Teixeira's translation much of the matter is by himself.

Marco Polo, however, who travelled in the thirteenth century, would appear, by his description, to have existed both upon the coast and the island, as the last is specially mentioned, and may have been considered a province. He describes summer houses built in the water, to which the inhabitants resorted in the heat; and also mentions the trade in "spices, pearls, precious stones, cloth of gold and silver, and all other precious things from India." In Teixeira's translation, or rather edition of Torunxa's chronicle, there are many interesting descriptive notes. We are told of "three overflowing springs of pure clear water, but as salt as the sea:" also "at the end of the island there is a little fresh water made use of to water the king's . . . orchards;" and again "the island affords much game, as gazelles, creatures like wild goats; adibes, which are a sort of foxes: turtle doves, and other sorts of fowls; and it is wonderful, that the island affording no fresh water but what has been mentioned, it is not yet known what these creatures drink. Some pretend that, being excessively thirsty, they drink salt water, and others have invented no less unlikely fables."

We also get a glimpse of the inhabitants :—

" Most of the Hormuzians are fair and well

shaped; the men polite and genteel, the women beautiful, . . . and all Mahometans: some Schyays . . . . others Sunnays . . . . Besides these, are many Portuguese Christians, Armenians, Georgians, Jacobies, ... Nestorians . . . . Baneans and Jews." In summer, " the terrible heat consumes all peccant humours with excessive sweat."

Early in the sixteenth century Don Mathias de Albuquerque took the city and founded a Portuguese factory. The fort they built, and which is still to be seen from the anchorage at Bunder Abbas, was quadrangular in plan, well-built and strengthened by a moat. It is said to be the best preserved Portugese fort remaining in the Gulf: and there are, or were, a quantity of ancient guns remaining about the ruin. In 1583, Mr. Ralph Fitch, merchant of London, and three companions having travelled to the Persian Gulf by Tripoli, Aleppo, and Bagdad, were seized by Albuquerque, and after having some of their goods forfeited, were sent on to India. In the account of his travels, he has left us an interesting account of Hormuz at that time. He describes it as the " driest island in the world "; and tells us that there is a Portuguese castle, wherein "there is a captain for the King of Portugal, having under him a convenient number of soldiers, whereof some part remain in the castle, and some in the town." There is also "a very great trade in all sorts of spices, drugs, silk, cloth of silk, fine tapestry of Persia, great store of pearls which come from the Isle of Baharim (*sic*), and many horses of Persia, which serve all India." He had an eye for female beauty, so that although the fair ones were no doubt closely veiled, our merchant adventurer found time to jot down that "their women are very strangely attired, wearing on their noses, ears, necks, arms, and legs, many rings set with jewels, and locks of silver and gold in their ears, and a long bar of gold on the side of their noses. Their ears, with the weight of their jewels, are worn so wide that a man may thrust three of his fingers into them."* In 1622, the English, allied with Shah Abbas, besieged Hormuz, and after a siege which lasted nearly three months, it capitulated, † and three years later the coast was handed over by treaty to the Persians, a treaty which the government of the

---

* Pinkerton's "Collection of Voyages," Vol. IX, p. 408.

† Hamilton says less than two months; and that the agreement was faithfully observed till 1680, when the English failed to keep the Gulf clear of insults.

nation made but little scruple of breaking. The same Shah soon after formed the port on the mainland, which before had been a fishing village of the name of Gombroon (said to mean, the shrimping village), and it was now named Bunder Abbas.

About this time Hormuz seems to have been in the zenith of its magnificence, and Sir Thomas Herbert in 1627 describes, " houses furnished with gilded leather, and India and China rarities. Buzzar rich and beautiful, splendid churches, and castle regularly and strongly fortified."* The remains of the reservoirs for water, fragments of mosques and the town, are still to be seen. The population, once forty thousand, is now reduced to a paltry three hundred, who migrate to the mainland during part of the year.

Gombroon, now Bunder Abbas, rose to take the place and trade of Hormuz, in which it only partly succeeded. English, French, and Dutch factories were established, and the remains of some or all are still to be seen. Towards the end of last century it was under the rule of the Sultan of Muscat, as before mentioned, and it was not until a quarter of a

---

* See Curzon : " Persia and the Persian Question."

century ago that the Persians obtained the full
power over it.

We left Bunder Abbas on the evening of the
29th, and as we were not going to Muscat, it
was a three days' voyage to Karachi. After that
port the British India steamers, having regained
British seas, resume British activity, and go a
respectable speed to Bombay, which they reach in
about fifty-six hours. As we steamed out of
Bunder Abbas, I thought I had never seen such
a lovely scene anywhere. Jinao, Shimal, and the
islands lay wrapped in a purple haze, and behind
them the sky was lit with the pale orange glow
of departed day. To the ship stretched the placid
sea, bright with the reflection of sunset. It looked
a perfect fairyland, and nothing could be more
inexpressibly beautiful. It was hard to believe that
such a fair place could be anything but healthy.
As the darkness fell, the sea was illuminated by
innumerable phosphorescent gleams, each of which
glowed for a second, and died.

During the three days to Karachi, we got distant
views of the Persian and Baluchistan coast. Some
parts had the most astonishing outline, jagged and
serrated like a saw's edge. In a few places the

shapes were strangely fantastic, peaks like light-
houses sticking up side by side. Queer items of
natural history were met. A sea-snake, about four
feet in length, with a yellow body with dark bands
and a flat tail like a fish. Here I first made
acquaintance with the flying-fish, which, when they
were first pointed out to me fluttering away from
the bows of the ship, I refused to believe were
anything but small sea birds, until one of them
accommodatingly flew on board and dispelled the
illusion. One day we sighted a great many of
these, an enormous black-fish, and a big turtle, all
in a quarter of an hour. The latter was rolling
about placidly, fifty miles from land, and apparently
quite unconcerned about his wife, who was no doubt
keeping his tea warm on the shoals of the Baluchistan coast. The heat and damp increased, and
sleeping below deck became very trying, but the
dews were so heavy and continuous, that it was
difficult not to get soaked to the skin when sitting
on deck in the evening. On the 3rd May we anchored in the harbour of Karachi, and I was at
last back to European civilisation. With this my
story must come to an end. In a few days more I
reached Bombay, which, as the monsoon was

brewing, I found too hot to be pleasant. The thermometer fluctuated between 91 degrees and 98 degrees in the hotel hall, which in the muggy climate of Bombay is an uncomfortably high temperature. A week later, having seen the principal

A TOWER OF SILENCE AT BOMBAY.

sights of that city, I took my passage home, and arrived in London on June the 8th, the only remarkable thing about the voyage being the singular weather we encountered in the Red Sea. The steamer *Damascus*, an "outsider," but well found and most comfortably fitted in every respect, carried a full cargo, and was low in the water. We passed Bab el Mandeb on the 20th, and on the 21st a strong head wind which was blowing, increased to half a gale. On the following night the wind became stronger, and all the passengers (myself included), who were sleeping on deck, were, like Pharaoh, overwhelmed, and sent flying below in soaking pyjamas. In the morning it was blowing a full gale, and being so low in the water, we kept continually shipping heavy seas both fore and aft. Sheep-pens and boats were washed loose, and went thumping against the forecastle and bridge. A duck-pen was smashed in, and several birds were drowned, while others came swimming down aft, and clamorously demanded accommodation in the saloon. The decks fore and aft were continually flooded, and everything was in an indescribable state of confusion. On the night of the 22nd everyone slept below, and as the cabins were still disagreeably hot, I occupied a choice position on the saloon table until I found myself rolling off, when I retired beneath. For several hours we were compelled to slow down to half-speed, so that when observations were taken on the following morning,

we found we had covered but one hundred and
sixty-eight knots. The gale abated the following
day. This was curious weather to experience in
the Red Sea, the breezeless heat of which we had
all feared. On the whole, however, I think drown-
ing is an agreeable alternative to roasting.

APPENDIX.

I.—Itinerary of the road between Scanderun and Bagdad.

II.—Khans on the pilgrim road to Kerbela, and on the road to Hillah, with the distances from Bagdad in hours.

III.—Abu Nawas, the jester of Harun al Rashid.

IV.—An Astrolabe purchased at Bagdad.

V.—Chaotic weights and measures.

VI.—Balbi's journey from Bagdad to Busrah.

VII.—Hamilton's account of Busrah.

VIII.—Romance of the Persian Gulf.

APPENDIX.

I.

ITINERARY

OF THE

ROAD BETWEEN SCANDERUN AND BAGDAD.

(The halting places are printed in capitals.)

Right.	On the Road.	Left.	Hours from each stage.
	SCANDERUN.		
	Beilan.		$2\frac{3}{4}$
Plain and Lake of Antioch.	KARAKHAN.		$6\frac{1}{4}$
	Amurath's or Murad's causeway—Kara Su.		$1\frac{1}{2}$
	Hammam Khan, (sulphur springs.)		$3\frac{1}{2}$
	A stream.		$8\frac{1}{2}$
	AFRIN Khan and river.		11
	Khan and tell		$5\frac{1}{4}$
		Tel el Fadr (village).	$6\frac{1}{4}$
	ALEPPO.		$10\frac{1}{4}$
Deir (village).			1
	JEBRIN (village).		3
	Villages and tells at intervals.		
	Very large tell.		$3\frac{1}{4}$
	Stream running south.		$4\frac{1}{2}$
Salt lake called Sabbakh or Subkhet el Jebul, some distance away.	Ditto.		6
	DEIR HAFR (village).		$7\frac{3}{4}$
	Small stream.		
		Mounds called Madum, on a plain.	$2\frac{1}{4}$
	First sight of Euphrates.		$5\frac{3}{4}$

Right.	On the Road.	Left.	Hours from each stage.
Khan and mud fort.	MESKINEH, camp on river bank.		$7\frac{1}{2}$
Kalah Balis, (Old Meskineh) castle and minaret. Half mile distant.			$\frac{1}{2}$
	SHEIKH GHANA, an ancient tell, from summit of which Kalah Jaber, and Abu Hureira are visible.		7
Abu Hureira, ruins of mosque, etc.			1
		Kalah Jaber in Mesopotamia, ruins.	$1\frac{1}{2}$
	Wady.		3
	HAMMAM on edge of Euphrates—no village.		$7\frac{1}{4}$
		Rakka on the east bank of river.	$4\frac{3}{4}$
	Remains of an ancient canal : sight at same time Tel el Munkhir (or Menakhir).		$5\frac{1}{2}$
	Tell and Muslim cemetery.		6
	One hour later road cut up by wadies.		
	SABBAKH. Police fort.		$10\frac{1}{2}$
	MOGLA? A backwater of the river. Mud fort.		$7\frac{1}{4}$
	CAMP at mouth of two desert wadies, on river bank. The river winds very much here.		$7\frac{1}{4}$
	DEIR, Town.		6
	Part of the plain covered with pottery: no mounds.		3-4

Right.	On the Road.	Left.	Hours from each stage.
Saracenic Castle of Rahaba about three-quarters of an hour off road.			$7\frac{3}{4}$
	MAYEDIN, village.		$8\frac{1}{4}$
		Mound called Ushareh (El Ashar?) perhaps one hour distant.	3
High cliffs.			5
		Ruins of Salahieh. Castle of Salah-ed-din.	8
	SALAHIEH, mud fort.		$9\frac{1}{4}$
	Small stream.		$1\frac{1}{4}$
	Remarkable conical hill, perhaps artificial.		$4\frac{3}{4}$
	ABU KEMAL, mud fort and village of hurdle-built cottages.		$6\frac{1}{4}$
	Wady Sheikh Jebur.	(Tell) Sheikh Jebur at mouth of Wady.	$3\frac{3}{4}$
		Extensive ruins called Sur, three-quarters of a mile distant.	4
	Large wady.		$4\frac{1}{2}$
	EL GEIM or KEIM, mud fort.		6
	Wide and shallow wady.		$2\frac{3}{4}$
	Wady.		$4\frac{1}{2}$
	Wady Sofra.		$5\frac{1}{4}$
	Wady Zella.		$6\frac{1}{2}$
	NAHIA, mud fort.		8
	Large wady.		1
Jebel Khushga.	Wady Khushga. Many Nahuras on this part of the river.		3
	Ruinous sheikh's tomb.		$5\frac{3}{4}$

Right.	*On the Road.*	*Left.*	*Hours from each stage.*
		Rhowa, village with fort on left bank of Euphrates.	6½
	ANAH, town.		7½
	Wady containing lake of stagnant water.		2¼
	Wady Fahmin, very rough travelling.		6½
	HADITHA, village.		12
	Sheikhs' tombs, and quarries.		
	Wady with stagnant water.		1¼
	Wady Sagreidan.		3
	WADYBAGDADI, no village or fort.		8¼
	Wady with water.		4¾
	Wady.		5¾
Mazarre: Large sheikh's tomb.			6¾
	HIT, town. Ancient mounds. Bitumen springs.		7¾
	Salt marsh.		2¾
		Sheikh Waiss, a wali.	7
	KALAHRAMADI, town.		11
	Ancient canal.		
	Mud hills about here, also swamps.		2
	Marshes and swamps.		5½
	Cultivated land.		
	Marshes.		
	FELUJA. Ferry and bridge over Euphrates. Village on east bank.		9¼
	Cultivated plain on right.		4¼
	The first Babylonian canal is reached, after which they are frequent.		7¼
		Ruin called Nimrud, or Akar Kuf.	9½
	First sight of Bagdad and Kazemein.		10½
	Marshes and swamps.		12
	BAGDAD.		14

II.

KHANS ON THE PILGRIM ROAD TO KERBELA, AND ON THE ROAD TO HILLAH, WITH THE DISTANCES FROM BAGDAD IN HOURS.

Khan Khirr, 1 hour 10 minutes.

Kiahya Khan, mentioned by Buckingham, 2 hours.

Khan Ez Zad: Khan i Zad (Layard), and Assad Khan (Buckingham). Large brick caravanserai. Dismantled and unused 1892, but in use in time of Buckingham. 4 hours.

Khan Mahmudieh, like Ez Zad, with Arab village : 5¾ hours.

Khan Birumus, or Bir Yunus (Buckingham), called by Turks Orta Khan. Unused 1892. 7¾ hours.

At about eight hours from Bagdad the road bifurcates, one track leading to Hillah, the other to Musseyib, and Kerbela. On the latter

Khan Scanderieh, or Iscanderieh, with Arab village and coffee house. Buckingham, riding to Babylon, was misdirected and got to a khan called Mizrakjee Oghlou, east from here about three miles. He describes it as a well-built khan. Finding his mistake he retraced his steps to Scanderieh. Mizrakjee Oghlou Khan would seem to be also upon the Kerbela road, and possibly was built to accommodate the overflow of pilgrims. I did not see it, but being unaware of its existence I made no enquiries. 8¾ hours.

Musseyib, town and khan, 11 hours.

Kerbela, 17½ hours.

On the road to Hillah :—

Khan Haswa, with a few huts and coffee house, within sight of Scanderieh, and same distance as it, from Bagdad, 9 hours.

Khan Nusrieh, 10½ hours.

Khan Haji Suleiman, mentioned by Buckingham, who describes it as an inferior establishment, 10½ hours.

Khan Mahawil, Mohawil (Buckingham), from which the ruins of Babylon are first sighted, 12 hours.

From Mahawil to Hillah is about 3¾ hours riding by the ruins of Babylon without stopping ; 15¾ hours.

III.

ABU NAWAS, THE JESTER OF HARUN AL RASHID.

Many stories are still in circulation in the East about this personage,
who is a sort of Will Summers of Oriental history. The
following examples were told me by a Syrian—

ABU NAWAS AND THE PLATE OF SOUP.

Abu Nawas was one day waiting on his master, the Caliph,
at dinner. By accident he spilled on the neck of Harun a drop of
the hot liquid. The Caliph, in wrath, turned, and drawing his
sword was about to strike off his head, when the jester nearly
blinded him by pouring the remainder of the contents of the
plate over his head. "Wretch," said the Caliph, "for what did
you that? Speak before you die." "O, my master," answered
Abu Nawas, "if I had lost my head for spilling but one drop of
soup upon your neck, all the people would have said you were an
unjust and oppressive master; but if you slay me for pouring a
plate of soup over you, none can blame you for oppression; therefore upset I the plateful of soup over your head."

The next story has its point in certain play upon words and letters.

ABU NAWAS AND THE LADY KHALISA.

There was a certain damsel in the household of the Caliph
Harun al Rashid, of whom Abu Nawas was jealous, because she
was the Caliph's favourite. One day the Caliph presented her
with a valuable necklace, which so irritated the jester that he
wrote upon her door :—

لَقَد ضَاعَ شِعرِي على بابكم كما ضاع عقد على خا لصه

"Is not poetry thrown away upon your door,
As a necklace is thrown away upon Khalisa."

When the offended fair one had read this couplet, she ran with
tears in her eyes to tell the Caliph, who in great wrath came to
examine it with his own eyes. During her absence Abu Nawas
altered the meaning of the couplet by rubbing out the lower limb
of the letter "ain" ع in the word "daa" (ضاع) so that it
became ء the sign "hamza"

لَقَد ضاء شعري على بابكم كما ضاء عقد على خا لصه

> " Does not poetry shine upon your door
> As the necklace glitters on Khalisa."

The Caliph seeing this, rebuked Khalisa for summoning him, as in the couplet there was nothing but what was flattering. Khalisa, whose power of punning, although her feelings were hurt, seems to have been equal to the jester's, replied :—

" Now that its eyes (عين "ain" an eye) have been removed, it (the verse) can see " (*i.e.*, can be understood).

ABU NAWAS AND THE ASSES.

Abu Nawas obtained leave from his master to seize, as a sort of tax, one ass from every man in the district who feared his wife. He accordingly went forth into the villages, and from every man who was known to be afraid of his spouse he demanded an ass, taking one here and one there until he had a large drove. One day the warders at the town gates saw a great cloud of dust rising from the plain, and they said to each other " Lo! what is this ; " but when the multitude which caused the dust approached the town, they saw that it was not an enemy, as they feared, but Abu Nawas driving before him a great drove of asses, which he had seized from the hen-pecked husbands in the country round. Abu Nawas entered the city and approached the palace, and as he did so the dust floated up in a cloud, and entered the chamber where the Caliph was sitting, so that it made him sneeze. The Caliph demanded the meaning of this, and, on being told, sent word to his jester to attend in his presence, and tell him how he had fared. So Abu Nawas went to the Caliph, and proceeded to describe to him his experiences, and " O, my master," said he, " there was at such and such a village, a lady so beautiful that you should send for her to the palace. Her hair is as the raven's wing, her eyes like the desert gazelle's, her lips like the seal of our Lord Suleiman, and her whole form of willowy grace." And so he proceeded to describe in detail all the varied charms and beauties of the lady to his master. Unfortunately, however, as the jester continued his catalogue of charms, the Caliph glanced at the window opening into the ladies' apartments, and there he saw the round black eyes of the Lady Zubeidah, which were shining with a very unpleasant light, while her beautiful lips were pursed up in anything but the smile Harun was so fond of. He turned hastily

to Abu Nawas and said " Hush ! hush ! do you not see the Lady
Zubeidah listening to us. Speak another word at your peril."
" Then, O my Lord," said Abu Nawas, " you must give me two
asses, for you are a king, and it is very evident that you also are
afraid of your wife the Lady Zubeidah."

IV.

AN ASTROLABE PURCHASED AT BAGDAD.

(*See Frontispiece.*)

Examples of the instrument called the astrolabe are now by no
means common, either European or Oriental, so that it may be
of interest to describe as briefly as possible the small but beautiful
specimen I purchased at Bagdad. It is of bronze, composed of
ten separate parts, which were known in English instruments by
the names of the mother,* the plates or tables (four in number
in mine), the net (rete or spider), the pin, the rule, and the horse,
all of which have also their proper Eastern names. An astrolabe
thus constructed is called in English " planispheric," in Arabic
" musattah," *i.e.*, superficial.

The chief part, the " um " (mother), is a disc of bronze $3\frac{1}{2}$
inches in diameter, one side of which has a circular depression,
into which fit the plates and spider. At one side (the south
side) is the apparatus for suspending the instrument when in use.
This is a projecting and ornamented portion, the " kursi," or
throne, and attached to it by a pin are two rings called the
" urwah " and " halqa." The " kursi" is beautifully engraved on
both sides with a floral arabesque.

I will now describe the various parts, and symbols engraved on
them. Of these the back of the astrolabe ("zahr al usturlab "),
which is the reverse of the disc containing the " um," is the most
elaborate.

It is divided by two cross lines into four quadrants; that

---

* One side of this portion only is, speaking correctly, the " mother," b it
as no distinctive name seems to have been applied to the whole of this, the
largest part of the instrument, it is probable " mother " was used in this
sense.

which falls perpendicularly from the "kursi" is the north and south line (the "kursi" at the south), the other the east and west line. The S.E. quadrant contains on the edge the ninety degrees of altitude numbered. This is the arc of altitude; within this the quadrant is divided by sines and cosines. The whole is called the quadrant of the canon, or of altitude.

The S.W. quadrant has the arc of altitude as the last. Within, a smaller quadrant is marked off, which is the arc of the obliquity of the ecliptic. In the S.W. quadrant, also, are the Zodiacal signs in Arabic, and the parallels of the signs of the Zodiac. There are also, cutting these, the arcs of the azimuth of the kibleh, *i.e.*, of the altitude of the sun when it passes over the azimuthal circle of the kibleh at Shiraz, Bagdad, Isfahan, and Tus, which arcs are marked with these names, and the meridians of the different latitudes. Two inscriptions are engraved in this quadrant for explanation.

The two northern quadrants must be taken together. They are divided into seven semi-circular compartments and a rectangular one in the centre. The outermost contains the shadow of feet and the shadow of fingers. The next is marked with the degrees of the shadows.

Of the five remaining we will take the centre first. It is marked "al buruj," and contains the twelve Zodiacal signs in Arabic, beginning from the east. The third from the outer edge is marked "al kawakab," (the stars), and contains the five planets, arranged five to each sign.

The fourth from the edge is "al hudud," (the limits), *i.e.*, the number of degrees of each sign allotted as the limits of the planets.

The sixth is "al wujuh" (the faces of the planets), each of which is the third of a sign, or 100 degrees.

The last, or seventh, has "al manazil," or the twenty-eight lunar mansions.

The square table is the square of the shadows inverted and level, showing the scales, the natures, and names of the signs of the triplicities, and the planets having dominion by day and night in the triplicities. The use of the two quadrants just described was chiefly astrological. Beneath the square of the shadows is the name of the maker, Haji Ali, and at the base, or north end of the north-south line, is the date, 1125 (A. H.)

The front of the astrolabe is the "um" and the "hajrah," or rim. The latter is divided into the 360 degrees and twenty-four other compartments, containing symbols I have not been able to decipher.* The depressed space of the "um" is occupied by two tables of cities with their latitude, longitude, and "inhiraf." The longitude is measured in the same way as on the great astrolabe of Shah Husein and other Oriental instruments, and according to Mr. W. H. Morley, is reckoned from the old meridian of the Fortunate Islands. The "inhiraf," the same writer says, is an arc of the horizon intercepted between the meridian of any place, and a vertical circle passing through the zenith of such place, and that of Mecca, such circle being called the azimuth of the kibleh. The table commences at the top of the instrument and reads from right to left, in which it differs from most Oriental instruments, which read from left to right. The outer table contains twenty-three names, the inner eleven. For convenience sake the order is reversed in the table as shown on page 472 :—

The plates "safaih" are made to fit into the "um." They are four in number, each engraved on both sides. Of these eight sides, seven are similar. Each of these is divided, by the south-north line, or line of the midst of heaven, and the horizontal line, or line of east and west. Besides these, they have the circles of Cancer and Capricorn, the equinoctial line, and a segmental line dividing the heaven above from that beneath the earth. Above the last are fifteen circles of altitude, "almucanteras," each representing six degrees, and numbered from 6 to 90 † on the zenith. These are crossed by thirty-six incomplete arcs of azimuth, "sumut," numbered 10 to 90, in four batches respectively.

---

* In most Oriental astrolabes this part is numbered 1 to 365 by fives. In European instruments there are the letters of the alphabet denoting 24 hours.

† It is therefore a "sudsi" *sexpartite* instrument. The "tam" *complete* has 90; "Nisifi," *bipartite*, 45; "talathi," *tripartite*, 30; "khumsi," *quinquepartite*, 18.

OUTER TABLE.

The Cities.	Mekka.	Medina.	Bagdad.	Busrah.	Shiraz.	Shuster.	*Kharfadqan?	Isfahan.	Kashan.	Kum.	Rei.
Long.	77·10	75·20	82	84	88	84·30	84·30	86·40	86	85·40	84·21
Lat.	21·40	25	33·25	30	29·36	31·4	34	32·25	34	34·45	35
Inhiraf.	0·0	27·10	52·15	37·19	33·8	35·24	38	40·29	34·31	31·54	37·26

The Cities.	Kazwan.	Saweh.	Hamadan.	Sennan.	Damghan.	Bostam.	Shirwan.	Nishabur.	Meshed.	Herat.	Merv.	Candahar.
Long.	85	85	83	88	91·30	89·30	91·30	92·30	92·30	94·20	97	107·40
Lat.	36	35	35·10	36	36·20	36·30	36·5	37	37	34·30	37·40	33
Inhiraf.	27·34	39·16	32·34	36·17	38·15	39·43†	44·12	45·6	45·6	44·8	42·30	75·5

INNER TABLE.

The Cities.	Tabriz.	Ardebil.	Anrwan.‡	Shirwan.	Maraga.	Kanja.	Bardi.	Lahijan.	Astrabad.	Amol.	Sari.
Long.	82	82·30	89·15	84·30	82	83	83	84	89·35	87·20	88
Lat.	38	38	38·30	40·50	37·20	41·20	40·30	36·10	36·50	36·15	37
Inhiraf.	15·40	17·1	36·20	20·9	36·17	15·49	36·27	29	18·48¶	35	36·44

* This town is written خرفادقان Kharfadqan? on the astrolabe of Shah Husein كلبايكان Kulpaikan. It is difficult to imagine that both represent the same town, but I can find no other town approaching the name in these latitudes.

† This is 83 on the astrolabe, an evident clerical error for 43.

‡ Is this meant for Amrwan, lat. 36. a little south of Astrabad, and close to Damghan?

¶ 88 on the astrolabe; clerical error for 48.

These bearings are of course anything but reliable. They are only approximate. The above table should be compared with the much more lengthy table of towns on the great instrument of Shah Husein (see "Description of a Planispheric Astrolabe constructed for Shah Sultan Husain Safawi, King of Persia," &c., by William J. Morley, 1856). Thirty-one of the thirty-four towns given on the Bagdad Astrolabe occur on that of Shah Husein, of which only eight exactly coincide in bearings.

From Cancer radiate twelve arcs, the planetary, temporal, or
unequal hours. Another series, cutting these at the equinoctial
line, and numbered 1 to 14, are the equal or clock hours or 24ths
of time, between two sunrises.

There is also given on each plate the latitude at which the
plate may be used, and the duration of the longest day at such
latitude. These are subjoined, with the names of the towns on
the tables situated on the same latitude.

LATITUDE.	DURATION OF LONGEST DAY.	TOWNS.
Plate I.	hrs. min.	
29	13·12	Shiraz.
Plate II.		
32	14·7	Isfahan, Sari.
34	14·36	Herat, Kharfadqan, Kashan, Kum.
Plate III.		
38	14·39	Tabriz, Ardebil, Anrwan,
37	14·38	Nishabur, Meshed, Merv, Maraga.
Plate IV.		
36	14·28	Kazwin, Semnan, Damghan, Bostam, Shirwan, Lahijan, Astrabad, Amol.
30	13·56	Busrah.

It is worth notice that the space on the second side of Plate II.
is shaded where the latitude and duration of day is given, which
is not the case on the other plates. This renders it probable that
the instrument was constructed at one of the four towns.

On Shah Husein's astrolabe the duration of longest day for
the various latitudes differs a trifle in four cases out of six.

The reverse of Plate I. has a different combination, being
called the "safihah al afakiah," or plate of horizons. As an
almost identical plate is described in Mr. Morley's book, it is
unnecessary to describe it here.

The next and last of the larger parts of the instrument is the
"ankabut," the spider, or the rete or net, as it was called in English
examples. This is a skeleton plate, of which portions are cut away,
leaving an inner and an outer ring, the circle of Zodiac and the
tropic of Capricorn. Within both project numerous points called
"shaziahs," each marked with the name of some star, the position
of which is at the point of the "shahziah." The zodiacal circle

is marked with the signs and degrees. At the top between Sagittarius and Capricornus is a pointer, "almury," and opposite it near the outer circle is the "mudir," a small knob to turn the plate by.

The following is a list of the twenty-nine stars:—

Inside the Zodiac :—

(1.) Ras al hawa, the head of the snake-catcher (ras al haque) α serpentarii.

(2.) Unk al hayah, the neck of the serpent, α serpentis.

(3.) Nasr tair, the flying vulture (al thayr), α Aquilæ.

(4.) Fum al faras, the mouth of the horse, ε Pegasi.

(5.) Ridf, the follower (arrided, arrioph), α Cygni.

(6.) Nasr waki, the falling vulture (vega), α Lyræ.

(7.) Nayir fakah, the luminary of fakah (munir malfecare, alpheta), α coronæ borealis.

(8.) Ramih, *i.e.*, Simak-i-Ramih, the supporter of the spear-bearer (al ramech arcturus), α Bootis.

(9.) Makib al faras, the shoulder of the horse (scheat alpheratz), β pegasi.

(10.) Kaf al khasib, the stained hand, β Cassiopeiæ.

(11.) (Ras al) ghul, the ghul's head (algol), β Persei.

(12.) Ayyuk, the kid (capella), β Aurigæ.

(13.) Zahr al dhub, the back of the bear (dubhe), α Ursæ Majoris.

Outside the Zodiac :—

(14.) Qalb al aqrab, the heart of the scorpion (antares), α Scorpii.

(15.) Simak al azal, the sustainer of the unarmed man (azimech, spika virginis), α Virginis.

(16.) Janah al gurab, the wing of the crow (al gorab), γ Corvi.

(17.) Qalb al asad, the heart of the lion (regulus) α Leonis.

(18.) Qaidah (butiah), the base of the cup, α & β Crateris.

(19.) Fard al shajah, the solitary one of the serpent (alphard cor Hydræ) α Hydræ.

(20.) (Shira al) shamy, the Syrian or Damascus dog-star, (Algomeisa, Procyon) α Canis Minoris.

(21.) Shira Yamany, dog-star of Yemen (alhabor sirius) α Canis Majoris.

(22.) Rijl al Yasra, the left foot of Jauza (rigel al geuze) β Orionis.

(23.) Yad yumny, the right hand of Jauza (bed al geuze) α Orionis.

(24.) Ain al thur, the eye of the bull (aldebaran) α Tauri.

(25.) Musafa nahr, the interval of the river, δ, ε, or ζ eridani.

(26.) Sadr qitas, the breast of the whale, π ceti.

(27.) Fum qitas, the whale's mouth, γ ceti.

(28.) Danab qitas, the whale's tail, β ceti.

(29.) Saq sakib (ma), the leg of the water carrier (scheat) δ aquarii.

Of the remaining parts the rule is divided longitudinally by the "line of faith." Near either end are erect plates, called "the tiles," through which are holes to take observations. To use the instrument any or all of the plates are placed in the "um," with the spider on the top. The pivot is passed through them by the hole which is in the centre of each, and is then secured by the small ring and wedge.*

The chasing and engraving throughout this instrument is of the most minute and delicate character. Though purchased at Bagdad, I was told it came from Kerbela.

Those who wish to know more about Persian and Oriental astrolabes should consult Mr. Morley's work above referred to, without which I should never have been able to decipher the one just described. For the use of the astrolabe in mediæval England no better work exists than Chaucer's "Treatise on the Astrolabe," edited by the Rev. W. W. Skeat for the Chaucer Society.

V.

CHAOTIC WEIGHTS AND MEASURES.

I have mentioned the perplexing currency of Bagdad. The following report shows the condition of the weights and measures :—

---

* The rule is "idadah," the pivot "qutb," the wedge "faras," and the ring "fals."

The *Journal* of the Board of Trade quotes from the *Journal* of the Constantinople Chamber of Commerce a curious account of the weights and measures in use in Bagdad, in Turkish Arabia. The metric decimal system, which was decreed in Turkey in 1870, has not been adopted by the people of Bagdad, and there, as in other parts of the empire, the old weights and measures are used. The foreigner recently arrived in the town knows nothing about them for a long time, and is liable to be easily duped by the servants and shopkeepers. Thus, for example, he should know that when a cook speaks to him of an ocque of meat, a large ocque is to be understood, for bread, meat, butter, rice, vegetables, fruits, and other comestibles are sold by the large Bagdad ocque, which is equal to about two-and-a-half Constantinople ocques. The grocer, on the other hand, who probably considers himself more progressive, sells his articles by the Constantinople ocque. Wheat and dates are sold per tarar of 20 vesnes of about 78 ocques, whilst for wood, lime, plaster, &c., there is used a tarar of 20 vesnes of 50 Constantinople ocques. For wool, the men of Bagdad, equivalent to about six Bagdad ocques and 12 Constantinople ocques, is in vogue. The jeweller calculates by the métkal (miskal), which is equal to one-and-a-half direms. Tissues are sold, according to their kind, by the halebi pic (26¼ inches), bagdadi pic (29½ inches), or Persian pic (40 inches). Persian furriers, before cutting a stuff which they have purchased, always make certain that the measure is a fair one by the following process:—Taking in the left hand one of the two ends of the ell, they hold it near the nose and stretch the other arm as far as they can. This length should correspond to a drà Chah. Some singular customs are in vogue for the weighing of certain goods. There is, for example, the calculation made for gall nuts. After having weighed the goods in mens of six ocques, the mens, net weight, are reduced at the rate of 12 for 10, which result is further reduced at the rate of 31 for 30, and what remains is converted into kantars at the rate of 30 mens for one kantar, the price being stipulated per kantar. It is difficult to understand the origin and reason of this obscure arithmetic. The little wine coming from Diarbekir and Kerkouk, which is consumed at this place, is sold by weight—that is to say, by the Constantinople ocque. Milk is sometimes sold by weight, but generally it is sold by the bottle and half-bottle, it being of little importance whether the receptacle is large or small, the difference is made up as required by a larger or smaller addition of Tigris water.

VI.

BALBI'S JOURNEY FROM BAGDAD TO BUSRAH.

Gasparo Balbi's journey from Bagdad to Busrah, at the end of the sixteenth century, is remarkable as containing place names which do not occur on modern maps. I do not pretend to identify them:—

" The 13th of March, 1580, they departed from Bagdet towards Balsara, embarked in the Tigris, a river seeming like Nilus, not so endangered with shelves and bodies of trees as Euphrates. At Elmaca the river divided into two, one running after into Euphrates, the other to Balsara. The inhabitants on the right hand are Arabs, on the left Gurgi. On the 18th, they came to Cher. There are many lions and Arab thieves. There are also many keepers of oxen, sheep, and goats. Thence to Encaserami, where each mariner cast in a biscuit for devotion to a holy man there buried. Hitherto both in Euphrates and Tigris they had good air; but there they began to have an ill scent of the river, very noisome, and they were in the night endangered with a kind of whirlpool, and were fain to call to their consorts, which towed them out. The next day they came to Casale, a Saniak's residence, where the Persian river Maroan disembogueth. There the tide was first encountered from the Persian Gulf. A little beyond at Calætel, they fasten their barks when the tide riseth, which otherwise could force them back. The champaigns are well inhabited. They entered Corns, and a little beyond encountered a piece of Euphrates, joining with Tigris, where abide many soldiers with a Saniak, to prevent thieves, which by hundreds in a company used to rob. Here the river (which in some places had been like Brent) was as large as Nilus, and well inhabited. At certain times it is here so hot

that many die thereof ; and in this voyage four persons wearied
with heat and travel sat down to refresh themselves awhile,
and were overcome by a hot wind which strangled all four.
On the 21st they arrived at Balsara."—Pinkerton's " Voyages,"
Vol. IX., p. 396.

" At Elmaca, where the river divided into two," must refer
to the Shat el Amara or el Hai, which branches off at Kut el
Amara. Cher may be identical with Ischahriyé, marked on
Kiepert's map, but of which I have no further knowledge. The
holy man is probably Ali Sharki, or Gharbi. The Persian river
Maroan must be one of the mouths of the Kerkha ; and the
fact that the tide was first felt there points to that at Ezra's
tomb. Corns is of course Kornah.

VII.

HAMILTON'S ACCOUNT OF BUSRAH.

In Captain Alexander Hamilton's travels there is an account
of Busrah, containing so much of interest that I reproduce here
an extract. His journeyings are printed in the eighth volume of
Pinkerton's " Collection of Voyages and Travels," London, 1811,
under the title, " A New Account of the East Indies ; being
the Observations and Remarks of Capt. Alexander Hamilton,
who spent his time there from the year 1688 to 1723 ; Trading
and Travelling, by Sea and Land, to most of the Countries and
Islands of Commerce and Navigation, between the Cape of Good
Hope and the Island of Japan."

" Bassora is the easternmost city or town in the Turkish
dominions, standing about two miles from the famous Euphrates,
and has a small river that washes its walls on the west side, and
discharges its waters into the Euphrates. This city stands about
thirty leagues from the sea, and, it is alledged, was built by the
Emperor Trajan, and had the honour of being the birth-place of
another Roman Emperor, Philip, surnamed the Arabian ; but at
first it was built along the side of the river, and the vestigia of
its ancient walls are still to be seen from the aforesaid rivulet, a
league down the banks of Euphrates, which disembogues her

waters, by four or five mouths, into the Gulf of Persia ; but none navigable for ships of burden but that channel that leads to Bassora. At the city it is a short mile over at high water, and it keeps about the same breadth to the very mouth of it.

The river abounds in fish, but none good, except a small shad about the bigness of an herring. And there is great plenty of wild fowl, such as swans, geese, duck, teal, wigeon, and curlews ; and the fields have plenty of partridge of several kinds, plover, snipes, doves, pigeons, and large larks, whose flesh is very savoury, and their wild notes grateful to the ear. They have also birds of prey, as eagles, many sorts and sizes of hawks, and kites, crows black and white, and it is observable that the black keep the Arabian side of the river, and the white the Persian, and if any presume to interlope into another province they raise the *posse*, and drive them back to their own territory.

There is great plenty of small tortoise in the river ; but none eat them, because they are forbidden in the Levitical law, to which the Mahometans adhere much in point of eating. They have also many species of wild beasts. Wild swine are very numerous, and their flesh is sweet and juicy, but no fat to be seen about them. And the peasants come often to town to invite Christians to kill them ; for they make sad havoc of their corn and roots. And if a Christian kills any they'll bring them to their houses on asses or mules for a very small reward, notwithstanding there is a positive command in the Alcoran that forbids them to touch swine's flesh.

They have plenty of black cattle, wild and tame, and good milk; but they make but scurvy cheese of it, and no butter, because they make the fat of their sheep's tails serve in their kitchen instead of butter, and they keep no tea tables for the consumption of fresh butter. And coffee, which is much in use, is the constant companion of a pipe of tobacco, which is taken by the ladies as well as gentlemen. In the desert, which is very near the town, there are wild camels, horses, asses, goats, lions, leopards, panthers, and foxes, which they hunt on horseback, with sword and lance, and on foot with fowling-pieces. They have plenty of delicious fruits, as pomegranates, peaches, apricots, quinces, olives, apples, pears, nectarines, and grapes that are

as sweet as the juice of the sugar-cane, and their spirits are so
weak that they'll produce neither wine nor vinegar; but the
most plenty and useful of their fruits are their dates, which
support and sustain many millions of people, who make them
their daily food, and they are wonderfully nourished by them.
Bassora exports yearly for foreign countries above ten thousand
tons of dates, which employ abundance of seamen for their
exportation, besides many more poor in gathering and packing
them in mats made of the leaves of the date tree, and likewise in
drying them. I bought about one hundred and sixty pound
weight of wet dates for 2s. 3d. sterling, and sometimes they
are cheaper.

Bassora was many years in the hands of the Persians, who
gave great encouragement to trade, which drew many merchants
from foreign parts to settle there, and particularly from Surat,
in India. But in the year 1691 a pestilence raged so violently
that above eighty thousand people were carried off by it, and
those that remained fled from it, so that for three years following
it was a desert, inhabited only by wild beasts, who were at last
driven out of the town by the circumjacent Arabs, who possessed
it about twelve months, and were in their turn driven out by the
Turks, who keep it to this day; but its trade is very inconsiderable to what it was in the times that the Persians had it, and the
reason is that the Turks are very insolent to strange merchants.

There are many Jews in Bassora, who live by brokerage and
exchanging money; but the Turks keep that set of people very
low, for reasons of state. There are also about two hundred
Christians of the Greek Church, but no priests of that com-
munion, wherefore some Roman missionaries officiate there. The
Greek clergy are very indifferent about gaining proselytes, and
to nourish their flocks will not run the risk of martyrdom, so
they keep none of their priesthood at Bassora; but when I was
there three Roman priests of the Carmelite order had the super-
intendency of that church. These sanctified rascals were a
scandal to Christianity by making a tavern of their church; for
having more indulgence from the government than the Mahometans in moral matters, they abuse it to the vilest uses, in selling
arrack, which they distil from dates, and procuring birds of

paradise for the use of their customers. The Mahometans again are strictly forbidden the drinking of wine or distilled liquors, both by their ecclesiastical and civil laws ; for the heat of the sun and the dry sandy soil create such a dust choler in their brains, that when they are heated by drinking strong liquors they become furious and mischievous to one another, and in those mad fits wound and kill their fellows. Those scandalous priests had been often reprimanded by the government for abusing the indulgence they had, but to little purpose, for their trade was very gainful ; but upon a drunken quarrel between two seamen of mine, wherein one was dangerously wounded with a knife, and the other, for fear of punishment, turned Mahometan, being a Portuguese Christian, the bashaw sent an officer and soldiers to enter the church and all the houses appertaining to it, with orders to break their stills and jars, with the rest of the distilling utensils, and to pour out all the arrack they found on the ground, which was accordingly done ; and in the search the soldiers met with a fine silver watch and about four hundred Spanish dollars, which they carried off with them. The priests petitioned the bashaw to have the watch and money restored ; but were answered that they preached much on the contempt of worldly riches, and if his soldiers had made them practise what they preached they ought to be thankful, and to let the despicable money continue in hands that professed their love of it, and knew much better how to use it than priests, and so dismissed them with threats of harder penalties on their next transgression ; but the sweets of worldly gains soon made them forget the admonition given them by the bashaw, as well as their heavenly promises and oaths made at their admission into their holy order ; and like a dog to his vomit, returned back to their old trade of debauching Christians, Jews, Mahometans, and Pagans with liquors, and set up stills for that purpose once more."

I I

VIII.

ROMANCE OF THE PERSIAN GULF.

That there is still room for romance in the Persian Gulf may be
seen from the following, which appeared in the " Times " of
October 4th, 1892 :—

"The Indian papers brought by this week's mail contain a
remarkable story of shipwreck and privation. The steamer *Simla,*
which arrived in Bombay from the Persian Gulf on September 2,
had on board two brothers named Lavy, belonging to Mahé.
They were engaged in carrying produce from one island to
another of the Seychelles, using for the purpose a small schooner
of about 25 tons burden, which had but one sail. On June 21
it left Port Victoria with six persons on board, all French, on a
short voyage round the island, with four days' provisions only.
Shortly after leaving they encountered bad weather, which prevented them from making for land. Four days after leaving port
the jib sail was carried away by the force of the storm. By this
time they had been blown well out into the open sea, and were
drifting out of the track of vessels. They divided the food and
water into small allowances, and took it in turn to keep a lookout
and endeavour to keep the craft's head to the sea. On the 19th
day after starting their provisions became exhausted. More than
one of the castaways drank the sea water, and seven days after
the provisions had given out one man died from hunger and
exposure. Two days later another died, but on the third day land
was sighted. The boat drifted on the shore, where it afterwards
sank. Shortly after they crawled on land another of their number succumbed to the protracted privations. During the time they
were at sea they must have drifted at least 1,300 miles in their
open boat, as the place where they landed was subsequently
found to be Rashoor or Ras Madruka, a deserted point on the
Arabian coast. While the three survivors were searching for
some fruit and water they were surprised to see coming towards
them a solitary Bedouin, who, instead of ill-treating them, as they
expected, offered them dates and water. The three men eagerly
drank of the latter, and the two Lavys also devoured the dates,
their first meal for eleven days ; but the exertion was too much
for their companion, who shortly afterwards died, making the

fourth death since the voyage began. The Bedouin, finding they were incapable of walking, placed them on the backs of two camels which he had with him, and travelled a short distance to a place in the desert, where he found a tree, under which he made them lie down. Here he remained for three or four days, trying to find out where they had come from. Conversation, however, was not possible, but after a time he mentioned the word Muscat, and the elder Lavy, knowing that there was such a place on the Persian Gulf, signified that they would like to be taken there. On the fourth day of the sojourn in the desert, finding they had regained a portion of their strength, he placed them again on the camels, and set off, himself walking. After a journey of twenty-two days he led them before the British Consul at Muscat, to whom they gave an account of their adventures. The Consul handed to the friendly Bedouin as reward a large sum of money. After remaining at Muscat for three days the *Simla* called, and they were placed on board and given a passage to Bombay. At the expense of Government they were to be sent back to the Seychelles, *viâ* Aden."

INDEX.

A

Abbas ben al-Ummar al-Ghani, Emir of Anah, 208

Abdallah ibn Ali, sanctuary called, 406, 407

Abdin Rezak, on the heat of Muscat, 429

Abraham, traditions of, 68

Abu Hureira, 140, 141

Abu Jafar al-Mansur, founder of Bagdad, 286

Abu Kemal, village of, 190, 191

Abu Nawas the Jester, Appendix III.

Abu Obeidah, besieges Aleppo, 69

Abu rakab, the influenza, 54

Abu Risha (Arborise), Emir of Anah, 208, 209

Abu Sedra, grove and saint's tomb, 389

Adod ed-Daulah the Buyide, 289

Ainsworth, W. F., references to his works, 32, 39, 138, 141, 150, 167, 183, 184, 194, 215, 227, 245, 291, 309, 317, 400, 419

Akar Kuf, see Tell Nimrud

Albu Mohammed tribe, 394, 395, 403

Albuquerque, Don Mathias de, founds a factory at Hormuz, 453

Aleppo, The Azizia hotel, 47. Cookery, 52. Cholera, 54. Routes from to Bagdad, 55, 56. Servants, 57 et seq. Description of the city, 74-104. Traditions, 68, 69. History, 69, 70. Factories, 71, 72. Situation, 74. The river, 74. Dimensions, 77. Gates and walls, 79 et seq. Houses, 82, 83. Bazaars, 84. Mosques, 85 et seq. Citadel, 87 et seq. Khan el Wezir, 96, 97. Heraldry, 98, 99. Suburbs, 100

Cemeteries, 102. Sheikhu Bekr, 104. Population, 105. Manners, 106. Fanaticism, 107. Mr. Tyrwhitt Drake, references to, 107. Costume, 109, 110. Climate, 110. Boil, 111, 112

Alexandretta, see Scanderun.

Ali Gherbi, village on the Tigris, 389, 397

Ali Sherghi (Sherki), 389

Altone, an Oriental Christian, 167 et seq.

Amara, town of, 389, 398

Amir el-Omra, title of, 289

Amk, El-, the plain of Antioch, 35

Amurath's causeway, over the Kara Su, 39, 40

Amurath IV., his conquest of Bagdad, 298

Anah, town of, 206-209. The inhabitants of, 208. Ibn Haukal, on, 208. Ralph Fitch on, 208. Gasparo Balbi on, 209. Anatho, 209.

Anazeh Arabs, 134, 148, 185, 190, etc. Costume, 149

Antioch, plain of, 35, 39

Arabs, cupidity of, 226

Arak drinking, 53

Arms, coats of, at Aleppo, 98

Astrolabe, purchased at Bagdad, Appendix IV.

Azizieh, a village on the Tigris, 389

B

Babylon, Ruins of, 316 et seq. The Mujelibe, Mukallibe, or Makloube (of Buckingham and Rich), 317, 323. Of Layard, 322. Of Ainsworth, 325. The Babel, 317-319. The Kasr, 321-323. Of Rich and

Ainsworth, 321. Description of, by Layard, 322. Amran ibn Ali, 324. Buckingham on, 324. Al Heimar, 326. Buckingham on, 326. The mounds in general, Rich on, 325.

Bagdad, Routes to from Europe, 2; fro n Aleppo, 55. Account of the City, 241-300. Situation, 242. Bridge at, 244. Walls destroyed, 245. Gates, 245. Dimensions, 246. Old guns at, 247. Roads and houses, 248, 249. Heat at, 250, 382. Coffee Houses, 251. Bazaars, 252, 253. Shopping in, 254, 255. Currency, 256. Mosques, 257-259. Medrasseh el-Mostan-serah, 259. Tomb of Zubeidah, 260-262. Kazemein, 263-267. Mosque of Imam Musa el-Kazem, 266. Population, 269. Inhabitants, 270-275. Churches, 275. Climate, 276. Trade, 277. Modern state of the town, 278. Post-office, 279. Ramazan, 280. Hotel, 281. Date mark, 282. History, 286-300. Floods, 380

Baghdadieh, a fort, 389

Bahrein, 438-440. Pearl fishery of, 439. History, 440.

Balbi, Gasparo, on Rahaba, 183. On Anah, 209. Account of Hit, 220 n. On Tell Nimrud, 235. His journey from Bagd d to Busrah, Appendix VI.

Baldwin, his siege of Aleppo, 70

Ballums, canoes on the Tigris, 398, 400, 412

Baluchistan, remarkable coast line, 456

Barber of Bagdad, 283. Shop of at Aleppo, 85

Barkiarok, Sultan, 290

Barmeki (Barmecide) Wezirs, 287

Bathing, danger of, while travelling, 157, 191

Beetle, an ingenious, 192

Beilan, village of, 32

Beirut, town and port of, 20 et seq. Disgusting scene at, 21

Belfante, Mr., 27

Beni Lam Arabs, 397

Benjamin of Tudela, Rabbi, his account of Bagdad, 291. Of the Birris Nimrud, 342. Of Jews at Hillah, 335, etc.

Berœa founded by Seleucus Nicator 69

Birris Nimrud, the mound of, 336-349. Described, 340. Layard on, 340 n. Theories about, 343. Account of Benjamin of Tudela, 342. Opinions of Rich, Buckingham, Oppert, Rawlinson, Layard, and Ainsworth, 343. Sanctuary called Nebbi Ibrahim at, 346. Traditions of Abraham, 346

Bitumen springs, 220, 221. Use of bitumen and naphtha as a weapon (Tarikh Mirkond), 221 n.

Blunt, Lady Anne, her "Bedouin Tribes of the Euphrates" referred to, 135 n., 141, 166, 277 n.

Bombay, 458

Bostani Kesra, the ruins of Ctesiphon, 389

Brickmaking, at Musseyib, 356. At, Kerbela, 374

Buckingham, J. S., the traveller, references to his writings. On Tell Nimrud, 236. The walls of Bagdad, 245. Conical tombs, 262 n. Khan ez-Zad, 304. Khan Iscanderieh, 309. Population of Bagdad, 269. Its climate, 276. Ruins of Babylon, 317 et seq. Birris Nimrud, 343

Buggalow (baghlah), 390, 428

Bukhit, the katterji, 128, 129; meaning of the name, 129

Bunder Abbas, town of, 448 et seq. Old guns at, 448. Great heat of, 449. Prevalent diseases, 449. Bab el-Belao, 449 and n. Exports, 450. Population, Hamilton on, 450

Bursif, Borsiph, Byrsia, Borsippa, 343

Burton, Sir Richard, reference to his works, 169.

Bushire, town of, 432, et seq. European shop at, 434. "Bajirs," at, 434. Water supply, 436. History, 437

Busrah, 411-419. The creek at, 413. Condition of the town, 414. English spoken at, 415. History, 416, 417. Trade, 417

Button, Aleppo, a boii, 111, 112

Buyide dynasty, 288-290

Buyuruldi, a passport, 67

C

Cairns of stones, (seoulchral?) near Wady Fahmin, 212
Cairo, 8-16. Dole at tomb of the late Khedive, 10 et seq. Moolid of Sitti Zeyneb, 14 et seq.
Caliphs, Al-Mansur, 286. Amin, 287. Motasim, 287. Mustain, 287, Mutazz, 287. Mohtady, 287. Moktader, 287. Al-Radhi, 288. Mostader, 290. Kaim, 290. Nasir, 292. Mostanser, 292, Mostasem, 293. Ali, 368. Muavia, 368. Omar, 416
Canals, Babylonian, 222, 234, 315
Caravanserais, 304. See also Khans.
Causeway, from Auranitis to Carrhæ, 150.
Chaldæan Christians as sailors, 387
Chause, chiaus, chouse, etc., a Turkish officer, 72. Mr. G. A. Sala on, 72 n.
Cherrid, an irrigation appliance, 164
China pots, used for kohl, 443
Christians of Bagdad, once subject to oppression, 294
Commander of the Faithful, title of, 288, 289
Costume, at Aleppo, 109. Of muleteers, 129, 130. At Bagdad, 272.
Ctesiphon, ruins of, 379 and n, 392
Currency, Turkish, 19. At Bagdad, 256. At Busrah, 415
Curzon, Hon. G., references to his work, "Persia and the Persian Question," 262 n, 268, 368. Hormuz, 455.

D

Darga Beg, title of governor of Bushire, 438.
Date mark at Bagdad, a boil, 282
Deir, town of, 161-176. Lack of provisions at, 164. Cultivation, 164. Cherrids, 165. Inhabitants, 165. History, 167. Woodfuel fishing, 170. Mounds near, 178
Deir, village near Aleppo, 118
Deir Hafr, village, 122. Khan at, 124
Desert, fear of by townsmen, 172
D'Herbelot, reference to, 286 n.
D ala river, 389, 391
Durwish, howling, at Sabbakh, 154. Wandering, 188

Dysentery, 157, 209

E

Elephantiasis, in the Persian Gulf, 431, 449
Ezra, tomb of (El Ozeir), 389, 407, 408

F

Factories, European, at Scanderun, 25. At Aleppo, 71 et seq. At Busrah, 417. At Kharak, 432. At Bunder Abbas, 455. At Hormuz, 453. At Bushire, 437.
Farur, island of, 442
Feluja, village, 231, 232. Ferry, 232.
Filaria Mendenensis (or Dracunculus) the Guinea worm, 431
Fitch, Ralph, his description of the Tell Nimrud by the name of the "Tower of Babel," 235. His description of Bagdad, 297. Of Hormuz, 453.
Flints, worked, found four hours south of Deir, 179. Near Wady Skeikh Jebur, 193.
Fow (Fao), quarantine station, etc., 425.
Frogs, at Aleppo, 75
Fauna, of the Euphrates, 202.

G

Gearv, Grattan, references to his "Through Asiatic Turkey." Tell Nimrud, 236. Date trade, 277. Population of Hillah, 335. On Tragedy of Husein, 373 n. Traffic of the Tigris, 395. Revolt of the Madan Arabs, 405 n
Geim (or Keim) El-, fort at, 195. Ghazu, 195-199. Ptolemy's Agamna, 195
German travellers murdered at Deir, 166
Gilded plates on Shiah shrines, 267, 268 and n
Ghazu, an Arab foray, 191, 195 et seq
Ghenghis Khan, 292
Gombroon, 445. See also Bunder Abbas
Gul Bushi, mound of, 40
Guns, old, at Bunder Abbas, 448

H

Haditha, village of, 213

Hamadi the Akam, 131. Costume, 131

Hamdanide Sultans, the capital of, 69

Hamilton, Capt. Alexander, on Bagdad, 300. On Bunder Abbas, 450. On Hormuz, 454. His account of Busrah, Appendix VII.

Hammam Khan, 41. Sulphur springs at, 41

Hankliz, Al-, an eel at Aleppo, 75 and n

Harun al Rashid, puts to death El-Kathem, 263. The Caliphate under, 286

Hashi, the, a north-east wind, 430

Hassan, see Sayyid Hassan

Haudaj, the, a litter, 148

Hebbet es Sinah, the Aleppo boil, 111

Heraldic devices at Aleppo, 98

Herbert, Sir Thomas, on Hormuz, 455

Hieroglyphic formula found in heraldic devices at Aleppo, 98 et seq.

Hillah, town of, 329-335. Description, 334. Population, 335

Historical sketch of Bagdad, 286-300

Hit, town of, 217-221. Ancient mounds of Is, 219. Bitumen springs of, 219. History of the springs, and accounts of travellers, 220 n, and 221

Hormuz, island of, 451-456. History, 451 et seq. Description in the Tarikh Mirkond, 452. By Marco Polo, 452. Factory, 453. Fort, 453. Sir Thomas Herbert on, 455

Hotel at Aleppo, description of, 49

Hulagu, destruction of Aleppo by, 70. His conquest of Bagdad, 293, 296

Husein, the Tragedy of, 373 and n. 492. His death at Kerbela, 368-370, References to accounts, 370 n

I

Itinerary of steamer's route from Bagdad to Busrah, 389

Itinerary of the road between Scanderun and Bagdad, Appendix I.

J

Jago, Mr. T. S., British Consul at Aleppo, 54 et seq.

Jaleel, a boy of Aleppo, 33, 51, etc.

Jebels, Bakhur, 447. Bustaneh, 442. Hamrin, 597. Jinao, 446. Kushga, 203. Khamir, 447. Shimal, 447. Simon, 44. Turanjeh, 442

Jebul (Sabbakh el Jebul), a salt lake, 121

Jebrin, village of, 118

Jews, at Aleppo, 105, 106. At Bagdad, 273 et seq. At Deir Mahariz, 142. At Hillah, 335. Their pilgrimage to Ezra's tomb, 408

Jisr Gerarah, on the Tigris, 391

Julian, the Emperor, his halt at Antioch, 69

K

Kaif, 173

Kait Bey, Sultan, arms used by, 99

Kajaweh, the, a litter, 305

Kak, a hard biscuit, 64

Kalah Balis (Barbarissus Barbalissus), 137. History, 138

Kalah Jaber (Dauser Dabanas, etc), 140, 142

Kalah Ramadi, town of, 224, 225

Kalah Salah, village of, 405, 406

Kara Khan, village and khans, 35, 36

Kara Su, Amaurath's causeway over, 39, 40

Karun river, 420, 421. The Bahmeshir channel, its natural outlet, 422. A trade route, 425

Katterji Bashi, the head muleteer, 117

Kazemein, 263-267. Its mosque, 266. Gold-plated domes at, 267

Kellek, a raft, 203

Kerbela, the pilgrimage to, 303, 306, 371. The pilgrim road to, 308. Our host's house, 363. The mosque of Meshed Husein, 364, 366. Of Imam Abbas, 364. Kerbela stones, 366. Fanaticism at, 367, 368. A place of pilgrimage, 368. The martyrdom of Husein the origin of the pilgrimage, 368 371. Corpse caravans, 372. The town, 373, 374

Keubbé, a preparation of meat, 41

Khabur river, junction of with the Euphrates, 180

Khafaja Arabs, 347

Khali i, the "sword of God," his siege of Aleppo, 69

Khans, Appendix II., Kara Khan, 35.
Afrin, 42. El-Wezir, description
of, 96 *et seq.* At Deir Hafr, 122,
124. At Deir, 161. Khirr, 302.
Ez-Zad, 304, 305. Mahmudieh,
305. Haswa, 308, 309, 310. Birunus, 306, 308. Iscanderieh, 309,
378, 379. Nasrieh, 313. Mabawil,
314, 352

Kharak, island of, 432

Khosru II., Aleppo burned by, 69

Kiff el Yahudeh, the traditional
tomb of Ezekiel, 341

Killi, a Persian game, 436

Kishm, island of, 446, 447

Kniphausen, Baron, director of the
Dutch factory at Kharak, 432

Kofa, circular boats, 231, etc.

Kornah, the traditional Garden of
Eden, 410

Koss, the, a south-east wind, 430

Kubabs, a preparation of meat, 52 *n*

Kuh Hormuj, a mountain, 432

Kut el Amara, a village, 389, 396

Kuweik Su, the river of Aleppo, 74

L

Ladies, Syrian, 37, 38

Layard, Sir Henry, references to his
writings. The ruins of Babylon,
321 *et seq.* His description of a
building on the Kasr, 322, 323,
and *n.* The Birris Nimrud, 343.
Ctesiphon, 379 *n.*

Leben, a preparation of milk, 52 *n*, 145

Levinge bed, description of, 3

Lingah, town of, 443. Unsanitary
condition of, 443. Inhabitants,
443. Birkehs, 444. Lawlessness
of, 444

Lizard, a species of *gecko*, 132 and *n*

Locusts, said to be killed by birds, 354

M

Madan Arabs, revolt of, 403 *et seq.*,
412

Madum, mounds called, 132

Mahadi, town of, 291

Mahdi, see Sayyid Mahdi

Mahmud of Ghizni, besieges Bagdad, 289

Marco Polo, his account of Bagdad,
294 *et seq.* Of Ormuz, 452.

Marshes near Bagdad, 238

Mattara, a leather water-bottle, 64,
192

Matting encampments on the Tigris,
397 and *n.*

Maundrell, Henry, his account of
salt works at Jebul, 121

Mayedin, village of, 183

Medrasseh el Mostanser, founded,
292

Meskineh, on the Euphrates, 135

Midhat Pasha, his tramway, 263

Mirage, effect of, 178, 179

Mir Mahenna, sheikh of Kharak,
432

Mir Naser, sheikh of Kharak, 432

Mizal, sheikh of Mohammerah, 420,
423

Modein, Al-, the twin cities, 393

Mogla, Lake, (?) 157

Mohammed, Haji, the Akam, 130

Mohammed ibn Hassan, tomb of,
355

Mohammed of Kharazm, 292

Mohammerah, town of, 420 *et seq.*
Canoes at, 421. Fisheries, 421.
History, 423.

Mongols, at Bagdad, 292 *et seq.*

Montefik Arabs, 394 and *n*

Months in which the Kerbela pilgrimage is most usually performed, 371

Moryson, his description of Scanderun, 25

Mosques at Aleppo, 85 *et seq.* At
Bagdad, 257 *et seq.* At Kazemein, 266 *et seq.*

Mosquitoes, at Kerbela, 375

Mouth of Hell, a name of Hit, 219

Muiz ed Daulah, Sultan, the Buyide,
289

Mules, sore backs of, 160. The cry
of, 187

Muleteers, Agreements with, 160.
Hardihood of, 175

Musa el Kathem or Kazem, Imam,
death of, 263. Mosque of, 266

Musseyib, town of, 357-362, 378.
Pilgrim traffic in, 358 *et seq.*

N

Nahr Huseinieh, a canal to Kerbela,
373

Nahr Salah (the Pallacopas ?), an
old outlet of the Euphrates, 419
and *n*

Nahr Sares, an old canal, 227

Nahura, a water-wheel, 103

Noah, traditional residence of, at Deir, 167

Nur ed Din, Aleppo rebuilt by, 70

Nusirieh Arabs, 355

O

On ebn Jaffa, Nebbi, tomb called, 362

Ophidium Mastacembelus, a fish of Aleppo, 75

Outfit for the journey, my, 3, 4

Owlad Muslim, domes near Musseyib, 355

P

Pass, mountain, between Scanderun and the plain of Antioch, 32, 34

Pearl fishery at Bahrein, 439

Persian Gulf, 420 *et seq.* Geography of, 427. Piracy, 428. 447 *n.* Climate and winds, 429, 430. Formerly a land-locked sea, 446. Romance of, Appendix VIII

Pigeon Post, between Bagdad and Busrah, 417

Pilaf, an Eastern dish, 52 *n*

Piracy in the Persian Gulf, 428, 447

Pococke, Dr., on the dimensions of Aleppo, 77

Politeness of the Persians, 351

Post, Camel, from Damascus to Bagdad, 280

Postal services, between Bagdad and England, 279

Q

Quarantine on the Syrian Coast, 9

R

Rahaba, Saracenic castle of, 180-183. "Rehoboth on the river," 183. Notes on history of, 183

Rahaba al-Malik ben Tauk, 185

Rakka, a distant view of, 151

Ramazan, 221, 226, 280

Rauwolf, the traveller, on Rahaba, 183

Red Sea, rough weather in, 459

Reshire, 435

Rhowa, village of, 204

Rich, C. J., references to his writings; the ruins of Babylon, 317, 318, 325. The Birris Nimrud, 343

Rochette, Reference to "Hist. des Colonies Grecques," 24

Russell, Dr. Alexander, references to his "Natural History of Aleppo." On Scanderun, 25. On the Kuweik Su, 75. His list of the gates of Aleppo, 79. His plan of Aleppo, 78. On an ancient conduit there, 103.

Russian Travellers at the Birris Nimrud, 338

S

Sabæans at Amara, 400 and *n.*

Sabbakh, on the Euphrates, 152

Sabbakh or Subkhet el Jebul, a salt lake, 121. Maundrell's account, 121

Saour, a sort of fish, 421

Saheili, the, a south-west wind, 430

Saklawieh Canal, 292, 302

Salah ed din captures Aleppo, 70

Salabieh, ruins of, (Rahaba al-Malik ben Tauk), 185

Salt lake at Jebul, 121. Salt at Hit, 219

Samida and Samargha, marshes of, 399

Sand storm at Salahieh, 186

Sarab (mirage), 178

Saud ibn Munshid, sheikh of the Madan Arabs, his revolt, 403

Sayyid, meaning of the title, 330

Sayyid Hassan, 329, 330, 333, 349, etc.

Sayyid Mahdi, 363

Scanderun, town of (Alexandretta), 24-30. Willebrand of Oldenburg, Rochette, Russell, Morysoo, and Van Egmont, on, 24, 25. Hotel at, 27. Present state, 28

Sea snake in the Persian Gulf, 457

Selim, Sultan, Overthrow of Mamluks by, 70

Seleucus Nicator, founder of Berœa, 69

Shahid Husein, a tragedy, 373 and *n.*

Shah in Shah, the title, 289

Shah Ishmael Sophi, capture of Bagdad by, 297

Soammar, fellahin of the tribe of, 354

Sharks, in the Karun river and Tigris, 421

Shat el Arab, descriptions of, 410, 425

Shat el Khud, 399

Sheep, the Black and White, Turco-
man hordes, 297
Sheep-skins, inflated, used for swim-
ming, 153
Sheikh Ghana, a tell called, 140
Sheikh Jebur, tell and wady, 193
Shemal, a north wind, 430
Shiah shrines, precedence of, 368 *n*.
Shohr, name of a fellahin tribe, 137
Shrines, Shiah, see Shiah shrines.
Shuster, natives of, tradition of
their origin, 422
Stano, Mr. F. F., 63 *et seq*.
Subzabad, 435
Sulphur springs at Hammam, 41
Sur, ruins at, 194 and *n*.
Sura, 227
Surieh, ruins of, (Thapsachus), 150

T

Tahir, General of Mamun, his siege
of Bagdad, 287
Takht-i-Khusrau, the arch at Ctesi-
phon, description of, 392
Takht-i-rawan, description of, 124,
125
Tancred the Crusader, 138
Tarikh Mirkond, Teixeira's trans-
lation of, edited by John Stevens,
221 *n*., 286, 290, 291 *n*., 296, 451 *n*.
Description of Hormuz, 452
Tavernier, on the Afrin river, 40 *n*.
Tells, el Fadr (a village), 45. Mun-
khir, 151. Nimrud (Akar Kuf), 234,
235, 236. Various writers on,
ibid. Sheikh Ghana, 140. Sheikh
Jebur, 193
Temperature in the Persian Gulf,
429
Tent used for travelling, 3
Teskereh, or Tethkireh, a passport,
67
Thapsachus, site of, 150
Thieves, Arab, 133, 222, 223
Thompson, Charles Robert, Monu-
mental inscription to, 102
Tib river, 399
Tigris, the. Steam traffic, 385.
Paucity of traffic, 395
Tigris, the steamer, foundering of,
187 *n*.

Timur Beg, (Tamerlane), Bagdad
taken by, 296
Togrul Beg, destruction of Bagdad
by, 290
Tragedy of Husein, the, 373, 402.
References to accounts of, 373
Tramway at Bagdad, 263
Tripoli, port of, 23
Turks, the, at Bagdad, 289

U

Ushareh, mounds of, 184

V

Van Egmont, on Scanderun, 25.
His travels, 26 *n*. On the cause-
way of Amurath, 39. On Aleppo,
70, 71, 73, 77, 79, 82, 113
Van Houting, Mr., director of the
Dutch factory at Kharak, 432

W

Water of the Euphrates, turbid, 136
Water, stagnant, preference of
Arabs for, 210
Wadys, formation of, 201. Sheikh
Jebur, 193. Sofra, 201. Zella,
201. Kushga, 203. Fahmin,
211, 212. Sagreidan, 214. Bag-
dadi, 215
Wali, a sheikh's tomb, 224. Mean-
ing of, 224 *n*.
Weights and measures at Bagdad,
Appendix V.
Willebrand of Oldenburg on Alex-
andretta, 24
Winds in the Persian Gulf, 430
Wright, Thomas, " Early travels in
Palestine " referred to, 291
Wulda Arabs, 141

Y

Yafa, town and port of, 17 *et seq*.
Yoghurt, a Turkish preparation of
milk, 52
Yusuf Antika, 283 *et seq*.

Z

Zabtiehs, or Turkish police, 145
Zobeide Arabs, 394, 396
Zubeidah, Lady, the tomb of, 260
et seq., 291

THE END